Julia Child's *The French Chef*

A production of the Console-ing Passions book series
Edited by Lynn Spigel

Julia Child's
The French Chef

DANA POLAN

Duke University Press   Durham and London   2011

© 2011 Duke University Press

All rights reserved

Printed in the United States of America

on acid-free paper ∞

Designed by C. H. Westmoreland

Typeset in Warnock by Keystone Typesetting, Inc.

Library of Congress Cataloging-in-Publication Data appear

on the last printed page of this book.

FOR JOHN AND JOANNA,

lovers of life

Contents

Acknowledgments

In undertaking to write about the cooking show as a very particular genre of popular American television, I encountered a warm and gracious community of scholars and writers in the area of food study who offered extremely helpful counsel and who were always ready to share research and reflection. Amy Bentley, John E. Finn, Darra Goldstein, Signe Rousseau, Joan Reardon, Laura Shapiro, and Andy F. Smith read the entire manuscript and brought their expertise in matters of American culinary tradition to bear on it in ways that were always rich in insight and suggestion. Laura, in particular, was so giving of her own findings and conclusions from the manuscript in progress for what would soon become her excellent biography of Julia Child. Additional thanks to her and Andy for inviting me to present my research on *The French Chef* in their Julia Child course at the New School University. Other scholars who have written on food, such as Gary Allen, Madonna Berry, Frances Bonner, Isabelle de Solier, Meredith Eliassen, Joanne Hollows, Sharon Hudgins, Zilkia Janer, Nathalie Jordi, Jessamyn Neuhaus, and Wayne Wooden all shared research materials with me and pointed me in important directions. Krishnendu Ray provided detailed comments on an early essay version of my initial thoughts on Julia Child. I first presented that essay as a talk to the Feast and Famine food studies seminar at New York University, and I thank all of the participants for their feedback and lively conversation. I also thank audience members who responded to other presentations of the material at the Society for Cinema and Media Studies, the Cinema Studies programs at the University of Pennsylvania and the Université de Montréal, the Department of Theater and Film Studies and the Wilson Center for Humanities and Arts at the University of Georgia, and Film and Media Studies at Arizona State University.

Within my home disciplines of film/media and cultural studies, I benefited from close readings of the whole manuscript by Sarah Banet-Weiser, Scott Bukatman, Jonathan Kahana, Tom Kemper, Anna McCarthy, Toby Miller, and Lynn Spigel. Lynn, as editor of the Spin Offs series of television books at Duke University Press, has been a great resource and a great source of emotional support. I also got useful insights or research leads from in-person conversations with William Boddy, Scott Bukatman, Larry Gross, Ernie Larsen, Anna McCarthy, Sherry Millner, Sue Murray, and Elizabeth Nathanson and from e-mail interchange with Jim Baughman, Marsha F. Cassidy, Margot Hardenbergh, Kristen Haring, Joanne Hollows, and Rachel Moseley, as well as the late and much missed Manuel Alvarado. The television scholar Ethan Thompson provided me with an essential reference from his own research on Ernie Kovacs (and I thank Diana Rico for additional Kovacs insight). The doctoral students Lisa K. Broad, Dan Gao, Alex Kupfer, Jinying Li, and Jaap Verheul were marvelous research assistants from semester to semester and tracked down leads with efficiency and productive creativity. I had an opportunity to try out my thoughts in a graduate seminar on Food TV, and I acknowledge the contributions of the students in that class—Emily Bajus, Jessica Connell, Min Han, Molly Hubbs, Sara McMonigle, Daniel Metz, Ying Xiao—and thank my department chair, Richard Allen, for enabling it to happen and, more important, for being so supportive of my scholarship and for being such a good partner in intellectual exchange. Carrie Welch at the Food Network hosted an illuminating visit for the class to the studio, for which I give great thanks.

Leah Weisse and the entire staff at the public television station WGBH in Cambridge, Massachusetts, readily made a treasure trove of *French Chef* materials available to me, as did the staff at the Arthur and Elizabeth Schlesinger Library on the History of Women at Radcliffe, where Child's papers are housed. The Schlesinger Library also provided me with tapes of Dione Lucas's television shows through interlibrary loan services. Trips to Cambridge were made especially enjoyable through the welcome of several hosts who put me up on research trips: Haidee Wasson and Charles Acland and Haden and Maria Guest. The trips were aided by an award from the Dean's Office, Tisch School of the Arts, New York University. I benefited also from a trip to look at the PBS holdings at the Library of Broadcasting, University of Maryland (special thanks to Tom Connors there).

The resourceful Karen Fishman at the Library of Congress's Recorded Sound division helped me in the discovery of rare audio recordings of the George Rector and James Beard television shows. The early TV enthusiast Bob Shagawat first cued me in to this material. It's been great to chat with him about this period.

Special thanks to the Culinary Institute of America, the Special Collections and Archives division of the Georgia State University, WAVE-TV, WOI-TV, KABC, and the UCLA Film and Television Archive for providing access to rare materials and granting permission to reproduce images in this book. For those images for which permissions were necessary, the institutions or individuals (or the people whose legacy they are now entrusted with) who granted those permissions are acknowledged in the captions to the images.

Deepest gratitude to William A. Truslow, Esq., and the Julia Child Foundation for permission to quote from unpublished materials in her papers and to reproduce select images.

Lurene Frantz, who in the 1960s wrote a master's thesis on Julia Child while *The French Chef* was still in its first run, most wonderfully shared with me her research and even offered originals of articles and other primary materials from the period. Donald S. Green provided a kinescope of an episode of a cooking show made in 1954 by his mother, Edith Green, and provided great insights about her contributions to the history of cooking on television. Betty Tolson talked usefully to me by telephone about her experience as the host of a cooking show on a local (Oklahoma) TV channel in the 1950s, and other veterans of the period, such as Arlo Grafton and Art Jacobson, contributed lovely reminiscences. Ruth Campbell and Jill Wolfson shared thoughts about two 1950s TV cooks, Chef Milani and Florence Hanford. The totally fun Jinx Morgan shared reminiscences by e-mail of her efforts in the 1960s to turn the cookbook for which she was co-author, *Saucepans and the Single Girl*, into a television series. The ever affable Galloping Gourmet, Graham Kerr, helped resolve a last-minute historical question. And Julia Child's first television director, Russell Morash, took time out of his schedule to be interviewed at length and explain in eloquent terms (he's a great raconteur) the conditions of public television and of filming techniques in the early 1960s for *The French Chef*.

Some paragraphs from this book appeared on the occasion of the release of the film *Julie and Julia* in a short essay "Television That Tastes Good: Julia Child's Culinary Pedagogy," on the superb Moving Image Source website of the American Museum of the Moving Image. Thanks to Dennis Lim at the museum for inviting me to do that piece. Some paragraphs from the discussion of James Beard's early TV efforts rework material that was published as "James Beard's Early TV Work: A Report on Research," *Gastronomica* 10, no. 3 (summer 2010): 23–33. My thanks to *Gastronomica*'s editor, Darra Goldstein, and the University of California Press for this first opportunity to present the research findings on Beard. Ken Wissoker and Courtney Berger at Duke University Press have been the greatest of editors: patient when need be, supportive always. And special thanks to Leigh Barnwell, editorial associate at Duke University Press, who aided immeasurably with some additional practical issues and helped shepherd the manuscript through its final phases. How great to work with an editorial team whose members are such food enthusiasts. As he did for my previous Spin Offs volume on *The Sopranos*, Neal McTighe saw this book through the production process with care and super-efficiency, and Sue Deeks was the most perceptive of copyeditors. Thanks to them both!

Conversations with my dear friend Giovanna DiChiro have always been fun and inspiring. (She was wonderfully patient while I made an overly complicated lobster recipe from *The French Chef* cookbook.) My mother-in-law, the fun Marie Sturken, fan of the *French Chef* series in its original run on PBS, continues to be ever intrepid in her voracious desire to experience more and more of the culture of our world.

Leo-Andres Polan has now taken to helping out in the kitchen as "little chef" to "papa big chef." At every turn, he brings new delights into my world. Marita Sturken fills each day for me with inspiration and intellectual and emotional riches. She lived through this book with loving support and attention.

I dedicate this book to two of the finest people I know. John Epstein and Joanna Hefferen bring a strength of being to life that allows them to experience its every richness in every moment. They are fun; they are smart; they are courageous. They are models.

Julia Child's
The French Chef

Julia Child's manual labor

1 The Difference She Made

An episode of a TV cooking show begins. The first few instants of the initial shot have a bare-bones simplicity and directness and even a whiff of the generic about them. In close-up, on a baking tray on a kitchen counter, we see a large metal pot bottom side up and arranged around it a circle of baked ladyfingers. The edge of someone's hand, a woman's hand with a wedding ring on one finger, is visible at the top of the image, and in a moment the camera, by pulling back from its close-up and shifting a bit to the side, will reframe the scene to bring the hand fully into view as it picks up one of the baked goods to show off to the spectator while the credits fade in over the image. This is the beginning of "Introducing Charlotte Malakoff," episode 65 of Julia Child's *The French Chef.*

The shot, in black and white, offers a very limited depth of field that both renders the background soft and blurry and concentrates attention on those hands energetically going about their business. Except perhaps for the somewhat specialness of the food item being presented (Frenchified baked goods), this appears to be cooking pedagogy (and cooking television, in particular) at its most basic—pared down to its most fundamental state as the encounter of human intent, instruments (in this case, bare hands), and a foodstuff on which controlled and calculated demonstrations and transformations will be enacted and presented to an audience. It's a lot like what viewers already would have seen often if they watched daytime television in the 1950s and 1960s.[1]

But almost from the first instant, a voice has kicked in—that notable voice, the voice of Julia Child. "Under this silver drum is Miss Charlotte

Malakoff, who with the support of 'Lady Fingers,' " she declares bouncily and cheerfully, "is about to take part in an intriguing dessert drama today on *The French Chef.*" From the start, then, we're not simply in a prosaic site of quotidian cookery. Quite the contrary: We are in a special place that is totally Julia Child's, a joyful, even wacky, world for which she sets the terms. This is a voice that commentators for years have strained to try to find words adequate to describe its special quality: Is it a breathless warble? Is it a lilting and lifting vibration? Is it shrill or sonorous? Is it composed of snorts and grunts or of eloquent enunciations? Is it vulgar or marked rather by upper-crust emphases that resonate with the speaker's social origin in the moneyed world of white-bread Pasadena, California? One is tempted to imagine that this voice is unique and inimitable except that hearing it seems to lead so many listeners to feel impelled, precisely, to imitate it. Maybe the fact that no one else has this voice makes so many people want to assay its imitation (the most famous being Dan Ackroyd's hilarious impersonation of Child on *Saturday Night Live* in 1978, which led a whole generation of television viewers who never had watched her shows to feel still that they knew Julia Child; of course, we now can add to the notable attempts at mimicry Meryl Streep's star turn as Child in the fractured biopic *Julie and Julia*, for which she was nominated for an Oscar).

In the opening scene of "Charlotte Malakoff," Child's voice qualifies the anonymous image of culinary activity and turns it into something special, something personified, something *embodied*. And along with that voice comes further embodiment as the camera pulls out of its initial close-up to reveal Child herself in all her larger-than-life presence of personality. A strapping, six-foot-two-inch bundle of vivacity and boundless energy and enthusiasm, Julia Child commands the scene, her posture a blend of confidence and control *and* a comical wavering as if she were both sure of the culinary mission before her but vulnerable to a catastrophic loss of control at any moment. This presence, this personality, along with the quite visible tensions she embodied between control and chaos, would make all the difference for American television in the 1960s—indeed, for American culture more broadly in that decade—and it's fully there on display in the first few seconds of Child's "Introducing Charlotte Malakoff."[2]

Embodiment

In fact, any episode of *The French Chef* could serve as a reminder of why Julia Child became so key to the cultivation of modern American lifestyle and leisure culture in the latter part of the twentieth century. On the one hand, as I've learned, you only have to start showing a clip of her to students, colleagues, or friends, and the infectious laughter and enjoyment kick in. She stands for a quite particularly American embodiment of boisterous fun. On the other hand, many viewers clearly were getting something more than mere comedy by watching her: They were being offered lessons in a whole way of living and being and doing. And that too was her importance to her times.

Julia Child's pedagogy was of a generous, open sort. Against dogma, but also against mechanical and slavish obedience, Child didn't simply enumerate ingredients and recipe steps and then order her audience to follow her blindly. Instead, she took the time to clarify why things could—or in some cases, certainly should—be done as she was doing them (and why this or that variant would or wouldn't be as good). She made sure viewers knew the logic of her kitchen practices and could learn to judge them from within. Take, for instance, episode 45 of *The French Chef*, "Artichokes from Top to Bottom." Here, in just the first four minutes, one learns about the seasonality of artichokes, about the parts that make up the vegetable, about the best way to buy it (what to look for and what to avoid), about the different varieties of artichoke, and about the most typical way to cook them. In the remainder of the half-hour show, one also is taught the steps in cooking artichokes in non-standard ways, what *not* to do (for example, the water shouldn't be salted because this is bad for the vitamins contained in the artichoke and gives the vegetable a bad flavor), how to avoid discoloration (rub the artichoke with lemon), how to make artichoke dishes particularly attractive for when company is coming over (and even what plates to buy if one is doing such entertaining regularly), how to incorporate culinary etiquette into the presentation to invitees (for example, you will be "nice to your guests" if you remove the choke at the center of the vegetable before serving), how to make a sauce to fill an artichoke bottom and what main dishes it might accompany, and how to do all of this in the intimacy of the home yet with a professionalism that shows respect for food and for its preparation. There's constant humor along the way, but it is always linked to Child's assumption and acceptance of a fundamental instructional mission geared to careful and logical explanation.

The French Chef, we must then acknowledge, was, quite simply, based on good, effective pedagogy, even with all the larger-than-life, entertaining spectacle bound up in the dynamic figure of Julia Child. As Child's book editor, Judith Jones, notes, Child's teacherly talents centered on her clear and careful explanation of the logic behind technique (not just what to do but why to do it that way); on her reasoned analysis of ingredients (not just what they were but what each one contributed to the recipe and why they were recommended); on her clarification of what results to anticipate in each step of the culinary process and, importantly, on her willingness to pinpoint risky moments when a recipe might go wrong; and, most of all, on her honesty in showing that she could still make mistakes but then could offer suggestions about how either to avoid them the next time around or make do with them once they happened. Her TV show, for all its showmanship, also provided clear-cut instruction of a particularly compelling sort.[3]

During her first years in France—where she had accompanied her husband, Paul, when he took up a post as a cultural attaché for the U.S. government in Paris, and where she decided to make it her life's mission to soak up as much practical training and lore about French cooking as possible—Julia Child had frequently encountered a dogmatism that held that the culinary accomplishments of this most reputed of national cuisines had to be brought about one way and one way only. She had even been warned that only men could aspire to the summits of haute cuisine, and that rankled her. Child knew she loved the food and felt passionately that she could, to cite the title of her first book, "master" it. To her mind, French cuisine had a perfection of taste that could be felt in an instant—namely, the precise and punctual moment of tasting where one experienced a supremacy of achievement and, literally, internalized it. Reliably, Julia Child's autobiography replays that recurrent trope of the American visitor to France who has a special meal that, in a veritable epiphany, is a life-transforming lesson in culinary purity and intensity of taste.[4] At the same time, Child held emphatically to the idea that there might be any number of paths to such perfect taste moments, and there should be no hoity-toity dogma about the process. As we'll see later, one might even achieve genius in the kitchen with commercial products such as mass-manufactured broths or stocks as long as they were used (or doctored) in ways that made them French-like in taste. Indeed, in the specifically geographic context of America, her notion of "mastering the art of French cooking" frequently meant not cooking exactly as the French do but cooking in ways that would lead to results *comparable* to those of the French.

At the same time, it is worth noting that there could be a dogma of *low* cuisine along with the high, and this Child eschewed too—namely, the imposition of a compromised and compromising standardized American cookery promoted as a set of shortcuts and tricks one engaged in mechanically to get around the burdensome awareness that one's family had to be fed but that one really didn't like feeding them. In such terms, Peg Bracken's streamlined open-a-can-when-you-can approach to food preparation in the bestselling *I Hate to Cook Book* (1960) was no less dogmatic in its manner than the snootiest of French culinary academicians. For Bracken, anyone who needed to simply get the meals out—and for her, this meant most American housewives—should slavishly follow her instructions and not ask questions and not need to know the logic behind what she was doing. Like any good postwar science project, cooking became reduced to mechanical, engineered solutions to empirical problems in, in this case, the feeding of family. For example, if the fact that most months have thirty or thirty-one days meant that one needed to come up with that many dinners, then the reader should be given that exact number of step-by-step recipes to follow, one after the other, and should execute them without question or personal creativity. (Actually, Bracken provided only thirty such recipes, allowing that one could go out to a restaurant on the last day of months with thirty-one days; here, one was on one's own and had to order for oneself.) Insofar as *not* thinking for oneself was part of the conformist side of the 1950s into the 1960s, shortcut cooking of the Peg Bracken sort was easily a political expression of the times in encouraging an anti-intellectual obedience to authority in the service of domestic tranquility.[5]

In contrast, Julia Child's pedagogical procedure was steeped in a desire to explain and to gain her readers' and viewers' deep-felt assent rather than simply and dogmatically to order them around. Given the state of much American cuisine at the beginning of the 1960s—a canned, processed, artificially sweetened, and gummy cuisine—Julia Child's very insistence on eating tasty food with a sensual enjoyment combined with intellective understanding might itself have been an opening up of everyday American life. In her enthusiasm and her commitment, she stood out.

To be sure, some other culinary propagandists had been calling for an uplift of food in America through the mediation of hearty homespun cuisine and European distinctiveness in taste. On the one hand, new concerns for social status increasingly were impelling some American cooks toward a gastronomy that would be open to foreign influences (French by the beginning of the 1960s, Asian by the end) and thereby to new tastes both subtle and uniquely striking that would make one's fare take on aura and distinction. On the other hand, a recurrent desire to both document and celebrate American regionalist cuisine had found new proponents in the postwar period in figures such as James Beard and Clementine Paddleford, who extolled how local culinary fare could itself be a source of aura and distinction, enlivening mainstream food with accents of authenticity, vibrancy and depth of taste, social festiveness, and so on and substituting for mass-market standardization.

Paddleford, for instance, roamed the United States on journalistic assignment from 1948 to 1960 to sample the richness of American culinary byways and then to collect the relevant recipes in a joyous celebration of regionalism, the masterly and monumental *How America Eats*.[6] Across the nation, she found a diversity of tastes, derived both from local context and, significantly, from America's productive indigenization of all the cultures (for example, immigrant cultures) that had fed into its mongrel identity as a melting-pot nation. In a way, American cuisine, for Paddleford, was inextricably and eminently a foreign cuisine, and this gave it unique opportunities for gustatory excellence, but without dandified pretension. In the words of her biographers, "Her work focused on history and tradition and sought to undermine ideas that most people had about American cooking—that it had no authenticity, that it consisted of meals made entirely from packaged foods, that it was unexciting and uninviting—by bringing to life the people and the joy behind good home-cooked food."[7] There could be a vibrant, resonant American food for every taste, and the possibilities and promise went well beyond homogenized fare rendered bland by top-down standardization. To take just one example, the very last recipe in *How America Eats* is for chile rellenos (admittedly, with two of the seven ingredients from cans); it offers then a final assertion of Paddleford's willingness throughout her big book to tell Americans about aspects of their cuisine that all might not have known about but that were no less worthy components of their national culture. In addition, it is striking to see how often Paddleford's anecdotal accounts of her adventures with the diversity of American foods have to do with her encounters with it *at social occasions*. To be sure, her depiction of a gastronomically rich postwar America is often about basic home cooking, but it is also as much about parties and get-togethers and the desire to please others. This, again, is key to a postwar context in which meals increasingly are becoming outer-directed and all about status in the eyes of the world at large. It is then all about making American cooks aware of food preparations, many derived from foreign sources, that will add diversity and distinction to meals presented to invitees as they enter from that world into the home, and thereby open up domestic space to larger social influences and pressures. It is perhaps revealing, for instance, that Paddleford, like other food writers of the 1950s and 1960s such as Julia Child or James Beard or Craig Claiborne, speaks of an admiration for French cuisine, but that when she offers a recipe for cassoulet, it is one that comes from Cincinnati, Ohio. Even in the depths of her celebration of American heartiness, Paddleford seems of a piece with Julia Child and others who also mediate the foreign and the indigenously American in middlebrow fashion.

One difference between Julia Child and the other propagandists for a new, joyous potential for diversity in American cuisine was, of course, that Child made the break to television, the key postwar medium for instruction and for large-scale presentation of self and was thereby able to bring her gustatory message to the masses. James Beard, as we'll see in chapter 2, had no more than a short-lived local career in early television cooking. Paddleford's chosen medium was the newspaper article (and its collation into book form), where her lyric evocations of American landscape and her rich anecdotes could run wild, and, in any case, she had had a throat operation that would have made teaching through television impossible. The French-trained Dione Lucas did, as we'll see, have several TV series that attempted with great imperiousness to bring distinction through European cuisine to Middle Americans, but her demeanor was too stiff to mediate the rigors of instruction with a diverting air of entertainment. She never really took off as a television performer. Perhaps the vivacious and utterly captivating M. F. K. Fisher could have used her (by all accounts) striking presence and personality to captivate a broad public, but her commitment was to the literary word—to sensuous evocations of the glories of food, both local and foreign, through a honed mode of writing that made her one of America's great literary stylists (and not just in the realm of food). These were not TV personalities. Julia Child eminently was.

In Child's hands, *The French Chef* was a highly entertaining form of television. In its very desire to give reasons, to explain, to provide context (including historical accounts of ingredients and recipes and the famous people who had come up with them), Julia Child's pedagogy carried tremendous appeal. The lessons themselves were part of the difference she made. But clearly, of course, watching her was fun as well as instructive. She transformed the pedagogy of cooking on television.

As we'll see in more detail in the next chapter, from early in the history of the cooking-demonstration television genre, a set of conventions (somewhat malleable, to be sure) was put in place for filming the activity of cooking in the home kitchen. And, as we'll also see, *The French Chef* both inherited and adhered to these fundamental conventions even as Julia Child's personality gave them resonance and new vitality.

For educational television in particular, the imputed tension between functional pedagogy and audience-pleasing diversion was a constant issue. Were there ways for the sheer functionality of the cooking demonstration to be opened up to fun? Did it all have to be so utilitarian, so flatly sequential, so uninspiredly functional? From the start, cooking shows mediated an education provided by mere talking heads with seductive strategies for the leavening of entertainment. For instance, as the early history of cooking shows demonstrates, a chronological structure would feel less inexorable if it were filled by the antics of a comic chef or by a team composed of a "straight man" trying to get his recipe done and a stooge trying (whether intentionally or not) to fumble things up. Likewise, chronology could be interrupted by shtick or spectacle (even to the extent of a full-length song). In addition, the utilitarian exposition could be re-imagined as a fictional drama complete with suspense plots and narrative complications and engrossing characters.

Chronology, moreover, could be toyed with. For instance, by beginning a cooking demonstration, as Julia Child often did, with a glimpse of the finished dish that was promised to emerge at the end of the session, some cooking shows would offer a tantalizing "flash forward" that turned mere chronology into expectancy and promise. The anticipation of the ending, glimpsed this way in the beginning of the show, was rendered all the more intense and all the more fantasy-laden when the dish was not just anodyne fare but something new, something special (for example, artichokes or a Charlotte Malakoff dessert). To gaze on the seductive image of French food at the start of a cooking show was to be caught up in the uplifting offer of escape from the ordinary. This was not the flat unfolding of chronology but the promise —made from the start—of utopia.

With *The French Chef*, entertainment and instructional strategies came together in the force of a dynamic personality who cogently and consistently made cooking fun while never losing sight of the utility of basic instruction. There was still the unveiling of a demonstration offered in step-by-step succession, but it was rendered as an entertaining story in which a plucky, cheerful heroine confronted the odds (including her own fumbles and foibles) and energetically pushed her way to culinary success. Child was great at opening up the inexorable flow of chronology through moment-to-moment humor; through a recounting of background lore that, while keyed to the moment, also transcended mere immediate commentary on the utilitarian task at hand; through excessive and exuberant performance; and through a constant concern to anticipate and reiterate the wondrous pleasures that awaited at the end of the culinary process and that could be foreshadowed by sample tastes of the dish, step-by-step, as its flavors came together along the way.

Insofar as the goal always was to leaven mere chronology with the promise of wondrous gustatory payoff, one innovation of Child's television series, to my mind, was particularly consequential: namely, her physical displacement in the last moments of the show *from the kitchen*, where she had prepared the food, *to a dining room*, where she sampled it (and gave viewers the feeling that they too were participating intimately in this consumption and consummation, albeit symbolically). While today it might seem logical to end a cooking demonstration with the celebration of the act of eating in a space all its own, this sort of culminating activity seems unprecedented for the history of the cooking show up to *The French Chef*. At best, on this or that local daytime cooking show, there might be a guest (a visiting celebrity, for instance) who was on a promotional tour, had taken time out to participate briefly in a cooking demonstration, and would be given mouthfuls of the dish to sample as it came off the stove. Typically, the programs before *The French Chef* ended *in the kitchen*, where in most cases the instructor simply held the culinary results of the day up to the camera and did no tasting of it. The assumption here was fully utilitarian: What mattered most was not how a dish ultimately tasted and the pleasures that one might get from it but that the dish was completed and delivered in expedient fashion.

The dining-room scenes of *The French Chef* respect an overall chronology—since they follow the kitchen cooking and bring it to closure—but by ending *after* the mere completion of the recipe, I think they change the entire meaning of the act of cooking. In the history of the cooking show after this point, kitchen work is inexorably tied to consumption—and to the assumption that the pleasures of the table matter as much as the processes that have brought the wondrous food *to that table*. Utility is now extended into taste and enjoyment, and the mere functionality of the cooking demonstration is transformed into steps on the path to pleasure. In its own way, *The French Chef* prepares the way for later, more hedonistic cooking shows, such as Nigella Lawson's *Nigella Bites*, where the final scene often transpires long after Lawson has left the kitchen and where she now figures out an ultimate way to enjoy the fruits of her labor. For instance, she is shown sneaking down, late at night, to make a refrigerator raid on a dish she prepared much earlier and now snacks on in the dim light of the fridge's open door. Or she takes a dessert upstairs and lasciviously spoons it into her mouth as she dreamily lounges in a bubble bath surrounded by candles. In *The French Chef*, to be sure, the activity is less sensuous and certainly less surreptitious (and therefore less narcissistic). Child's dining room is right next to the kitchen, and the food is consumed just after it has been prepared in the kitchen, and she makes sure to include the viewer, if only vicariously, in her enjoyment. But this already is not a fully utilitarian sort of consumption, and it enables important, first televisual steps in thinking about food and about food preparation as more than functional and as more than mere necessity. It is now also all about pleasure and enjoyment.

The French Chef, then, offered suspense and drama, comedy and ribald physicality, mayhem mixed with professionalism. The show could be indulged in even by, or especially by, viewers who had no intention to cook as she did. No doubt, many of her fans never made her recipes or even watched the show as a *cooking* show specifically. It is worth remembering that both the first and second iterations of *The French Chef* —a black-and-white series from the early to middle 1960s and a color series at the beginning of the 1970s—took place in an age before video-cassette recorders (although, as we'll see, the second iteration was connected to an early technology of playback devices) and therefore didn't always encourage easy following along with the culinary pedagogy.

It is clear that many viewers watched not to turn themselves into cooks—or even to gain familiarity with cooking activities—but to see a funny, bubbly, and sometimes awkward character perform in her chosen televisual space. To take one anecdotal example, the garrulous, wise-guyish doorman for my apartment building tells me that he watched Julia Child religiously in the 1960s but never would have imagined cooking from her instruction—or from that of any other teacher, for that matter, since he had no interest in taking time to cook. For him, the appeal of Julia Child was that of a television performer and her particular realm of performance was pretty much irrelevant—except when she killed lobsters on-screen for one of the shows and pushed his squeamishness too far.

While Julia Child needs to be situated in a history of *cuisine* in America, she also belongs to a history of *television* and, in particular, to that common brand of nonfictional hosted programs popular in the 1950s through the 1960s and peopled by names such as Jack LaLanne, Zacherly, Officer Joe Bolton, Vampira, and so on. In a related register, Child's invitation of the spectator into her aestheticized realm bears comparison to the widely watched tour of the White House hosted by Jackie Kennedy in 1962, in which viewers (one out of every three Americans, in this case) were welcomed in hushed, even breathless, tones to partake of the secrets of hitherto unseen, mysterious locales (parts of the White House, that is, that had been off limits to the public) and to partake of art and elegance.

By accepting entrance into the television host's special realm, the viewer shares in privileged forms of knowledge and performs rituals of membership (for example, in the aptly named *Mickey Mouse Club*, with its incantatory songs and so on). Hosted programs of the 1950s and 1960s frequently provided in this way a sense of introduction into a secret universe, a place of intimacy—just the viewer and the presenter

"As soon as the technical difficulties have been cleared up, we'll return to Julia Child.."

Live TV, 1960s style. Cartoon by Henry R. Martin; courtesy Henry R. Martin.

in an inner sanctum of shared information and private codes and procedures. The host's actions entranced and seduced through a sense of whispered appeal to secrets that one was being taken into confidence about. One infamous incident occurred on January 1, 1965, when the kids' show host Soupy Sales suggested to the children watching him that, since their parents undoubtedly were still asleep after New Year's Eve revels, they should sneak into dad's wallet and mail him the green pieces of paper with pictures of presidents that they found there.

Like these other hosts, Julia Child in the same historical moment had her own breathlessness of invitation into her private space. As with them, the visuals of her televisual appearances had her looking outward toward the spectator and taking him or her into her confidence and into her way of being in the world. Julia Child's television work was very much of a piece with a moment in television in which hosting was presented as a gift to the spectator, a special and seemingly personal invitation to enter into the host's world for the duration of the show and live on its terms. Such hosts would then guide the spectator through the rules of life within these special and secretive televisual worlds and offer an active, energetic demonstration of their special talents (physical in the case of LaLanne; artistic/cultural and verbal in the case of Jackie Kennedy; culinary in the case of Julia Child). The demonstrations were often quite dynamic, exuberant, and therefore captivatingly watchable, even if one had no intention of trying them at home.

In frequent cases, the host's welcome specifically was an invitation to enter into an interior realm, a *domestic* one even, and the thrill was not that of television going beyond the everyday but offering a new look at an everydayness that often had not seemed worthy of representation. In other words, television, as a medium of the home but offering a "window on the world," might well venture from time to time into a "wild kingdom" (to cite the title of one noted program of exotic exploration), but it might also rest content with offering a better, closer, and richer look at forms of domesticity itself. Often, as a form of popular culture, television served to give instruction about, and fresh glimpses of, a simple quotidian world, but one that had perhaps fallen below the radar of the arts of high culture.

It's worth noting in passing that even the movies came to be affected by this televisual fascination with rendering quotidian realities that had been so invisible because they were so routinely ordinary and now were being opened to peering eyes. In 1960, for instance, Alfred Hitchcock used the technical crew and a writer from his television show *Alfred Hitchcock Presents* and played on his own reputation as that show's sardonic master of ceremonies in the film preview he shot for *Psycho*: this trailer involved Hitchcock addressing the camera/viewers and walking them through the private spaces of the Bates home and motel. A striking moment in the trailer has Hitchcock opening a door and conspiratorially closing it immediately with the hushed declaration that it's "the bathroom." Like the bold close-up of the toilet in the film itself, the trailer here is commenting on the very prudery by which American popular culture claims to engage with everyday reality but can't acknowledge basic bodily functions. Hitchcock is being cheeky, but he's also taking on the role of the realist who sees the world for what it is and wants others to do so too. Among other things, the 1960s were a period in which prudishness underwent change—in which popular culture came often to depict those aspects of everydayness that had seemed either too banal or too taboo to merit representation. One motif of the decade involved the discovery of the physicality of the flesh, the corporeality of being. Think, for instance, of the vastly influential last line from Susan Sontag's essay "Against Interpretation" (1964): "In place of a hermeneutics, we need an erotics of art." The call here is to engage in the world boldly with one's senses, to open up the body to experience, both earthy and transcendental.

Throughout this same historical moment, Julia Child would appeal in large part because of her willingness to get physical with food—to not imagine that just because French food was refined, its preparation had to be done in dainty fashion. This too revolved around a breaking of taboos of the seen and the unseen. Among the reasons many fans adduced for their ebullient admiration of her was the sheer directness of Child's actions with food. Not merely was she revealing what went on when French food was mastered, but she was showing how visceral that mastering had to be. In the words of Laura Shapiro's trenchant biography of Child, "Julia Child loved handling food. . . . Nothing made her gleam with pleasure like the prospect of getting her hands into the fresh and glistening flesh of an animal—a rump of veal, a goose, a suckling pig, a giant monkfish."[8]

Similar to Hitchcock's showing what happened behind the closed door of the bathroom (just as, at the beginning of the next decade, the TV series *All in the Family* would harp endlessly on Archie's bowel-movement issues), Julia Child was revealing what happened beyond the closed doors of the kitchen, and if it was always fun, it wasn't always pretty (live lobsters killed on-screen!).

At times, it must be said, there can seem to be something almost deliberately provocative, even humorously ghoulish, about Child's insouciant handling of the dead animals she works with in the kitchen, from the "chicken sisters" she prances about on her countertop to the whole pig whose carcass accompanies her through much of one episode (and whom she slaps affectionately on its naked rump at one point). This also is very much of the historical moment. The discovery of the sensual, the visceral, and the physical was also the morbid, if wry, awareness of mortal limits and the vulnerability of the flesh. It's there in the close-ups of the taxidermied Mrs. Bates in *Psycho*. It's there in Andy Warhol's Death and Disaster series (1962–63). It's there in the "What, me worry?" satire of *Mad* magazine (for instance, at a patient's deathbed, a doctor comforts the grieving widow and then whacks the husband on the head when it's clear he's not yet dead). It's there in the stick-in-your-craw jokes of Stanley Kubrick's *Dr. Strangelove*, where widespread killing is given comic treatment. It's there, as well, in the wave of "sick humor" comedians who filled the stages of smoky clubs and amused through wincing, sardonic sketches (Mort Sahl, Lenny Bruce, and so on). To my mind, there is a touch of the same irreverence toward life and death in Julia Child, who encouraged her viewers to find wry and ribald pleasures as they dove into the visceral tasks before them (or, at least, vicariously watched her doing the deeds). She had no compunction about letting viewers know what they were in for if they wanted to take the efforts of French cuisine all the way. That pig carcass stares at us like Mrs. Bates does with her empty eyes, or as another dead pig does in a celebrated film from the year *The French Chef* debuted: *The Lord of the Flies*. This was not always an age for the squeamish. As Hannah Arendt said of the revelations at the Adolf Eichmann trial, whose televising in 1962 brought the banality of genocide into the living room (complete, as Arendt noted, with kitschy commercial interruptions), one needs to understand that "the horrible can be not only ludicrous but outright funny." That is a very 1960s attitude.[9]

If part of the mystery of classic French cuisine had lain in the presentation of dishes that emerged from a kitchen hidden off-stage and that came to the table with the aesthetic perfection of the "well-mounted piece" (*la pièce bien montée*, in official French culinary terminology),

The French Chef went behind the scene to show the sweaty, fraught work that went on before the spectacle of final display of the finished, consummate product to the diner.[10] At the same time, it *was* important, as noted, that many episodes ended with Child plating her creation and carrying it through a door from the kitchen into the dining room, where she sat opposite a place setting with an unoccupied seat as if offering up the dish to a spectator who could fill in for the camera and for the off-screen guest it represented. This was a program not only about the grubby work of food preparation but also about the dream of its hearty consumption. There was the pleasure of the heartfelt labor but also of the gustatory payoff in the act of eating. Enjoy! This was also a very 1960s attitude. Think, for instance, of the Oscar winner for 1963, *Tom Jones*, with its famous eating scene that leads to sex but that is also a viscous, vibrant, virtuoso scene of sensual enjoyment and explosion in its own right (for example, oysters slithering down wide-open gullets).

Many fans wrote to Julia Child that they wished they could move into the space of the screen and join her in the meal; undoubtedly, this had to do not just with the seductiveness of this or that dish but with the entire narrative trajectory and visual rhetoric by which the plate was brought to the table and offered up to the first-person point of view of viewers invited into the televisual space. It mattered, as well, that the whole process to get the dishes to this wondrous moment at the dinner table was so physical. Central to Child's pedagogy was the notion that one learned by doing—and doing in a very physical way. As she puts it, for example, in the episode "Four in Hand Chicken" from 1964 (about how to get four different dishes economically from one chicken), "Everybody who's serious about cooking ought to know how to cut up a raw chicken." Two points are important here: First, for all of their kinetic spectacle, Child wanted her televisual actions to have educative import behind them (she was miffed when anyone spoke about her performance as just antics or clowning around); and second, she wanted that import to be embodied in actual practice rather than just remain ideational. So, in this instance, she believes you *need* to learn about chickens and that will best happen when you jump to the task with knife in hand. Her pragmatic pedagogy appealed thereby to an American investment in direct action, in a willingness to get one's hands dirty while getting things done. With the exception of some dieticians and health officials who complained about the reuse of tasting spoons or hand towels, and of some anti-alcohol campaigners who reviled the employment of wine on the show, most of the viewers who felt impelled to write to her were ardent fans and loved that Child was endlessly tasting the dishes, getting in close with the food.[11]

With a dynamic performance such as Child's, the very divide between education and entertainment in popular television turns fuzzy. Having fun with Child was itself pedagogical, whether or not one sought specifically culinary instruction. Viewers were learning, for instance, about the performative fun of television (especially public television's newfound ability to offer such fun after so many boring talking heads) and about its distinctive personalities, as well as gaining specific knowledge of cookery lore and technique. Viewers were also thereby learning about the seeming generosity of a new communications medium that offered them pedagogies and pleasures at the flick of a switch. By giving herself over fully, flaws and all, to the spectator, Child was echoing the medium's generousness of spirit in her own invitation to enter into her culinary sanctum.

Yet, even as Child prepared the way for later versions of the cooking show that are fully focused on the payoff of consumption, like, say, *Nigella Bites*, we might contrast the sense of communal tie between host and guest on *The French Chef* with the later, privatized moments in which someone like Nigella Lawson luxuriates. In her show, Lawson pretends not to be acknowledging the camera's presence and instead to be absorbed in her own thoughts and bodily pleasures (for example, that bubble-filled bathtub). *Nigella Bites* certainly includes moments of direct address and looks at the camera, but the show's visual stylistics participate in the pretense that we are merely (and surreptitiously) peeking in on a woman's pleasures that are all her own and not necessarily to be shared (or, at best, are to be shared by the special, often upper-crusty on-screen people who are already part of her world and are privileged enough to be invited to the parties that precede her final moments of private pleasure). This seems in keeping with the possessive individualism of the cultural moment that Lawson represents and that is all about making sure one's own needs and pleasures are met first and foremost. In contrast, there was a sense of givingness in Julia Child's historical moment that is less apparent in the later period of hosted television. If Child belongs to a legacy of TV hosts, it is necessary to see that such hosting was also about the seeming generosity of folksy, even middlebrow, experts whose mission it was to explain the world to those less knowledgeable. The 1950s and 1960s gave rise to a "cult of expertise" in which television figures served as popular teachers for all sorts of subjects, high and low. Undoubtedly, the process of invitation and initiation into Julia Child's world was less hushed than, say, that of Jackie Kennedy's White House tour, and perhaps less overladen with an aura of technocratic expertise than, say, *Mr. Wizard*, the highly popular and user-friendly science show that ran through 1964 (although Child would, like Mr. Wizard, become enamored over the years of all sorts of gadgets and technologies—ordinary kitchen items but also blowtorches and other gizmos), and it was accompanied by boisterous levity, rather than high-culture seriousness. Yet, like these others, she was a great, welcoming host.

Clearly, then, Julia Child mattered to the 1960s, but she did so in her own fashion and in her own realm of influence: as a domestic instructor, as an entertainer, as an adept of television performance, and, perhaps, as a cultural initiator who invited women and men to think differently about one aspect of activity in the home.

There were, indeed, lessons other than culinary to be gained from Child's television appearances, including lessons about how to watch television itself and enjoy its offering of can-do intimacy. This was also the pedagogy of this bit of popular culture. *The French Chef* asks the spectator to witness the *performance* of an identity or, more specifically, of the embodied identity that was Julia Child—what she referred to as "the performance of me" (a phrase the Child biographer Laura Shapiro adopts as the chapter title for her discussion specifically of *The French Chef*).[12]

Watching Child was often an eye-opening education about some of the expansive things a personality on television could do and could be—and could do and be in a venue, the home kitchen, that had often been assumed to be a site of non-adventurous domestic conformity. At the same time, it must be said, it is not necessarily the case that Child's performance of a larger-than-life selfhood, on display for all to witness, encouraged direct identification on the part of the viewer. One watched Julia Child, one enjoyed her, and perhaps one even imitated her, but that didn't mean that somehow one imaginatively set out *to become her.* Certainly, Child's non-dogmatic, chatty, and intimate approach to pedagogy made the spectator into somewhat more than a passive figure who simply had to do slavishly what one was told (unlike, say, the targeted reader of the *I Hate to Cook Book,* who was commanded by its author to be a routinized rule follower of the utmost sort). Child's personable offer of intimacy brought viewers into her world but in the guise of warmly, even heartily, welcomed guests, not as dogmatic copies of herself. Child offered up a personality that others might try to impersonate (as with that voice) yet could not incarnate. It is perhaps fitting that one episode, "Invitation to Lunch," has Child showing off a table setting in her studio-set kitchen (that is, not in the dining room) and announcing that the meal this time is going to be informal and served in the kitchen since a guest is coming to lunch— namely, "You," as she puts it, to you the spectator—who, of course, will not really be cooking (and not actually eating, even if fans often wrote that they felt they could almost touch and taste the food) but "simply" watching, with whatever degree of vital enjoyment and emotional investment, as Child does the cooking and runs the show. "You" the viewer are there with Julia but as her guest, not as somehow a version of herself.

One way to capture the difference Julia Child made in the American culinary landscape of the time is to resort to contrast and see what cooking instruction by means of visual aid was like at the beginning of the 1960s but without the lively, even wild means by which Child used television to embody cooking as a veritable way of life. In this respect, there is perhaps no document more curious—but also more representative and more revealing both of the stereotypes and, perhaps, of many of the actual practices of American culinary activity in the postwar period—than a cookbook that came out in 1960: *Knox On-Camera Recipes,* published by the Knox Gelatine company and designed to offer new takes on standard fare of the 1950s brought about by the addition of Knox gelatin to each and every recipe. For instance, that old stand-by, Waldorf salad, became "exceptionally fine" when transformed into a molded concoction dominated by a mass of gelatin into which were folded apples, celery, and pecans.[13]

Not all American food in the period was like this, but a lot was. The Knox cookbook is—in several ways, as we'll see—an oddity (in an age in which many cookbooks, like other mass commodities, turned to gimmickry to stand out from the crowd), but it is also of a piece with the clichés of commercialized food and its standardization in the period, and it thereby merits a closer look. There is, for instance, the insistent emphasis on the branded product, an artificial and engineered product at that, and one whose very commercial origin stands as the guarantor of its effectiveness and as the source of its appeal to the happy homemaker (or rather, an unhappy homemaker made happy by the introduction of such a shortcutting product into her life). Later, we'll see how such plugging of brand names was anathema to Julia Child. She tried to be in a very different world from one in which cooking was about often awkward attempts to get branded products into every recipe.

In addition, the Knox gelatin cookbook gives the idea that its branded product, while the result of the sort of wondrous scientific discovery in which postwar America had a deep investment, has a magical transformative power: Whatever the controlled, calculated experimentation that went on in the labs to perfect the product, the end result in the hands of the homemaker required little effort and just needed to be added to banal recipes to make them sing and zing with all the virtues of modern life at its best. There is little investment of self in the employment of such a product. One has simply to agree with it, deploy it, and watch the results magically appear. Here it matters that the product is a gelatin-based substance because gelatin itself (like its close cousin, Jell-O, so much an icon of the 1950s) seems eminently up-to-date (no matter how old the formula for it actually is). It resonates with an emphatic sense of modernity. Like plastic, like Plexiglas or Mylar and other translucent products of the period, gelatin combines transparency and substance and appears fully to be a marvel of modern manmadeness. Furthermore, gelatin possesses a sort of omnipotent ubiquity. In it, endless sorts of foodstuffs (fruit, meat, vegetable, and so on) can hover; gelatin thus becomes a perfect medium for assemblage of ingredients into the perfect postwar dish. Whether there were actually as many Jell-O fruit molds and other such concoctions in the 1950s and 1960s as the stereotypes of cuisine in the decade would have it, the very nature of the product—shimmering, radiant with colors that looked artificial, coagulative and agglutinative, and so on—made it seem appropriate to the age.[14]

Two central and striking traits of *Knox On-Camera Recipes* as a cookbook resonantly reflect the commodification and massification of everyday American life in this historical moment even as they seem to do so in unique, eccentric fashion. First, notably, the book presents its recipes as if they were coming to the audience *as a television show*. *Knox On-Camera Recipes* assumed as its conceit that home cooks were so used to getting their knowledge of the contemporary world from television that the short cookbook also should resemble a television show, even though Knox's book really had nothing to do with any actual TV program. Thus, within the static medium of a book, the visual format of *Knox On-Camera Recipes* sets out to approximate the experience of television viewing, even in the absence of any actual television show on which it might have been imagined to be based. On the one hand, the top of each page announced the recipe in large type and offered a color image of the expected, desired result; on the other hand, the rest of the page appeared in black and white and displayed a sequence of photos that followed the steps of the recipe and that were cropped specifically to evoke the shape of a TV screen. As the preface to the cookbook explains, "The pictures we have selected are the high points of the action that goes into making each dish. They are like 'still shots' taken from a TV film, and we hope they make each recipe much clearer . . . and easier to follow. We hope . . . that this, a new kind of recipe presentation, will result in a new kind of cooking success for you where it counts for most . . . around your family table."

Television, this cookbook seems to be saying to ordinary Americans, is our fundamental way of seeing, of knowing, of learning. It is our popular pedagogy. The cover of *Knox On-Camera Recipes* also amplifies this conceit that television is the most natural, the most appropriate, and the most efficacious venue for culinary education by picturing

Waldorf Salad

MAKES 6 SERVINGS • 103 CALORIES PER SERVING

Everyone enjoys Waldorf Salad. New on the salad scene is an exceptionally fine variation of this popular favorite.

INGREDIENTS

1 envelope Knox Unflavored Gelatine	¼ cup vinegar or lemon juice
⅓ cup sugar	2 cups diced tart apples
½ teaspoon salt	½ cup diced celery
1½ cups water, divided	¼ cup chopped pecans

1. Mix gelatine, sugar and salt thoroughly in a small saucepan.

2. Add ½ cup of the water.

3. Place over low heat, stirring constantly until gelatine is dissolved.

4. Remove from heat and stir in remaining 1 cup water, vinegar or lemon juice.

5. Chill mixture to unbeaten egg white consistency.

6. Fold in diced apples, chopped celery and chopped nuts.

TV cooking?

(in a color drawing) a young woman in housewifely garb standing on a kitchen set while a production crew around the periphery films her from a studio filled with lights, microphones, and a television camera. The woman faces outward with her hands forming a circle around the food she is offering as she smiles pertly. (Purists will notice that there is a mismatch between what her hands are shown to be doing in this long view and what they are up to in the close-up view on the television monitor in the scene.)

While in this way the cover of *Knox On-Camera Recipes* gives body to the figure of the television cook, it is a relatively generic, identity-less one. This could be any housewife (and, in any case, it's a drawing, not a photograph of any real woman). Moreover, when one turns past the cover to the recipes themselves, the full-body image of this anonymous housewife is left behind, and the discrete, televisually cropped photos that break each recipe down into key steps offer only close-ups of the cook's *hands* performing the tasks. Here, the second striking particularity of this cookbook enters into play. The assumption is that the specific identity and personality of the Knox cook are irrelevant to the food preparation itself. You don't need to know the cook; you just need to see her hands at work. If these anonymous hands can do it, so can anyone's. In contrast, remember that while *The French Chef*'s "Introducing Charlotte Malakoff" episode showed us, in its first image, a close-up of hands, it immediately overlaid them with a distinctive voice and then expanded the field of perception outward to insist on the inescapably distinctive presence and personality of Julia Child.

The sort of image of anonymous labor purveyed by the gelatin cookbook offers a common understanding of the work of the housewife cook in the period of the 1950s into the 1960s. Her activity was imagined essentially as a manual task, sometimes even an onerous one, as Bracken's *I Hate to Cook Book* might have it, but whether pictured as easy or as burdensome, cooking had little to do with any emotional investment of self. Personality had little role to play in the kitchen, which was, instead, a space where one had to go about the mission at hand with, at worst, resigned submission or, at best, a perky cheerfulness (like the generic housewife on the Knox cookbook cover) that might be little more than a self-deceiving masquerade assumed to paper over the fact that cooking was a dirty, burdensome business, but someone had to do it.[15]

Visually, Julia Child's *The French Chef* puts us in a fully other universe, and the results—in terms of entertainment, the emotional connection between viewer and performer, and the very meaning of the act of cooking—are astounding. Her personality matters absolutely to the task at hand. Yet it must be admitted that while Julia Child always unflaggingly extolled the brisk pleasure she felt that cooking should entail and emphatically rejected any notion of cooking as a loathsome burden, not everything about the world of Peg Bracken and the *Knox On-Camera Recipes* was foreign to her take on culinary activity. Child, for example, accepted the possibility that in some cases commercially prepared products (such as canned goods, pre-made mixtures, frozen foods, and so on) could be substituted for similar foodstuffs made from long preparation. The caveats, though, were several. Above all, there had to be no sacrifice of taste. For instance, any ersatz quality to the store-bought item had to be remediable through creative additions by the cook. Thus, to take one example, canned stock was an acceptable substitute for the homemade variety, crafted through long simmering of hand-chopped vegetables and carcasses, as long as one added spices and seasonings to make the commercialized product taste natural and take on accents derived from personal intercession and initiative. As important, shortcuts enabled by commercial products were permissible as long as they didn't substitute for the whole activity of culinary preparation and imply thereby that cooking was indeed a pleasure-less burden to be avoided or foreshortened whenever possible. Child believed fundamentally that cooking should be enjoyed, and she believed, more generally, that the best means to a person's self-realization in any domain, culinary or otherwise, was through energetic engagement in vital activity, not through avoidance of it. In an art such as cooking, something certainly happened to the objects at hand—literally at hand insofar as one engaged in manual activity to transform things—but something also happened to the subject engaging in the actions: By leaping in with one's full self, one's full bodily engagement, one took pleasure and one grew as a person. To shortcut the culinary process would be to shortcut the cultivation of self.

Bodily display

With the debut of her first television series, *The French Chef*, Julia
Child's personality came into its own to make a claim for an un-dogmatic culinary pedagogy. While there are obvious continuities from her
first hit book, *Mastering the Art of French Cooking* (1961), to *The French
Chef* (1963 and after), there are also differences, and they have to do in
large degree with popular television's technique of embodiment and
creation of celebrity, even for someone like Julia Child, who at first look
might not have seemed—or might not have imagined herself—destined
for stardom.

As majestic as *Mastering the Art of French Cooking* was in its historical moment, one can read it in vain for any biographically specific
glimpse of the larger-than-life personality of Julia Child herself. Certainly, the book is written (in fact, co-written) with enthusiasm and an
engaging energy that is personable and even personal, but no specific
personality emerges from behind it. If one didn't know Julia Child, one

Tasty literature. 1960s cartoon by Gus Arriola;

courtesy Mona Arriola McNamara.

couldn't really imagine her from her book. But once one has seen Child on *The French Chef*, she is impossible to forget.

Let's return, for instance, to the episode "Introducing Charlotte Malakoff" and compare the specific moments in which *Mastering* and this *French Chef* episode each admonish the viewer not to buy ladyfingers from the store but to make them from scratch. The book certainly expresses an editorial point of view, an entire philosophy of homespun cookery, but stylistically it does so in a relatively commanding and somewhat dry, impersonal fashion:

> *Warning*
> Do not attempt any dessert calling for a mold lined with ladyfingers unless you have ladyfingers of premium quality—dry and tender, not spongy and limp. Inferior ladyfingers, unfortunately the only kind usually available in bakeries, will debase an otherwise remarkable dessert.[16]

Conversely, the television rendition gives us an outpouring of adjectives as Child dramatizes her heartfelt horror at store-bought ladyfingers (all of this, of course, in a voice that goes up and down in register as she sputters out the words): "This loathsome, horrid, limp, soggy thing that's called a ladyfinger and they're just, they're just absolutely disgusting, and if you use them in any decent dessert, it just wouldn't [here she gropes for the right words] . . . I mean it just wouldn't go. But if you make homemade ladyfingers like this, which are nice dry little cookies made out of sponge-cake batter, I think that ladyfingers will mean a delight to you." The dialogue, of course, is keyed to engrossing visuals in which this strapping woman leans over, first to bend a limp, store-bought ladyfinger back and forth, then to demonstrate triumphantly how the home-baked variety breaks in crisp, visually pleasing fashion. Everything is physicalized and dynamized—both Child's demonstration and the televisual presentation of it through camera placement, movement, and editing. Moreover, through the full course of the episode, the television version of the recipe gives us humor, suspense, dramatic personification of food, odes to personal pleasure (when trimming the ladyfingers, Child says the ends should be saved for the chef's own degustation), anecdotal digression, displays of gustatory delight, vivid demonstrations of the kinetic working of gadgetry, and dynamically physical presentation, all of this wrapped up in the inspiring performance of a chipper and plucky personality who confronts a challenge with simultaneous can-do effortlessness and lots of physical exertion. (When she does something that really requires force, Child is often wont to emit a quite vocal "Erp.")

Revealingly, the visual aid that *Mastering* as a book employed to accompany its text was itself depersonalizing. *Mastering* used drawings that Paul Child sketched from photographs he had taken of his wife's culinary activity but that focused on her hands doing the various tasks, with no full-body view (again, that sort of depersonalization that comes from an emphasis on the literally manual task). Visually, we are indeed not far here from the *Knox On-Camera Recipes*. Moreover, these drawings are angled from the approximate point of view of the chef himself or herself, as if to put the spectator directly into the active role. As Julia Child would explain the technique in introductory comments to a later volume, *From Julia Child's Kitchen*: "Notice when you look at the illustrated directions on how to carve a roast chicken, or how to toss an omelette or to form a loaf of French bread that you are looking at the picture from the angle at which you will be doing the work."[17] In other words, in her cookbooks, Child emphasized not her own personality but a more anonymous manual dexterity.

Interestingly, in her original thoughts for the visual style of the *French Chef* television series, Child had imagined a camera placement behind her and somewhat peering down over her shoulder, which would have put the camera/spectator more directly in her position and which therefore would have been closer to what the drawings in *Mastering the Art of French Cooking* set out to accomplish. Thus, as she wondered in the memorandum that she had drafted for WGBH-TV in 1962 to explain her proposal for the television show that would become *The French Chef*, "Could camera shoot over the cook's shoulder so that everything is viewed as from the cook's view? (Camera work on recent TV heart surgery program, 'Breakthrough' was especially good from detail point of view)."[18] Revealingly, Child persisted in her desire for first-person camera, long after the more exteriorized visual style of *The French Chef*, where the camera faces her and never adopts her point of view (except perhaps in overhead shots looking down into a dish), had clearly proved to be a tremendous success. As late as 1973, when she shot some lead-ins for the BBC, which was testing six episodes of *The French Chef* for the English market, she talked about over-the-shoulder, first-person point of view as a missed opportunity, one that she clearly had longed to try out and now was militating for anew. As she put it, wistfully perhaps, "On our TV [series], we have a cover camera and a close-up camera, and also overhead mirrors for the close-up camera (not successful entirely since they do not reverse the image). I am used to tipping pots and so forth toward the camera to show what's happening. But if we could do some shooting over the shoulder, so the viewer could see operations as though he were doing it himself, that would be far the best system. Because of budget and lighting problems, we've never been able to try this out."[19]

Yet, contrary to Child's persistent feelings about the best way to film her cooking (i.e., from the cook's own point of view), it may well be that the more exteriorized perspective that her television series ended up adopting, with the camera generally facing Child, better helped foster viewers' engagement in the televised action, the culinary process, and the physicality of it all. As the history of cinema bears out, putting the camera in the position of a first-person point of view, as Child had wanted to do, actually may tend to distance the spectator from emotional connection with the camera as character, since it can seem forced and unusual (such as, for instance, in the notorious failed film noir experiment *The Lady in the Lake* [1946], where the camera is supposed to approximate the point of view of Philip Marlowe but instead comes off as a gimmick, and a clumsy one at that). By settling on a set of camera positions external to Child, the visual rhetoric of *The French Chef* actually makes her performance more visceral, more direct, more involving, and, in a way, more "first person."

I will have occasion at various points of this study to talk about Julia Child's own sense of modesty (despite her evident flamboyance of presence and performance), and her self-effacing side was no doubt at work in this desire to have no more than her hands shown on-screen. But along with modesty, there was—especially at the beginning of her television appearances—the possibility quite simply that Child had no conception of how interesting and compelling a television personality she could be. As her biographer Laura Shapiro recounts, Child was dismayed by her first appearances on television and throughout her career she persisted in worrying about the impact she was having as a television figure. The idea of not being visible by having the camera adopt one's point of view is in keeping with this modesty and anxiety about her person and personality.

Nevertheless, *The French Chef* moves away from veritable identification with the chef's point of view by putting the camera outside the action and by offering frequent full shots of Julia Child herself (and close-ups of her hands, but again from a removed point of view). The camera stays back from her, exterior to her. It often keeps more than a bit away from her as well, as if too much facial closeness would betray the intimacy that is fostered when one can see her in full form as a fully engaging personality. Indeed, in the rare (and generally unintended) instances in which the camera gets too close to Child's face, she goes all squinty; the perspective flattens her visage; and everything seems a little off. (In contrast, today's cooking shows centered on voluptuous women are often all about getting in very close indeed, as when we see every sinuous, sensuous swallow down the gullet by Nigella Lawson, Rachel Ray, or Giada De Laurentiis.) It is also the case that the camera stays in front of Child (or, at most, to the side of her), almost never crossing an imaginary line that might put it and the spectator in Child's own perceptual field.[20] In contrast, we might think of a more recent cooking show, *The Iron Chef*, where the camera is all about getting into the stadium with the performers to accompany them in their frenetic activity and even to seem a close participant in their efforts. But the intense proximity in *The Iron Chef* is not necessarily the same as intimacy and the sense of knowing a person, and it may well be that *The French Chef*'s sober maintenance of somewhat distance from, and exteriority to, its performer actually increases the impression of psychical closeness to her and emotional complicity with her.

In this way, of course, Julia Child's presence made all the difference for *The French Chef*. Think again of those first moments from "Introducing Charlotte Malakoff." On display is a pedagogy that is heartfelt (all those adjectives that pile up to describe just how bad store-bought ladyfingers are), that seems spontaneous (the groping for the right words that implies this is an authentic performance of self, not a rehearsed script), that is intimate (the spectator is addressed, directly recognized as a "you" out there in TV land but also as a "we" who shares Child's own experience of bad commercialized food), that is accessible (ladyfingers can be analyzed into a few everyday ingredients with which everyone is already acquainted), and that nonetheless knows with some sophistication and some surety of purpose (manifest in that emphasis on how the wrong foodstuff in a meal "just wouldn't go") that there are standards in which tasting good merges with having good taste, to use two terms that Charlie the Tuna, the cartoon spokesperson for one (in)famous commercial product, was having trouble sorting out starting with his first appearance in 1961, the year before the pilot episodes of *The French Chef*.

If the ultimate goal of *The French Chef* was to produce pleasurable and good-tasting food, the path to doing so should be pleasurable and involving as well. In Child's hands, the functional and temporally progressive structure of the cooking show—a recipe followed from beginning to end—offered not just a raw chronology but a narrative, a story that gave consequence and resonant meaning to the chronology of actions, and this created a sense of drama. For example, there was much suspense. Would Child be able to pull off a dish in the allotted time? Or, more pointedly, what disasters or setbacks might she encounter on the way to her inevitable comic kitchen triumph? From the start, as the extensive fan mail Child and WGBH received attests, viewers liked watching a show that had errors and imperfections. They liked the very fact that mistakes occurred; they liked that Child admitted her weaknesses (for example, in "Charlotte Malakoff," she declared herself untalented at spooning out ladyfinger batter and admitted she preferred to use a canvas bag with a snout); and they liked that she tried to repair the damage done when she could. Child's own manner mixed firmness and confidence with the constant implication that she was really only one step ahead of the game (if that much) and that things could fall apart (sometimes literally) at a moment's notice. Even Child's tremulous voice seemed to signal a certain vulnerability and a somewhat less than total grasp of the situation as she groped for words and as she breathily gasped in search of composure.

Viewers liked that a person whose very appearance on the public medium of television made her special was not so special that she wouldn't sometimes make mistakes, admit them, and set out to rectify them. This too was a major part of the instruction and a major part of the charm. For instance, at one point in "Charlotte Malakoff," Child says to add a few drops of almond extract to a batter and then gives the measure as "a quarter of a cup." A few moments later, she returns to this instruction and apologizes, with a self-deprecating, wry smile, by saying that she meant "half a teaspoon." Child's mistakes were also part of the drama of the show. How would she triumph over upsets—since she always did triumph in the end—and turn mistakes into positive lessons? This awareness that there always is the potential for disaster is yet again a way in which the cooking narrative becomes something more than a dry chronological account.[21]

Also contributing to the sense of an unfolding drama was the fact that this drama had its full cast of characters—not just Child herself but all the foods with which she was working and to whom she gave endearing personification. For instance, the presentation of "Charlotte Malakoff" as a veritable stage performer with a sidekick ("Lady Fingers," with the naming punning on aristocratic titles) transforms the narrative of cooking from simply rigorous instruction into a theatrical play with lively characters. If Child liked to show off food items because of the sheer pleasure in a sensuousness of touching, the physicality of direct contact with food as something intently visceral, she also possessed a dramatizing impulse that led her to turn ingredients into active and cherished participants in a gripping story. In Laura Shapiro's words, "The food seemed to be a live, spontaneous participant. Julia welcomed it warmly and gave everything she had to the relationship, parrying with the food, letting it surprise and delight her, very nearly bantering with it."[22]

By treating the food items as characters—sometimes even as people—Child was making them players in a play, and she was the stage director. For example, in an episode on sauces, she talks of Béarnaise and Hollandaise as siblings who come from the same stock (pun intended) but end up with different personalities. It's perhaps a similar sort of anthropomorphizing that leads her also to say that one of the sauces must be vigorously beaten as one beats a recalcitrant child(!). Or, as she puts it elsewhere in the episode, as a good postwar liberal, "Egg yolks are like people. They want to be understood; otherwise, they act like hoodlums and beatniks."

Offering a dramatically good show was always a primary goal. For example, in the upside-down mold whose content was not yet visible in the "Introducing Charlotte Malakoff" episode, there was the immediate production of suspense: What was under there? What did it look like? Years before the much less pedagogical cooking show *The Iron Chef* had secret ingredients rise out of the floor within clouds of fog while battling chefs looked on with awe, Child was already playing with the appeal of mystery, the slow reveal, the hidden substance gifted with aura. To cite another example, mentioned earlier as good pedagogy because of all the instructive lessons it packed in, her artichoke show began in close-up with its title ingredient obscured under opaque netting, which Child then dramatically pulled away as she ebulliently announced this unusual and even somewhat exotic and mysterious vegetable. It's worth noting, though, that in that specific case, the artichokes that were dramatically unveiled were ones in the process of being cooked (in other words, not yet a finished dish). In contrast, the Charlotte Malakoff hidden under the silver pot was a completed dish, and in

its status as a predictive depiction at the show's beginning of the anticipated end result, it stood as an enticing promise, an annunciation of
the dreamy payoff to this suspenseful drama. Even though the cooking
demonstration fundamentally takes place in a present tense that ad-
heres to chronology, many episodes of *The French Chef* operate under
the sign of a bountiful future held out as the reward to which the
kitchen labor will lead if all goes well. We are shown the end result *at
the beginning* to give us a glimpse of the utopia that awaits one at the
terminus of one's progress as a culinary pilgrim.

To reiterate, the fundamental difference that Julia Child's show
brought to culinary culture was that it rendered personality—or, at
least, her personality—indispensable. It was not merely that Child was
a presence on her show; more emphatically, she was, in the fact of her
presence, clearly making of her very material embodiment an argument for a way of life lived fully and joyfully, lived corporeally. To take
just one more example, when she outlines alternative methods for
congealing the eggs on a show about omelets—simply shaking the pan
physically with one's hands until the eggs form together *or* mechanically shaping the eggs with fork or spoon—and then tells the viewer
that the shaking method is the best, her justification is not that it leads
to better taste or is more efficient but that it is more "fun." *Fun*, indeed,
may be the most recurrent word on *The French Chef*. Given what so
much instructional television had been like before she came on the
scene, a commitment to fun like the one she demonstrated could also
make all the difference for the medium's promise as popular pedagogy.

The utility of Julia Child's televisual demonstrations had to do, then,
not just with things culinary, such as the usefulness of the recipes and
the techniques for which she offered instruction. There were multiple
levels of enjoyment and benefit, including that of sheer aesthetic con-
templation. The presentation of the seductive and inviting French dish
was in itself an instruction to the viewer in how to look at television and
how thereby to appreciate the excellence both of the thing viewed (the
food) and of the medium of viewing (this wondrous new box that could
bring such images into the home). In a study of postwar hobbyism,
Steven Gelber asserts, "By mid-decade [of the 1950s] only reading and
watching television were more popular forms of recreation than do-it-

yourself among married men."[23] In the 1960s, however, a television show such as *The French Chef*, airing on public television, could make the very act of TV watching seem a form of do-it-yourself activity and could combat notions of television viewing as wasteful and slothful.

Might not the very fact that one could take pleasures from TV watching itself be a pedagogy of sorts—the lesson that in some part of this particular historical moment, enjoyment (and, in particular, enjoyment through the mass medium of television) mattered and might readily be at hand? In the early 1960s, the demonstration of someone having fun could be a life lesson, an instruction in a way to perform one's being in the world.[24] Julia Child's public entrance on the culinary scene coincided with the beginning years of the Kennedy administration, and she and the president (whom she revered) shared a sense of Americanness as grounded in demonstrations of energy and vitality. The Kennedy White House set a national tone that became a key aspect of the early 1960s moment in America—a sense of life as fun, energy, and action (for example, the elegant Jackie Kennedy complemented by John playing football on the White House lawn and promoting images of youthful "vim and vigor"—key words in his public discourse).[25]

In a sharp essay, Scott Bukatman has suggested that the capacity for direct, vibrant action is a centrally defining trait of personality in American popular and high culture of the postwar period—what he refers to as a "mythos of physicality."[26] Bukatman too is dealing with U.S. appropriations of European culture similar to Julia Child's odes to the American potential for "mastering the art of French cooking." In Bukatman's case, the focus is on both MGM's attempt to render the life of Vincent Van Gogh in its splashy film *Lust for Life* and the equally "splashy" efforts, after their own fashion, of the "action painters" of abstract expressionism. Bukatman reiterates the famous argument of Serge Guilbault (in *How New York Stole the Idea of Modern Art*) that postwar America, within the context of new geopolitics, needed to show the world that it had culture as well as military might on its side, and this involved a co-optation of European aesthetic traditions to its own ends. A key part of the process involved representing Parisian ventures in the arts as effete, artificial, decadent even, compared with American efforts, which were taken to be earthy, direct, and authentic.

Biographers of Julia Child like to talk of her as a Californian and a Bostonian, but it is also worth remembering that her father's side of the family came through Illinois. Child possessed some of that strapping, no-nonsense, enthusiastic vitality and even boisterousness of the larger-than-life Midwesterner. The Frenchness she offered up on television was Americanized to the core. Much of the cultural work that an action figure such as Julia Child performed in the period was to mediate an American go-getter, frontier spirit and a European concern with aesthetic refinement. Out of this mediation would come a sense of the rarefied realm of high culture (in this case, haute cuisine) as itself an arena for Americanized action, physicality, personal immersion in the arts of making, and so on. In her book on how American popular television of the 1950s and 1960s was more receptive to modern art than the rampant early 1960s cliché of such television as a "vast wasteland" would have it, Lynn Spigel argues that American television was able to be open to modernist styles and modernist experimentation precisely because it found affinities with those aspects of modern art that could be assimilated to mythic American qualities of directness, innocence, authenticity, and so on. As she puts it, "Although Abstract Expressionist painting seems the direct opposite of the variety show's populist 'boffo' appeal, leading art critics valued precisely the same formal qualities in painting that the leading television critics valued in variety shows: liveness, kinesis, spontaneity, and presence."[27] Overwhelmingly, these were the very virtues that viewers found in Julia Child. There is, for instance, a striking regularity to her fan mail in its terms of praise: honesty, directness, simplicity, forthrightness, willingness to plunge in. These were virtues that she brought to cooking and to television with every bit of her being, with every bit of her body.

As with action painting, what mattered in French cooking in the American style was not just the final result but the process by which the skilled fabricator had built up an aesthetically vibrant object through bold, dramatic, visible actions and exertions of energy. Indeed, in the black-and-white episodes, the completed dishes often have a smeary look to them that may even be said to resemble the messy canvases of the abstract expressionists. Like the paintings, the culinary concoction is built up step-by-step, and the viewer can see all the labor expressed vividly in the final results.

Throughout this study, then, I will outline the appeal that Julia Child's performative actions in the realm of cuisine held for the 1960s, particularly as they appeared in the popular medium of television. Child is very much a key figure of her age, but she hasn't so much been analyzed as admired (the two are not incompatible, of course), and there is little attempt to place her show in the history of the medium of television.[28] From the earliest moments of celebrity and adulation that came with her book *Mastering the Art of French Cooking*, and then with her television series *The French Chef*, a lot has been written about Julia Child, little of it scholarly in intent. It is striking, for instance, to realize that there have been few attempts to analyze and examine as a cultural icon this personality that so many Americans took to heart.

No doubt, this is, to a large degree, understandable. Child was a figure of rambunctious and infectious spontaneity, and there is a risk that any *study* of her could lose sight of that and dissolve her into a mere symbol of larger forces. There are reasons, then, for the lightness of much of the writing on Julia Child. The very intimacy that so many readers and viewers enjoy with her encourages a discourse of appreciation and admiration in which anything too analytic, too probing into the reasons for her appeal, would seem bothersome. Julia Child was the sort of beloved figure of contagious enthusiasm and inspiring personal empowerment whose joyful approach to the arts of living fans want to share, not intellectualize. For example, famously (or infamously, depending on your point of view) when one Child fan, Julie Powell, assumed as her life goal of the moment to undertake every recipe in *Mastering the Art of French Cooking* in a year's time, and post on a blog how her attempts wove into the ups and downs of her personal life, the initiative could easily stand as an indulgent oddity of the electronic age in which the Internet allows anyone to advertise his or her tastes, desires, and pleasures by means of anecdotes. But it could also seem inevitable that someone would want to do this. Powell's claim to link her own identity to Child's, made even in the title of the book she published based on her experience, *Julie and Julia*, is perhaps only an extreme version of the impulse that leads so many fans to attempt impersonations of Child as if she were a figure whom one eminently and endlessly needs to embody, if only in imitation.[29]

Of course, most of those who engage in mimicry around Child do so with awareness that it is a game. Child was generally too distinctively zany to inspire that sort of celebrity fandom that is about merging one's own life with the object of one's veneration. One might imitate Julia Child for the fun of it, but one doesn't set out to become her (even *Julie and Julia* is about how Powell's imitation of Child's cooking worked to very different ends in a very different life context). Intimacy with Child was often tempered by a sense of her as a cultural eccentric; here, we have a second reason that there hasn't been much in the way of critical analysis. Child could come across as a figure of fun-filled campiness, and there's the assumption that a phenomenon of that kind is sort of self-explanatory. In other words, it's assumed that Child entertained America because she was entertaining, and no more explanation and analysis need be ventured.

Of course, there's *always* a risk of over-interpretation when the scholar approaches popular culture and searches for its meanings, but surely the fact that certain figures come as celebrities to captivate the populace in a particular moment in history could be something we might want to explain and seek some cultural lesson about. The common rejoinder to serious analysis of light popular culture is that such culture is "just entertainment," but then it becomes all the more compelling to wonder why we would invest—monetarily, psychically, emotionally—so much in something that is "just" that. In the case of Julia Child, the general reluctance to want to understand why we take pleasure in our popular culture no doubt is amplified by a specific resistance to taking seriously—and assuming the cultural meaningful-ness of—things related to the world of food. Food is just too physical and too trivially ordinary to seem worthy of cultural explanation.[30] Along with an anti-intellectualism that is wary of explaining our every-day world, there is also a snobbish intellectualism that assumes that only certain things—supposedly higher parts of the human experience, such as the mind at the top of the body, rather than the crass functions such as digestion lower down—are appropriate for advanced critical thought. In its own way, this intellectualism is also anti-intellectualist in its dogmatic assumption that some things not merely should not be studied but *cannot* be studied to any productive end.[31]

As Roland Barthes famously observed in "The Myth Today," the popular assumption about popular culture is governed by tautology: that that sort of culture is what it is, obviously, and needs no analysis.[32] Food is food, and it is better eaten than thought about, especially by intellectuals. Julia Child was enjoyable because she was enjoyable, and nothing more needs to be said. (And if anyone dare say anything more, it can only be an example of academic overkill.)

Obviously, tautologically, fun is fun. But why something comes off as fun and why a particular culture needs fun when it does and in the form in which it does are already questions of a society and its values. It is to such questions that I devote the pages of this study. What about *The French Chef* made it work as it did in its historical moment? How did it compare with previous efforts toward a televisual pedagogy of the kitchen? What did it mean that, through the electronics of the small screen, an energetic woman came into American households and talked about an activity typically of the home (cooking, that is) but in ways that might transcend the immediate limits of domestic space, insofar as her cooking lessons were also life lessons about social mobility, about the discovery of foreign culture, and about a personal enjoyment and fulfillment that promised to go beyond domestic drudgery? Child was offering not just the steps of a recipe but any number of additional insights: about the purposes of this or that technique, about the values (aesthetic and gustatory) of this or that food, and about the wonderful and distinct and elevating qualities of the glorious country (France) from which much of the gastronomy derived. And she was offering insights also about modern American ways of living. This makes her very key to her times and very much deserving of critical analysis.

Studying Julia Child, then, means looking at larger contexts in which she was inscribed—and it means comparing her version of television celebrity and popular pedagogy with other popular cultural practices of her time. But it also means looking at Child's television work itself in detail and capturing the specificity of her appeal within the historical moment.

In a famous assertion in *Search for a Method*, his philosophical reckoning with the status of biography in relation to broader social theory, Jean-Paul Sartre cautioned that the poet "Valéry is a petit bourgeois individual, no doubt about it. But not every petit bourgeois intellectual is Valéry." Sartre was reminding the social critic that, in trying to figure out the place of any individual in his or her times, the need also exists to capture what is irreducible about that individual (even as he or she does in fact sum up something about the times).[33]

To turn Child into a mere mirror of her moment would be to miss the special ways she had something particular—and perhaps peculiar—to contribute to that moment, something that resonated with it precisely because she was like no one else. It is thus by invoking what was seemingly unique about Child and her television series that we can best understand why her performance and pedagogy resounded so strongly and so particularly in its time. She was unique, she was different, and that very much made her an icon for the American 1960s.

The following pages, then, chronicle how Julia Child came to make such a difference in American cookery, in American television, and in American culture. The next chapter provides a history of cooking demonstrations on American television before *The French Chef* in order to continue clarifying just what was so particular and different about her in ways that came so much to resonate with the times. Chapter 3 concerns French food, popular television, and popular television's presentation of French food and what these meant for the debut of *The French Chef* in 1963. This sets the stage for chapters 4–7, which chronicle the show's creation, its day-to-day production, and the history of its run across two iterations (a black-and-white version in the 1960s and a color version in the 1970s). Finally, chapter 8 returns to cultural theory: I examine the worldview that the typical kitchen set of cooking shows establishes and how Child's particular take on culinary demonstration offered both the comfort of reassurance and the excitement of open-ended adventure to Americans of the 1960s.

2 Television Cookery B.C. (Before Child)

The television kitchen is as popular as the kitchen in your own home.
—Ellen Pennell, *Women on TV*, 1954

Programming is a subtle art understood by some of the best French chefs,
and their method of arranging cuisine deserves study by TV personnel
interested in the mystic business of determining how to please the public.
—Carroll O'Meara, *Television Program Production*, 1955

When I mentioned to friends and colleagues that I was writing about Julia Child and *The French Chef,* they reliably would say how much fun she was and what a great research topic she would be. Then they would add, as a secondary assertion, "And she had the very first cooking show on TV, didn't she?" The assumption of her first-ness in cooking television is common. But in fact, kitchen demonstrations—both as segments in broader shows about the pathways of modern American everyday life and as full-length programs in their own right (usually a half-hour in length)—proliferated on both commercial and educational television from the immediate postwar moment, when broadcast television came back from the hiatus of war, up to the 1960s, when Julia Child made her mark. A few traces remain of these early shows in short profiles of this or that TV cook in local papers or in television trade journals, in the rare cookbooks by early television cooks, in bits and pieces of surviving film, in fan postings on the Internet, and in a very few scholarly studies.[1]

Insofar as this book is specifically about the differences Julia Child brought to both television and the pedagogy of cooking in America, the story of what came before her matters, because we see both how many of the conventions she worked with—and within—were established early on and how they were given new, breakthrough inflections when Child took them over to her own way of doing things. The difference Child made was a difference within a genre that had become quite commonplace—in the sense of seeming to be everywhere on commercial television at the time and of seeming to have become quite banal, trivial even. Beyond the sheer historical interest that the early history of cooking's encounter with television can hold for the researcher into the past of everyday American popular culture, it is also worth trying to reconstruct the history of the cooking show before *The French Chef*, since the very fact that there were so many such programs can help us understand something about the particular success of Child's show and what that success signifies culturally and historically. Earlier, I argued that, through her energetic personality, Julia Child brought a new dynamism, sense of fun, and dramatic visuality to television cooking. Clearly, *The French Chef* had special virtues that made it stand out, many of them no doubt intrinsic to the show and to the ways Child offered her own particular take on the practices of the kitchen when seen on TV.

Today's explosion of cooking shows in an astounding variety of forms—game shows, travelogues, reality shows, and on and on—has made it seem, perhaps, that there are unlimited ways to film culinary activity. But if the intent is to capture acts of everyday cooking that will indeed have instructional import, there are probably specific compositional set-ups, narrative trajectories, styles of filming, and so on that make more sense than others. Almost inevitably, it would seem, the television cooking demonstration is impelled to adopt a fairly sober, fairly transparent, fairly teacherly style of exposition. After all, if instruction is the point, there should be little that interferes with the conveyance of the content of that instruction. There's even a name for this in the food TV business: the basic, purified genre of cooking instruction is termed "dump and stir," which suggests a pedagogy reduced to the barest representation of the barest of kitchen activity.

Whatever the variants, large or small, there is a regularity to the look and action of postwar kitchen cooking shows (and it remains in quite a number of today's programs, despite the extent to which they overwhelmingly submerge the pedagogy beneath glitzy showmanship and seductive visual effect). Some of this is a regularity of content: To the extent that the goal is to teach something about what to do with food by cooking it (in whatever recommended fashion), it perhaps predictably makes sense to plunk a person in a kitchen and simply film him or her going through the act (although one can imagine a more minimal form—for instance, the crawl of worded instructions on the screen with no live action). The visual style of the typical television cooking demonstration will logically then be functional and utilitarian, as the camerawork seeks to convey each step in the chronological unfolding of the instructions for the recipe. Here, though, there *can* be alternative ways to capture the action. For example, to the extent that cooking involves both hands-on contact with food and utensils and broader bodily actions—such as putting preparations in an oven—there may be options for a greater or lesser field of visual action, from close-ups on hands to full body views. When personality comes into play, choices about what to show come to matter very much, as we'll see in chapter 5, when we look closely at the visual style of *The French Chef*.

At the same time, it must be said that some visual traits of *The French Chef* probably would not have seemed that different from the look of many other cooking shows airing at the time. Conventional ways of showing kitchen activity on television were codified from the advent of such programming. Thus, from early on in the history of the cooking show genre, the preferred visual presentation was to have the cook, with or without assistants, standing in a kitchen either before or behind a table or counter and against the back wall of the kitchen at which there was a sink, more counters, hanging appliances or utensils, and so on. Within this basic setup of the cook in the kitchen going through the lesson plan, there could be variants, some of which might not seem all that consequential as we look back on them. For example, some shows filmed the host against the flat back wall of the kitchen (often with the side walls at each edge of the television frame), while others positioned her or him in the angle formed by the kitchen corner. Each of these offered different compositional patterns, and, as later episodes of *The*

French Chef would best demonstrate, a moving camera could bring into play both setups as the dynamic Child bounded from one part of the kitchen to another and the camera followed her from center to corner and back again. The two choices—the cook viewed frontally against a back wall, or placed within the corner of the kitchen so that the composition was more diagonal—became so conventionalized that, by 1954, a manual on careers for women in television could describe them as the U-shape and L-shape options.[2]

In the immediate postwar years, the idea that the new medium of television might be particularly suited to intimate yet publicly available instruction in the arts of the home took hold very quickly. As early as 1949, for example, the manual *How to Write for Homemakers* included a short section on writing for television alongside other, more traditional media (such as the homemaker newspaper column). As the authors cautioned for the case of television, "Your big problem is, and always will be, to plan programs that will be most acceptable to the people who own television sets. . . . Who looks at it? If it's a daytime program, the homemaker sees it; if it's an evening one, Dad, Mother, the youngsters, and perhaps the neighbors, look at it. . . . If your telecast goes on in the evening, you'll want more entertainment value, more show business, more fun. . . . You need to have a natural, friendly, outgoing personality that you have built up throughout your life."[3] An accompanying drawing—of a mom, a dad, and a daughter, it would seem—all watching a cooking demonstration together suggests it was already commonly assumed that the imparting of culinary skills in particular would be central to television's instructions in everyday life. Cooking was typically what might be on, and it could be taken to sum up the television viewing experience. Likewise, advice that "showing the finished casserole or salad or dessert at the beginning attracts interest and tempts the casual tuner-in to stay through the show"[4] clarifies enduring conventions of TV cooking (such as beginning with a glimpsed promise of the wondrous end) that had been put in place very early on.

Postwar complaints by critics that too many cooking shows were appearing that resembled television offerings from *before* 1945 imply that there were a noticeable number of cooking shows in the rare

11.

Telecasts and Radio Scripts

How To Write
For Air-Wave Audiences

RADIO AND TELEVISION are commonly
thought of as being closely related. Actually their
techniques are quite different, although both are
sent out over the air waves.

In radio, the home economist or homemaking
commentator *talks* about a certain kind of sunsuit
or salad or soap. In television she *shows* the sunsuit
or salad or soap; shows how to make it or use it.
Let's consider television first, then radio.

Telecasting a demonstration is a good deal like
making a motion picture with sound transcription.
That is, you stand before the camera and the micro-
phone, demonstrating skills, talking as you work.
The difference lies in these facts:

(1) In a live television show, your range of action
before the camera is limited. In a motion picture the
scene may shift from market to exterior of house
to kitchen; from kitchen to dining room and back

[133]

An early recognition of food-TV

programming that did show up on commercial television from the late 1930s into the war, when television programming was virtually experimental, sporadic in nature, and seen by a very small number of viewers in limited viewing situations. During the war, for instance, programming that offered instruction in occupational therapy was piped into Veterans Administration hospitals, and this may well have included cooking shows.[5] One manual of introduction to the new medium of TV, Judy Dupuy's *Television Show Business*, published in 1945 just at the transition from wartime to postwar conditions, refers explicitly to several cooking demonstrations that aired on General Electric's local station in Schenectady, New York, WRGB, during the early 1940s: a segment on preparing banana dishes from 1940 and one on canapés from 1942, as well as a series of four installments in which an instructor named Consuela Kelly, whose story is now lost to history, "prepared a full meal right in front of the cameras."[6] So cooking instruction entered American television early on indeed.

By 1950, education journals were even extolling the special virtues of television as a most potent means of everyday instruction in domestic arts. For example, an article in the *Extension Service Review* reported on the ways in which a show on a commercial station, *The Food Basket*, which aired on Boston's WBZ-TV, resembled extension courses at colleges and universities in its careful, step-by-step demonstrations of shopping and then preparation of the food purchased.[7]

Not surprisingly, in 1952, when Margaret McKeegan, a student writing a thesis on homemaking television programs, sent a survey to the 108 television stations then on the air, 72 of the 82 that replied indicated they had homemaking shows, virtually all of them declaring that cooking demonstrations were their primary offering in the genre (and in extensive fashion: the average number of cooking episodes at the stations was more than five per week). Sixty percent of the respondents had *permanent* kitchen sets in their studios. Revealingly, though, only a fourth of the respondents said they also had dining-room sets. The emphasis on the pleasures of consumption that would be so central to the set design of *The French Chef*, where the kitchen was right next to a dining room, was not yet present in the early shows, where all that mattered was the homemaker's efficiency in getting food made and not the enjoyment that ensued from eating it.[8]

Representative of such early cooking shows, especially in their origin in homemaking instruction by means of mass media, is a half-hour offering that appeared from Monday through Friday at 11 A.M. on KFMB in San Diego: *What's Cookin'*, hosted by Marjorie Hume. *What's Cookin'* was cosponsored by the local butcher's union (a branch of the AFL-CIO), and each Tuesday a butcher would come on the show to explain how to get the most from various cuts of meat, poultry, and fish; on the other days, Hume showed basic ways to prepare nutritious courses and full meals for the family. Such demonstrations as the butcher's visits were typical of a concern in many of the early shows to deal not only with cooking but also with judicious shopping and food preparation—in other words, with aspects of the process that came as much under home *economics* as cookery. Also typical of *What's Cookin'*, and a sign of its practical intent, was the possibility for viewers to write to the station and (for ten cents) get a copy of a desired recipe.

In the beginning postwar years, many television stations and their programmers felt lucky to have anything to put on the air at all. Indeed, in the earliest postwar moments, the scarcity of available content meant that many stations were off the air for much of the day. Cooking shows were an easy, generally cheap way to fill up airtime; as Marsha Cassidy notes in her history of 1950s daytime television, they were indeed among the first kinds of daytime offering to be added to most TV stations' programming. In this regard, it is noteworthy how many manuals about the practice of television production during the early years assumed that a kitchen set would be an inevitable, permanent part of any studio setup.[9]

It would seem that the majority of cooking demonstrations on postwar television came from unassuming, even average, figures such as home economists or Midwestern housewives who claimed to represent to the people their own cooking preferences and presented instruction about preparing common fare in bare, utilitarian style. There were in fact dozens of these types of shows on the air, usually broadcast locally, and generally with no one bothering to keep copies of the programs for posterity.

Such television food demonstration—and household-hints programming, more generally—picked up on a similar daytime tradition in radio, especially local radio, throughout Middle America, in which women who were supposed to be little different from their listeners explained how to make all-American dishes with efficiency and economy and healthfulness but also, when possible, with appetizing taste. The goal was not primarily to introduce new foodstuffs to audiences. At best, there might be instruction about a dish that this or that housewife didn't know but, as an average American, should have had in her repertoire. Both radio and television were reacting to new domestic arrangements in the twentieth century in which more women were marrying young, moving away from their parents to new regions of the country, and therefore lacking in the experience of basic cooking and fundamental household lore passed on from generation to generation (taught, for instance, in one's own family kitchen by one's own mother). It is revealing in this respect that whereas some turn-of-century cookbooks hadn't included recipes for bread, as it was assumed that *any* young housewife necessarily would have learned bread preparation at her mother's side, later cookbooks not only included such recipes but went through each step with exacting precision, as if the young housewife of the later period couldn't be assumed to have any knowledge at all of the process. Like the cookbooks, by mid-century many radio shows and television series were spelling everything out and served as an education in a basic lore that housewives increasingly were felt to lack.

As early as the 1920s, in *Middletown*, their classic study of Middle America, the sociologists Robert and Helen Lynd had lamented the lessening of the family as social cement in modernizing America. Although the Lynds saw mass media generally as one of the culprits, many of the household radio shows were designed to compensate for the dissolution of family ties and serve as propitious substitute. This role for broadcast media intensified as both the Depression and the Second World War created conditions of scarcity, for which instruction about making foodstuffs go a long way, preserving taste even if one had to work with cheaper food substitutes, maintaining nutrition even with compromised ingredients, and so on, became quite useful to homemakers. For example, one popular radio show from the 1930s into the war period revolved around "Aunt Sammy," who was said to be Uncle Sam's feminine partner and whose mission was to complement Sam's work in recruitment for the war front with advice about economical management of the home front. Sammy dispensed pedagogy about floor care, laundry, nutrition, and vitamins; uses of leftovers; pest control; and so on. One part of her show, "What Shall We Have for Dinner?," was all about making quick, economical, and yet flavorful meals from everyday items.

It is likely that many of the daytime television cooking demonstrations of the 1950s followed common procedures and shared a basic set of conventions. The goal primarily was to tell young housewives how to do what ideally they already should have been doing. The instruction was in wholesome American food and was geared to explaining how to prepare it in ways that gave food flavor (but not too challengingly so), that were nutritious, and that did not require too much time or effort. Again, the impression conveyed was of a community of women in a shared situation, some of whom had a little more experience than others and who therefore were taking it as their task to impart it to their sisters so everyone could have the same skills. In many cases, while the household management show had a host, the assumption was that she was pretty much like her neighbors and that they, therefore, should be encouraged to send in recipes or hints of their own and even drop in to the station and offer their own advice. Thus, to take one example, the recipes for Trudy McNall's *Home Cooking*, which aired on WHAM-TV in Rochester, New York, on weekdays from 9:00 to 9:30 A.M. (and later, to 9:45), were printed in loose-leaf format so they could be mailed out to viewers biweekly. They were a mix of McNall's own recipes and ones sent in by viewers. For example, a single page has recipes for "Pat Martin's chocolate cake," "Helene George's maple syrup cake," "Bertha Everett's frozen lemon pie," and "Mrs. Peter Fry's pizza."[10]

Providing and caring for one's family was overwhelmingly the goal of the homemaker shows. As Bettie Tolson, who had a local cooking program on KMTV in Omaha, advised in a magazine article, "Keep in mind that food is primarily a family matter. Therefore, keep the family in mind when preparing menus."[11] Even though the mythology had it that postwar America was emerging from the deprivations of the previous decades into a period of abundance, the daytime cooking shows of the period still radiate a sense of thrift, economy, and anti-waste efficiency. Not all the instruction in the home economics shows came in the form of dry pedagogy, however. There might, for instance, be some attempt at folksy, regionalist humor, usually in the form of modest banter or, at best, home-spun cracker-barrel comedy: thus, Tolson recounted to me in an interview how she devoted part of one show to cooking a crow after a politician said he would eat that bird on her program if some campaign promise he made was not kept. The point was to stay in an all-American folksy realm.

Typically, the appearance of the daytime female cooks falls into two categories. On the one hand, there were older, homey, matronly women who looked, it could be said, like the stereotype of the caring auntie who is wise yet tender and dispenses advice with care and assurance.[12] On the other hand, there was the perky, cheery housewife who was pretty in a wholesome but not overly or overtly sexy way—much like the sitcom moms who figured in so many television series of the period (such as Donna Reed on the show named after her). Both types of cooking instructor offer images of women who bring security and comfort to a familial, domestic setting. As Erika Endrijonas notes, "References to home economics degrees, civic activities, numerous children, and, most importantly, grace and charm were what constituted a capable female cooking show host."[13]

As *Neighboring on the Air*, one chronicle of homemaker radio broadcasts in the Midwest, makes clear, many regional programs were sponsored by local businesses, and the homemakers who hosted the shows were expected to extol by name the foodstuffs or kitchen appliances the businesses provided.[14] In this respect, it is relevant that many of the early TV cooks had worked just before their television gigs as spokespeople for companies that specialized in household products, appliances, and utilities. In making the transition into television, these cooks were bringing along their skills not only in public presentation but also in a salesmanship that directly was about making specific branded items seem natural and necessary to the domestic setting.

Versions of the television cook: Josie McCarthy and Ruth
Kent. Ruth Kent photograph courtesy Special Collections
and Archives, Georgia State University Library.

Many of the home shows from the immediate postwar period up to the 1960s did not merely run commercials; they had sponsors whose products directly related to the televised activity at hand and that, therefore, they hoped would be used in the homemaking demonstration. To take a typical case, Mercedes Bates's *California Living*, which aired on weekdays on KNXT in Los Angeles, had multiple sponsors. A typical thirty-minute episode might be broken into a two-minute opening, a breakaway to a plug for Red Heart Dog Food, six minutes on baked halibut, one minute on a guest's salad dressing, a reminder that viewers could mail in for copies of recipes, six minutes on mock chicken legs, a breakaway to a plug for the Southern California Gas Company, six and a half minutes on cherry nut crumble, a breakaway plug for Best Foods mayonnaise, and an announcement of topics on the next installment.[15]

How to relate the cooking demonstration overall to the necessary moments of commercial plugging was a constant concern for the food shows throughout their early history. Could it be done without seeming crass? Could the products be woven into the course of the show in easy fashion? (One surviving episode of a mid-1950s show by Edith Green, a cooking instructor in San Francisco, has a striking moment in which Green invites one of the two cameraman into visibility on the set to eat the "Borden's Glacier Freeze" she has just plugged.)

A variety of strategies, in fact, were employed in cooking shows to mention sponsors' products. At one extreme, for instance, the hosts Chef Milani and Dione Lucas endlessly—and awkwardly—affixed brand names to every food item they cooked and to every appliance they cooked with. At another extreme, some shows tried to integrate the plugs into the demonstration by dramatizing fictional scenarios in which one person (the cook, usually) recounted to another (an assistant or other interlocutor) his or her personal discovery of the virtues of the branded product.[16]

For instance, James Beard's *I Love to Eat* (1946–47) combined direct plugs (such as discussing peach melba in a segment on fruit desserts and declaring it "a pity Madame Melba never knew about Borden's ice cream") with dramatized scenes in which commercial messages entered the flow of the story in characters' ordinary conversation to, it was hoped, more integrated effect. To be sure, the dramatizations still seem forced and give the impression that—in the case of *I Love to Eat*, at least—early television had not fully worked out the relation of salesmanship to showmanship. Thus, in an episode in which "George the deliveryman" appears, the phone rings. Beard, busy with his food preparation, asks George to answer it, and Elmer the Bull (husband to Borden's mascot, Elsie the Cow) is on the line with marketing ideas for the series, such as a juggler juggling the full line of Borden products, each enumerated with loving attention. In another episode, Beard tells a friend about a nightmare he had in which he forgot to mention all of the fine and wonderful Borden products on his show (which he then lists, thereby getting a plug in for all of them along the way).

In the daytime shows, with their often matter-of-fact, home-economics-centered instruction, there could indeed be lots of product promotion, but in the best of cases, sheer commercialism through the plugging of manufactured, branded items that promised to streamline and regularize culinary preparation was tempered by the shows' emphasis on regionalism, tradition, and personal touch. While much of the goal was to get homemakers to standardize their culinary efforts through modern, commercial products, homespun recipes and methods passed through generations of family members were also emphasized, as were hints on how to customize food and make it seem unique.

In fact, some of the daytime cooks had ambitions to do something more with their cooking or seemed to recognize that new social conditions of the postwar period were impelling homemakers like themselves to take on such ambitions. One constant motif was the need to teach viewers how to succeed in social occasions with meals for guests, and not just one's family, and therefore to serve food that not only was tasty but that also made a striking impression and solidified one's status vis-à-vis others in one's social orbit (or just above or just below). There was recognition of a new world of social obligations that assumed that food consumption was a socializing activity as much as a familial one and that the right (or wrong) effect conveyed by one's food could have consequential impact on one's standing. The homemaker of the 1950s who was most concerned just with getting her household through the day might still have faced the social obligations of church socials and community functions to which one had to bring dishes that would be held up to scrutiny by others. It is likely that some part of many of the daytime cooking shows dealt with preparation of foodstuffs that could succeed in this social arena. It is interesting in this respect to find Julia Child explaining in an early episode of the more upscale, night-time *The French Chef* that her recipe of the day, "Queen of Sheba Cake," would be perfect for a "committee meeting." Today, the phrase seems to have no context, but just after the 1950s, it would have resonated with familiar images of women's clubs, social meetings, and community organizations in which one met with one's neighbors supposedly to work together on some goal but where everyone really was judging everyone else.

One early example of a culinary instructor who moved between instruction in food for the family and a recognition that cooking also had its role to play in social occasions (as when guests were coming over) was Edith Green, who hosted the very popular *Your Home Kitchen*, which debuted in San Francisco in 1949 (initially as a show of general household hints, after which it turned into a series exclusively about cooking) before being given a national program in 1954.[17] Green early on had developed an interest in cooking that, by the 1930s, led her to offer culinary classes, often with French content (she had worked also as a French tutor and possessed a strong commitment to popular pedagogy), and then during the war to co-write a self-published, home-economics-oriented manual on ways to offer nutritious meals in a time of food restriction and rationing. Revealingly, Green and her co-author brought out a virtually unchanged edition in the postwar period (1952) as if even a period of supposed abundance was still one in which economy and efficient food planning had to matter as much as social spectacle and unbridled consumption. As the authors noted in both editions, the simultaneous missions for the cook should be to save time without sacrificing poise and to enhance food's nutritional value along with the visual charm of the plating, and all of this needed to be thought of together.[18]

This intent seems to have carried over into Green's television work, where the pedagogical content simultaneously involved meeting a family's nutritional needs in expeditious fashion while preparing stand-out dishes (for discerning guests but also for family who would be treated to quality meals) and while remaining efficient in the fulfillment of that mission. In the words of her son (in an e-mail to me): "Her style was to demonstrate as she had in her home to newly married young women, in their twenties, both the basics of cooking (eggs, etc.) and more sophisticated cooking of deserts, casseroles, crepes and the like. . . . This was serious cooking and teaching and learning about what mothers had to work with: limited funds, limited time, willingness to learn and present a meal that would be appreciated by the family and on occasion by others, be healthy, well-balanced, and meet special [health or nutritional] needs as they came up." Thus, a surviving episode of *Your Home Kitchen* begins with Green declaring that she hopes her viewers are in a festive mood, as she plans to give them instruction in a recipe that will be perfect for company: a chicken-with-mushroom casserole. As she explains, a casserole offers the advantage that it can be prepared in advance, then just needing a last-minute warming, so that one can limit one's time in the kitchen when guests start arriving. This dish, she advises, should be served along with two others that she prepared during the preceding days: an avocado mold and a creole cake (chocolate cake laced with coffee). All of this is in keeping with a general concern by Green that one use time efficiently—that even the seemingly ambitious dish be done in efficacious fashion. In passing, it's interesting to note that the days of the week form a sequence for Green so that each day's recipe becomes part of a larger offering, the full meal. Not all cooking shows integrated their individual episodes this way, but a number did, and they thereby turned the mere chronology of the passing days of the week into a serial narrative in which each episode added up to a coherent whole (even if, as in the case of the surviving episode of Green's show, cake making comes before casserole) and in which the Friday show might be all about summing up and presenting the full meal (just as the weekend itself promised pleasures after the weekdays' labor).

Indeed, while homemaking shows with a strongly utilitarian and domestic bent dominated television cooking, a variety of genres actually existed, with some diversity in the ratio of dry instruction to spectacle and entertainment. Some shows were offerings by notable personages,

Edith Green. Photograph courtesy Don Green.

such as James Beard or Dione Lucas, who set out to elevate America's cooking potential into something especially tasteful. Some programs were vaudeville-like and mixed cooking with comedy or music.

Confirming the sheer quantity and generic diversity of everyday culinary pedagogy by television chefs is the cookbook *Cooking with the Experts* (1955), edited by the television journalist William I. Kaufman, who most famously had been responsible in previous years for the collation *Best Television Plays of the Year*. (That Kaufman, a chronicler of the high accomplishments of early "Golden Age" television, felt it was merited to address the stereotypically feminized and lowly genre of the cooking show is noteworthy in itself in this regard.) In *Cooking with the Experts*, as Kaufman explains in a brief introduction, the reader has at hand a unique sort of cookbook that, instead of representing one chef's voice, brings together recipes from close to fifty chefs from television cooking shows from around the country (including the then protectorate of Hawaii).[19] Although the volume is primarily a catalog of those recipes, it usefully includes an end section of photos of the TV chefs, sometimes taken on their kitchen sets, along with brief biographical notices. These, plus the variety in the recipes themselves, offer a picture of the intersection of cuisine and television in the 1950s that confirms just how extensive that encounter was in the years before *The French Chef* achieved such notoriety. Some cooking shows had a comic edge; some were tied to famous restaurants; and at least one was hosted by a young couple (Ken and Lu Calfee, *Home Cooking*, WAAM, Baltimore) whose mission, it seems, was to teach adventurous fare to other young couples in the dynamic, status-seeking urban arena of postwar America.

Certainly, as the book confirms, a lot of postwar cooking was about homogenization and standardization, and even when it called for personal intervention and creativity, these were often in the service of a cuisine that was not about offering the new but providing the familiar, just done more economically, more nutritiously, more expeditiously, and, perhaps (but not as an absolute necessity) with a panache of attractiveness to make the ordinary newly palatable. Truth be told, the vast majority of the cooks on the early television shows (and in the survey of them in Kaufman's volume) were women with backgrounds in home economics and with agricultural experience through 4-H clubs and the like. Their strongest goal was to teach efficiently the preparation of wholesome American fare that didn't always need to be claimed adventurous to be deemed good and worthy of transmission to the viewers. As the blurb for Cordelia Kelly (who hosted *What's Cooking Today* at WFMY in Greensboro, North Carolina) in *Cooking with the Experts* aptly sums it up, "On the program Mrs. Kelly demonstrates methods of preparation of food, gives recipes, discusses kitchen short-cuts, interviews outstanding food authorities and by blending good food and good sense hopes that young people among her viewers, future homemakers, may grow sturdy plants from the seeds she sows."[20] Many of the TV instructors also had worked in health professions, and some even had nursing shows running concurrently with their television cooking demonstrations, thereby reiterating a connection between cooking and basic well-being. For example, Bee Baxter at KSTP in South Dakota hosted both *Operation Tender Loving Care* (a nursing show) and the *Bee Baxter Show*, a household management offering, which regularly included cooking demonstrations by Baxter and her guests. (She also had an agricultural show in which she introduced and interviewed enterprising farm families, although that seems unique among the home-economics offerings of the 1950s.)

But *Cooking with the Experts* also taps into a concurrent, if sometimes repressed, tendency in the history of American cuisine that celebrates regional richness, the vibrant authenticity of local foods and their contribution to an opening up of tastes beyond a single set of norms. It is noteworthy that if some of the recipes in *Cooking with the Experts* fit the cliché of a Midwestern model of Jell-O molds and ersatz creations cobbled together from cans, there are also intimations of redolent local cuisine, of a certain boldness with spices, of a celebration of new and atypical ingredients, of a budding discovery of exoticism, and so on. Thus, if the very last recipe in *Cooking with the Experts* (from Bee Baxter in Minneapolis) is for an iced coffee drink made from nothing more than *instant* coffee mixed with hot water, sugar, and a dash of vanilla extract (but exoticized already by its name—"Viennese Iced Coffee"), the first recipe in the book (from Marjorie Abel of KGMB-TV in Honolulu) is "Abalone in Soy Sauce" (with ingredients

Bee Baxter. Photograph courtesy KSTP-TV, Minneapolis.

such as garlic and ginger) and suggests that there was somewhat more variety and more daringness and inventiveness than the stereotypes of a bland, standardized, mass-produced American cuisine of the 1950s would have us believe.

In this respect, I find quite intriguing a photo, from the archives of WAVE-TV in Louisville, Kentucky, of Shirley Marshall, whose lifestyle show in the mid-1950s was *Ladies Fare*. In the blurb accompanying her photo in Kaufman's *Cooking with the Experts*, Marshall is described as a home economist whose program's "emphasis is not on fancy culinary arts but on how to make average food appetizing,"[21] and one can imagine her as representative of a utilitarian culinary philosophy that took cooking to be about simple provision for one's family. But in the archival photo, while Marshall wears the same simple summer frock that she is dressed in for her picture in *Cooking with the Experts*, now as she

Shirley Marshall. Photograph courtesy WAVE 3, Louisville, Kentucky.

looks toward the camera with a perky smile, she appears serving up a plate of food in front of an unidentified Indian woman wearing a patterned sari and with a bindi on her forehead. One wonders at the situation. Who is this guest? Is the food something the Indian woman has come to the program to show Marshall how to do, or is the guest there to be indoctrinated into American fare? How did this moment of proto-multiculturalism end up on Middle American television in this decade of supposed homogeneity of taste and cultural values?

Even with the home economists, then, there could be ambitions beyond utilitarian instruction in merely nutritious family meals done in timely fashion. For example, Corris Guy, who hosted *Tricks and Treats* on Friday afternoons at KTLA in Los Angeles, demonstrates the typical biographical background. She had been employed as a home economist for three utility companies, where her job was to demonstrate to the public the benefits of home appliances using their services, and had been the director of consumer services at the well-known Helms Bakery, where she eventually became a vice-president and for whom she wrote a small book of baking recipes. But beyond the home-economics background, Guy devoted many of her episodes to themed meals that appeared to be as much about social entertaining ("Hawaiian Luau") and status building ("Boss Comes to Supper") as about simply providing basic meals to the family.[22]

To the extent that cooking demonstrations gave glimpses of culinary diversity, this may have derived in part from a drive by the budding television stations of the 1940s and 1950s to offer programming that itself was diversified (especially when no one was really sure what anyone wanted to watch). Toward this end, a very common format for early television programs, first during the day and then at night, was the "magazine show"—either a half-hour or an hour long and composed, as its name might suggest, of several different segments, each on a particular topic and each understandable and consumable in and of itself. There might be cooking demonstrations, shopping hints, household management advice, fashion tips, and on and on.

As commercial television started up in the postwar moment, there was great uncertainty as to who would actually watch the new medium, in what ways, and to what ends. One common assumption was that television would be a daytime medium for women in the domestic sphere, and the magazine show initially was targeted at them. The magazine show could be held up by the television industry as a salutary form for daytime viewers. Many of the magazine shows' segments were devoted to a laudable pedagogy in the workings of everyday life (from household hints to success in the social world) in ways that made viewing seem useful both for the housewife and for the family (husband, children) who would benefit from the housewife's newfound skills. Magazine shows might include fictionalized, acted segments, and they might have moments of pure entertainment (musical acts especially), but for the most part they were geared to practical advice. The earliest postwar magazine show, WNBT's daytime *Radio City Matinee*, included, for instance, segments on fashion and hat buying, cultural events worthy of attention, home decoration and household maintenance, and so on. (One segment, notably, showed how to cultivate one's artistic talents through painting lessons from the instructor John Gnagy, who eventually got his own shows in the 1950s and became famous nationwide for his calm, quiet, do-it-yourself pedagogy.)

The idea behind the magazine format was simultaneously to give viewers the impression of a bounty of materials stuffed into a half-hour and to do so, in the case of daytime programming, in a manner in which any interruptions of viewing by household duties would not be irremediably damaging, because a missed segment would immediately be followed by another that promised to be equally rich in homemaking value. One of the most nationally successful of the early magazine shows was *The Kate Smith Hour* (which debuted in 1950), in which the famed performer sang, hosted guests from the worlds of entertainment and politics, offered household advice, and, once a week, did a cooking demonstration that could involve guests and might revolve around comic routines.[23] But even local stations got into the format of the magazine show. For example, at North Carolina's WBTV, Betty Freezor (not a made-up name) had the eponymous *Betty Freezor Show*, which ran for decades, with episodes that included sewing lessons, grooming hints, cooking demonstrations, interviews with visitors to town, and once a piano recital by Richard Nixon. Likewise, at Portland's KPTV, Barbara Angell's program, *What's Cooking?*, included lectures, cooking demonstrations, and interaction with guests. The invitees ranged from the mayor, who sampled Angell's pie, to a cheetah, which roamed the set and evidently brought breathless excitement to the moment. This latter sort of "guest" visit confirms how the magazine format was geared not only to practical instruction but also to sensationalistic entertainment that sometimes could seem far from pedagogical in intent.[24]

Indeed, as much as the structure of the magazine show came from the desire to cram as many helpful hints into the program as possible, the format was also inspired, it would seem, by programmers' wariness of talking-head instruction unleavened by strong doses of pure diversion. The goal, then, was also to get as much diversity and entertainment into the magazine show as possible.

As noted, *Radio City Matinee* at WNBT (flagship of NBC's fledgling television network) appears to have been the very first postwar magazine show, and it seems too that it had one of the earliest regular segments devoted to cooking demonstrations. *Radio City Matinee* debuted in early May 1946 with the chef George Rector, originally of New York's famed night spot Rector's, doing a culinary segment and using language that showed he was clearly targeting the "ladies," the presumed audience for such a daytime offering. At the Library of Congress the audio of one episode survives in which Rector made Welsh rarebit and presented the dish as serving the needs of social status and distinction more than that of mere sustenance. In other words, unlike many of the daytime radio shows for women that had preceded the advent of television cookery and that had been about instruction in typical dinner-table fare for the family, *Radio City Matinee* was participating in a soon-to-be-common postwar rhetoric of cooking as an activity of social advancement and status building. For guests, Rector explained, not just any recipes would do; the meal had to be something special, something distinctive—and for that, turning to things French was logical. Thus, Rector explained, the cheese he most recommended was Camembert, and he noted both that he had long been planning a cheese tour of Europe that the war interrupted (France as the deferred dream of culinary excellence that would become available to postwar America) and how he had won his wife-to-be's heart when he served her Camembert and strawberries on their first date (France as the embodiment of an exoticized romanticism).

Soon, though, the noted cookbook author and rising celebrity James Beard replaced Rector, and Beard's efforts eventually would lead NBC to give him a stand-alone show, *I Love to Eat*, which ran for about six months from 1946 into 1947.[25] The surviving audio for one of Beard's segments on *Radio City Matinee* (also at the Library of Congress) gives the impression of a teaching that is direct and straightforward and generally unfussy and functional. There is a process that needs to be demonstrated, so a commentary synchronized to the chronology of the recipe is the chosen structure. But Beard was able already to stamp some of his own perspective and noteworthy personality onto the food preparation. For instance, he made typically Beardian declarations in favor of authenticity and regional authority, such as when he noted that he was commonly asked whether the fish should be cooked with the head on and announced in favor of doing so, since "the people who cook better than any other people, the Chinese and the French, always serve their fishes like this, and why not follow their example?" Most important, Beard added to the functional unfolding of recipe steps a whimsy and affable jokiness of a sort that would stay with him through his life and that sometimes issued in corny quips and puns. For example, while stuffing an herb mix under chicken skin, he said that the recipe's name should be "Chicken, I've Got You under My Skin." But as silly as some of Beard's theatrics might have been, they were also of a piece with a deeply felt commitment to an idea and ideal of food (both its preparation and its consumption) as a source of pleasure, often of an ebullient sort. Thus, for all the functionality of his cooking demonstrations, Beard emphasized that any concern with efficiency and expediency in the kitchen could never take place at the expense of gustatory joy. Cooking was always about the delights of taste.

As Beard exemplifies, the magazine format thus offered a means to open up dry pedagogy to entertaining performance if one so desired (or the station so desired), and this could be achieved by a variety of means. For example, one could include relatively straightforward moments of instruction but conjoin them to sequences that were more purely about showmanship. Thus, in one of the earliest surviving recordings of a cooking show, *Chef Milani*, which aired in the morning on KNBH in Los Angeles, Milani cooks, but there are also cutaways to two musical numbers (a female accordion trio and Milani's own kitchen assistant, who sings a "A Dream Is a Wish Your Heart Makes"), and a visit by a young woman who has won a prize as Queen of Television Month (whatever that is). Despite the fact that the cooking segments take place in a somewhat domestic looking kitchen, with Milani's wife hovering in the background, the opening credits for *Chef Milani* offer a drawing of a restaurant bearing his name in blinking lights, and the conceit seems to be that we are entering into a nightclub-like commercial establishment where we will get not only the cooking but bountiful doses of entertainment.[26]

As another strategy, instruction itself could be subjected to the infusion or intrusion of entertainment instead of each being compartmentalized in its own sections of the show. That is, the two could be mixed

Chef Milani. Photograph courtesy Weddingspinster.com.

together in volatile blends. For example, at WTNH in New Haven, Pino and Fedora Bontempi hosted a show in which their dog wandered the set and Pino would keep interrupting his wife as she tried to cook, until she told him to go off and sing opera (Pino had been a professional singer) to soothingly accompany her activities in the kitchen. *Chef Milani* too was all about the staff milling around the kitchen set and pulling Milani into this or that comic sketch. (For example, his assistant drops a product on the floor, and Milani explodes into hot-tempered Italian invective, which the announcer then translates as commercial plugs for Hunt's, one of the sponsors). Yet another possibility was to have the chef be a showman himself or herself or have some tic or trait that was a source of comic entertainment and lightened up the kitchen instruction as it unfolded. For example, Mike Roy, who hosted *Key to the Kitchen* at KRCA in Los Angeles, was known for ad lib jokes, and Eddie Doucette, who hosted *Creative Cooking* at WNBQ in Chicago, recited original poetry while demonstrating cooking techniques.[27]

There is one seemingly unique case in which the distinctive personal trait was not comical so much as curious in its context: in San Francisco in the mid-1950s, there was a cooking show by the Mexican restaurant owner and cookbook author Elena Zelayeta, *who happened to be blind* and had her on-camera son, Billy, assist her with her television demonstrations. The premise of a blind cook doing a cooking show seems unprecedented, and unfortunately Zelayeta's efforts have left few traces in the historical record for us to know more about this unique case.[28]

More typically, the ideal trait to give a chef televisual distinction was some personal characteristic that above all made him or her funny. For example, Chef Milani had a notoriously thick Italian accent and hadn't fully mastered English grammar, so a great deal of humor came from his mangling of English. As Kathleen Collins notes, comic or performing chefs of this sort tended to be male, as if men could be shown in the kitchen only if they confirmed they were *playing* at being there. (Alternatively, as François Pope of Chicago demonstrated by always wearing a suit and tie on his cooking show and by appearing with his two boys, men could also show their supposed superiority to women's domestic work by displaying overtly formal professionalism.) But some women too worked to make demonstration television into a spectacle of sheer entertainment. This was likely the case, for instance, with the entertainer Jessie DeBoth, who had a cooking show on the ABC affiliate in Detroit. In the late 1920s and into the 1930s, DeBoth had been known in the city for paid-admission live shows about household management that she held at local theaters and in which she blended cooking demonstrations, comic patter, song and dance, prize giveaways, and the dispensing of household advice. (Evidently, she claimed to cover all topics except "how to wind the clock and put the cat out.")[29] She began her live performances in Detroit by running onto the stage in a flamboyant style, holding a flour sifter and yelling her trademark, "HiYo!" Given how that cry had branded her, it is likely that she carried this earlier form of vaudeville-like spectacle over into her television work.

Indeed, a listing for her TV show in an issue of *Time* magazine dated July 2, 1951, described her as a "veteran of newspaper cooking pages, who sports high-fashion hats while up to her elbows in flour, and wears the determinedly jolly air of a police matron speeding a departing inmate. When not badgering stray males from the studio audience by tying skillets to their shirttails, Jessie hammers home the virtues of her sponsoring products. Sample kitchen hint: don't sew up your turkey after stuffing it, use safety pins." Like Julia Child, DeBoth was over six feet tall, and clearly she used her size and her broadness of personality to craft an energetic self-image that turned home economics into exuberant spectacle.[30]

For shows that mingled comedy with culinary performance in this fashion, there was always a temptation to let the fun and entertainment override the instruction, as one sees in one of the most curious cases of television cookery of the 1950s. Starting in 1950, Ernie Kovacs, soon to be legendary for self-reflexive programs that deconstructed the codes and techniques of television from within, took over a seemingly unassuming cooking show, *Deadline for Dinner* (which, with his noted interest in wordplay, he quickly dubbed "Dead Lion for Dinner"), that had been running for a short time on NBC's WPTZ affiliate in Philadelphia. There are few traces in the historical record of just what Kovacs's version of the show looked like, but the available clues, as compiled and interpreted in *Kovacsland*, Diana Rico's authoritative biography of Kovacs, are enticing indeed.[31] While in the case of *Deadline for Dinner*, Kovacs seems not to have messed with the formal devices of television as much as he would in his later, well-acclaimed efforts for national networks, it does appear that he engaged in antics on the set to turn the staid world of culinary pedagogy into something zany and even subversive of its own best intents. In this respect, his humorous approach to cooking might bear some comparison to Julia Child's, where the narrative of food preparation is leavened by constant whimsy, wit, and wry commentary. Whatever "surrealism" transpired on the set of Child's *The French Chef* came not from playing with television stylistics or with effects created by camera trickery—in fact, her program was quite conventional and matter-of-fact in its use of the standard and stylistically functional conventions of instructional television—but from her own boisterous demeanor and manipulation of realities *in front of the camera*, such as the food she brought onto the set and often played with (for example, the so-called chicken sisters, whose carcasses she held up by the wings and pranced around on the kitchen counter). In like fashion, Kovacs appears to have built some comedy around conversations he had with the food he was working with, such as butchered turkeys, and his comic approach in this early show seems to have centered on the antics he engaged in before the camera's impassive gaze.

The story of *Deadline for Dinner* (hereafter, *Deadline*), as Rico recounts it, almost sounds like a media-world fairytale about being in the right place at the right time. Evidently, the regular host of the program didn't show up one day, and Kovacs, who was one of the station's hardest-working announcers, was asked at the last moment to step in. On so many local stations, performers and crews endlessly found themselves shuffled back and forth from one job to another, with little or no advance notice and no indication that they needed any talent other than the ability to keep things moving. This improvised scrambling to get things done appears to have paid off for Kovacs.

Kovacs, who had primarily been narrating Philadelphia prize fights for WPTZ, clearly flourished in a no-prep-possible/no-prep-necessary environment, and the improvisational skills that later so marked his appearances on national TV were evidently already on view in *Deadline*. For example, in one case, a guest chef didn't show up, so Kovacs threw together a bunch of ingredients for an omelet (supposedly instructing an aide to get whatever ingredients he could find but claiming to the television audience that what he was assembling came from a well-tested and venerable recipe) and said the resultant mess was the noted "Eggs Scavok" (an example of his wordplay: the word is his name backward).

Deadline aired on Monday afternoons on WPTZ after a movie feature, and eventually it expanded, it seems, to two days a week. The show typically had Kovacs as host interacting with various chefs, some of whom were invited guests, but one of whom appears to have become a regular: Albert Mathis, who was chef and manager at a local country club. This format followed a convention that was common to many comedy routines in the period, in which a star performer—in this case, Kovacs—served as a naïf, inexperienced in the byways of the show's subject matter, who then interacted with an expert professional who would try to school the emcee in the practices of the craft. (Earlier, *Chef Milani* had employed this structure with the emcee Lou Marcelle as the foil to the zany chef.) The structure, then, enabled a split between— but also a mediation of—serious pedagogy and disruptive comedy and seems in keeping with a vaudeville tradition widely available on post-war television in which a straight man attempts to instruct a dunce in the ways of the world (think of Bud Abbott and Lou Costello or Dean Martin and Jerry Lewis or George Burns and Gracie Allen).[32] Thus, it seems that the professional chef would talk the undisciplined Kovacs through the steps of a recipe, only to have his out-of-control student mess up at each moment. Chef Mathis evidently had a serious de-meanor but also a degree of slow-burn patience; he would simply go about his business, and then Kovacs would go about his own decon-structive version (but with Mathis ultimately succeeding, despite all the obstacles Kovacs put in his way). Joe Behar, the program's director, describes how the interaction between straight man and stooge worked itself out. The expert chefs "would show their most famous recipes and then when he [Kovacs] would try to prepare them he would create a mess. He did stay within the framework, however, and [viewers] could, theoretically, copy down what they were doing and make the dishes, so it wasn't a complete burlesque."[33] In other words, just as Julia Child later would spice up a rigorous commitment to effective culinary ac-tivity with humorous, even comically outlandish, setups but with the ultimate assumption that there still should be efficacious demonstra-tion of the art of cooking, so too did Kovacs's show seem to have revolved around a mediation of serious pedagogy and zany comedy rather than the anti-educative undoing of the former by the latter.

In 1951, just a day after NBC put one of his more typically comic vaudevillian shows, *Time for Ernie*, into national exhibition, WPTZ gave Kovacs another food show, *Now You're Cooking*, which was spon-sored by a natural gas company and contained plugs for gas cooking. *Now You're Cooking* adhered to the more typical format of the single cook alone in the kitchen—in this case, Kovacs cooking various simple recipes for housewives—and not enough is known today about the show to enable one to determine the extent to which Kovacs was able to turn his one-man stand into a propitious venue for his zany, improvisational comedy.

Kovacs's efforts in television cuisine represent a unique moment in the intersection of the two arts and form no part of a transmissible legacy.[34] But the wacky assault on a recipe's effective enactment resembles those demonstrations of domestic culinary ineptitude that would show up on so many comedy shows of the 1950s. (For example, Lucy Ricardo often wreaked havoc in the kitchen.) Beyond the cooking show as a specific genre of instructional television in the period, food was central to television's representation of everyday life, because success in its preparation signaled success in the domestic American dream and in the feminine mystique that held that women's culinary perfection in the home setting was key to marital and familial happiness and was, moreover, the foundation of one's perfection as an American woman. Failure said something about the limits of that dream and that mystique. It is not inappropriate that one of the most famous episodes of *Alfred Hitchcock Presents*, "Lamb to the Slaughter" (1958), from a story by Roald Dahl, has an abused housewife killing her husband with a frozen leg of lamb and then serving the murder weapon to the police detectives investigating his murder. Here, the housewife makes the perfect meal and does thereby seem to fit the feminine mystique she is supposed to fall into as a dutiful hostess, but she does so in subversion of marriage and in mockery of mainstream governmentality.

Kovacs and these kitchen subversives work to undo many of the domestic values the home economists built up in their mainstream cooking shows. For an example of the latter, take Kovacs's primary successor at WPTZ, who certainly appears to fit the idea and ideal of the daytime homemaker mold. From 1947 into the 1960s, Florence Hanford evidently achieved some local celebrity at WPTZ for a variety of cooking demonstrations that ranged from onetime appearances on other hosts' shows and culinary segments in broader domestic instruction programs to a stand-alone cooking show of her own, *Television Kitchen*, for which she hosted 1,005 live episodes.[35] A Wednesday afternoon offering, *Television Kitchen* was sponsored by the Philadelphia

Electric Company (before she went to WPTZ, Hanford had worked as a home economist for the company), and the overall claim of the show was that electric cooking was clean cooking, so Hanford never wore an apron. She would cook up to five recipes per episode, and viewers could write in for copies. One description of the program suggests that it involved a degree of pre-planning comparable, perhaps, to that of *The French Chef* (see chapter 5) and probably unavailable to more unassuming, lower-budget daytime cooking shows at smaller stations outside urban locales: "For her half-hour show, she planned a complete menu. She would list all the ingredients needed and any special type of plates required. She then tested every recipe herself. On Mondays, she would have a complete rehearsal to check the timings and appearance of the prepared recipes. Then they would have another rehearsal, preparing everything again. . . . On Wednesday, the actual day the show would air, she would repeat it all over again with yet another rehearsal." At the same time, the recipes seem much more Middle American than daring and foreign, as on *The French Chef.* Indeed, through the 1950s, the station (which eventually was renamed WRCV) would advertise Hanford's show as a quite domestic offering: "Every week you see a complete, perfectly balanced meal, appetizingly prepared. New, inexpensive menu ideas to suit every family's budget." A sample menu (from the show that aired on November 29, 1950) confirms this emphasis on all-American conventionality in foods that average audiences would likely already be comfortable and familiar with: "Baked Spareribs, Frankfurters with Sauerkraut, Mashed Potatoes, Vegetable Salad Bowl, Apple Lime Chiffon Cake." One particularity of the show that fans from the time remember was that Hanford appears to have used an on-camera assistant whom she would ask for ingredients or utensils and acknowledge by saying in ritual fashion, "Thank you, Mrs. . . ." (there were a number of such assistants over the years, all married women, thereby maintaining the domestic emphasis of the show).[36]

In the mid-1950s, another household hints successor at WPTZ to Ernie Kovacs's cooking shows was Mary Wilson's *Pots, Pans, and Personalities*, which aired in the same time slot that *Deadline for Dinner* had held and employed the magazine format. Wilson's show involved multiple segments to cover the cooking of recipes (some of her own creation and some sent in by viewers), the offering of household hints, and the hosting of noted guests and celebrities (on whom the culinary creations would be tried out). In many ways, Wilson's show again seems typical of women's daytime magazine-format television of the time. One rare photograph of her at work—standing in front of a camera and next to a table with food and condiments on it as she beamingly offers the actor Alan Mowbray a taste of hamburgers from her own recipe—resembles any number of cooking-show images from the 1950s in which celebrities who happened to be in town were recruited to give a few minutes of their time to spice things up in local daytime programming. The one intriguing distinction—one that might bring *Pots, Pans, and Personalities* a bit closer to the vaudeville aesthetic on which Kovacs, among others, would expand in the 1950s— was that Wilson's show included musical numbers (especially one in which *she* and a "singer-comedian" crooned a tune dedicated to a women's club from the area).[37]

Beyond the zany chef and the matter-of-fact home economics instructor, there were also cases, rarer no doubt, of television cooks who tried to make a difference by making food that was different—that is, food for special occasions, exotic food, and distinctive French food. One famous chef who tried in this manner to use television pedagogy to elevate American culinary taste—but who also compromised her imputed distance from U.S. commercialism by agreeing emphatically to plug sponsors' products—was Dione Lucas, an important symbol of French cooking in New York through the postwar period.[38] Lucas's first show, which debuted on a local channel in 1947 and then became a CBS national offering in 1948, was *To the Queen's Taste*, a title redolent of snobbish British investment in aristocratic value systems. It was broadcast from Lucas's own restaurant in New York and ran for more than two years. The show was sometimes also called *The Dione Lucas Show*, and when it went off the air, that name was used by Lucas on and off for her local daytime programs through the 1950s.

Lucas, an Englishwoman with some of that stiff-upper-lip aplomb that is so much a part of the cliché of the crusty British cultural snob, has been somewhat overshadowed in culinary history by figures such as

M. F. K. Fisher and Julia Child, who set out to mediate Frenchness for American audiences by means of sensuous enjoyment and a passion for life. Throughout the 1960s, nonetheless, Lucas was a doyenne of French gastronomy. Like Child, she had been to the Cordon Bleu cooking school, and like Child, she used her experience to offer classes in the culinary arts. With cookbooks, famed restaurants, and even, eventually, a line of kitchenware, Lucas became so key to the New York scene for French cooking that she was the person at the beginning of the 1960s who hosted the well-attended launch party for Julia Child and one of her co-authors, Simone Beck, when *Mastering the Art of French Cooking* was first published. (The story has it, however, that Lucas's noted drinking problems were well in play by that time, and she ended up not being much of a host, leaving it to Beck and Child to do much of the party prep.)

Marital problems had driven Lucas, who had two small children, to the United States and a chance for new opportunities. But there was always, it seems, a touch of desperation and depression to her, and most food writers, to the extent that they deal with her at all, see her life as somewhat tragic, a failed or missed opportunity. Like James Beard, Lucas began her television culinary pedagogy very early in the postwar history of the medium. As with Beard, her first efforts were broadcast in the evening (in her case, for a half-hour on Thursdays), which suggests a certain degree of prestige, but it also may say something about early postwar television, in which stations needed any programming whatsoever to fill up air time. In fact, *Variety*, in a brief notice for the show, asserted that daytime broadcast might have been more appropriate for it; *Variety*'s recommendation suggests that an assumption about the cooking show's pronounced affinity with the daytime schedule of the housewife had already been put into place. (Maybe Lucas's dryness of presentation made her program seem more like the home economics shows that filled up daytime television; or maybe *Variety* was accepting as given the association of any cooking whatsoever with daytime instruction for women.) In *Variety*'s words, "Under normal procedures … this type of show should be slotted for afternoon viewers."[39] In fact, Lucas's later, non-network shows all appear to have been daytime offerings, but this may have resulted from a fall from grace due to her noted personality problems rather than from a programming decision about where cooking shows generally belonged in the schedule.

Lucas certainly tried to bring to her culinary enterprise a high-society sophistication that might have seemed apposite for evening television, with its occasional forays into grace and cocktail-party elegance (think of *The Loretta Young Show*, with its eponymous host wafting through silky curtains wearing beautiful gowns). Lucas was all about crusty refinement of an evening-party sort. Evidently, for instance, she frequently began her in-person cooking classes with instruction in how to flute mushrooms for a decorative look, whereas typically a pedagogy in French cuisine might begin more prosaically with stocks and then sauces.

Lucas tried to offer elegance to the cooking show even in her own appearance. As the chef and food scholar Madonna Berry puts it in a rare scholarly study of Lucas's television work, "On the [surviving] 1953 cooking show she wears a fancy dress with a full skirt and [one-quarter] length sleeves, tight fitting bodice with darts and ruffles accenting the breast with just a hint of cleavage, a frilly, large bow, perfect make-up and a diamond ring. . . . The clothes she wore also reinforced the status of the foods she was preparing."[40] Lest this description make Lucas seem a sexpot, it is important to emphasize those aspects of her mien that were less about dazzle and frilliness than about no-nonsense assumption of the task at hand (a task that, to be sure, would likely include fancy socializing and the concomitant need to be dressy and elegant). Surviving episodes of her television shows offer a glimpse of her not as an extravagant bombshell but as a self-possessed, unruffled woman of poise with a bit of a hardened edge. Lucas's outfits signify dressiness, but they also speak of a professionalism so in control that it need not worry about the risks of kitchen soiling. (As Berry notes, Lucas wore no apron, and the implication is that, unlike the sweaty and grimy Julia Child, who endlessly wiped her hands on her apron, Lucas was above the messiness of the everyday world.) Even as Lucas emphasized cooking for status and social occasion—for example, she introduced her omelet show by saying omelets are a wonderful offering for luncheon guests—this was a deferred, even self-sacrificing, sort of entertainment in which the cook went about her business in no-nonsense fashion and denied herself any immediate pleasure for the later gratification, confirmed by her guests, that hers was a job well done. As Berry notes, Lucas did no tasting of her dishes along the way (unlike, say, Child, who emphasized the need to taste not only to check up on the recipe but to enjoy heartily the process of the flavors coming together), and the available episodes of Lucas's show end with her showing off the results but not partaking of them. This is quite self-denying in contrast to the tradition of self-reward through tasting and consuming that runs from Julia Child to Nigella Lawson, Rachael Ray, and Giada di Laurentiis.

This is not to say that Lucas's emphasis on restrained professionalism leaves no room for levity. Rather, the archived episodes offer moments of a wry, even sardonic, and yet controlled and crafted humor of the sort one can associate with British pretension to upper-classness. But even at her wryest, Lucas seems not to be a very dynamic performer, and her stabs at an authenticity of personality are marred by her willingness to serve shamelessly as a shill for branded products. For instance, on one show, when she has put an item into the oven to bake for a while, she goes so far as to recommend that the spectator use the waiting time in appreciation of something beautiful—such as a great landscape or the grandness of the Caloric Stove, which the viewer should be using to cook the dish.

As Lucas's case exemplifies, there undoubtedly already were glimpses in the cooking shows of the 1950s of the need to think about food, beyond home economics, as a spectacle of status and distinction meant to impress guests and bring cultural uplift, rather than as mere sustenance (however nutritious and tasty) for one's family alone. But Lucas's staid and even stilted performance meant that she offered a dryness of instruction that was really not so far ultimately from that of the home economists. This is again where Julia Child stepped in to offer an experience that overwhelmingly seemed worlds apart from what preceded it.

At the same time, for all of Child's energized rejection of cookery as mere domestic exercise to get nutritious but unadventurous food on the table, she inherited from the television cookery of the 1950s the emphasis on efficiency and speed and on an attendant sense of pressure and necessity. After all, her show managed, as had many before it, to cram a panoply of cooking demonstrations and culinary hints into a mere half-hour. True, it was also a fun-filled half-hour, unlike many of the dry home economics lessons that a number of the earlier shows undoubtedly imparted. But it was still a temporality governed by a sense of scarcity (in this case, of time) and of the pressures of the clock.

Nonetheless, the declared Frenchness of Child's show offered one essential difference. This was not food just as staple but as a transcendence of mere necessity alone: food that was fully socialized and no longer about domestic obligations; food that increasingly valued taste over mere sustenance; food that, it was claimed, went beyond the familiar and opened new gustatory horizons. It is striking, for instance—and a striking demonstration of how little Child needed in her historical moment to make her cuisine seem new and different from typical American fare—to watch Child propagandizing frequently for *garlic* as a special, distinctive, uplifting part of French cuisine. Through much of the early twentieth century, garlic, as Harvey Levenstein notes, had had a place in mainstream American mythology, but with negative connotations as a low-class immigrant food that ethnic groups such as the Italians consumed, to malodorous effect.[41] In contrast, Child introduced garlic (even her upper-crust accent made it seem of high caste: "*gah-lick*," she would enunciate) as a new and different ingredient that would add artistry to a dish. The negative connotations were also overcome by an emphasis on moderation (garlic more as a flavor enhancer than a foodstuff in its own right) and by crafty hints about ways to minimize the overpowering smell to bring out the more subtle (and therefore classier) underlying fragrance—for example, by boiling the cloves in milk, one could remove most of the low-class noxiousness and give garlic its true, high value. Elsewhere, garlic might not always have standing in the most haute of haute cuisine—there are stories about French food snobs turning their backs on supposedly refined restaurants that dared to include something as vulgar as garlic in their dishes—but Child's version of French cuisine was primarily focused on hearty bourgeois fare. There, garlic could have pride of place and could mediate between ostensibly more refined French food and ostensibly more banal American offerings.

There was much in Julia Child that was like the TV cooks that preceded her, but she was also about the little tricks, the little emendations, and the added flair that would transform everyday experience. Given the existing American mythologies of France as a source of epiphanous transformation, perhaps just adding garlic to a dish could indeed make a difference.

3 French Cuisine, American Style

INTERVIEWER: You are the only French person I know
who has told me he prefers American food.
MICHEL FOUCAULT: Yes. Sure. [*Laughter*] A good club sandwich
with a Coke. That's my pleasure. It's true. . . . Actually, I
think I have real difficulty in experiencing pleasure.
—Michel Foucault, ''The Minimalist Self,''
interview with Steve Riggins, 1983

Two CIAS began their postwar trajectories within a year of each other
(1946–47), and each in its own way had something to do with America's search for its place in the world as it emerged into new contexts of
home-front affluence accompanied by fraught global tensions. Each
CIA attempted in its fashion to solidify tranquility in the domestic
sphere through intervention in international arenas.

The first CIA is, of course, notorious. A reworking of the wartime
Office of Strategic Services (OSS), the Central Intelligence Agency had
as its mission to engage in covert operations throughout the world,
especially in what has been termed countries of the "middle ground"—
those nations whose commitments in the Cold War period were considered ambivalent and capable of tipping either way. But the other
CIA, the Culinary Institute of America, was no less connected to the
new values of an America moving out of wartime. Aided by the capital
that flowed out from the GI Bill, the New Haven Restaurant School,
founded in 1946 and renamed the CIA in 1951 (and relocated to Hyde

Park, New York, in the 1970s), targeted returning veterans and was intended to give them viable careers in high-end food preparation.[1] Predictably, indeed, it was French cuisine on which the CIA's pedagogy focused; through the period, as Patric Kuh and others have shown, it was French food above all that signified culinary distinction for Americans.[2]

Yet there was always the sense that the mission was not just to perfect French cuisine but to show its adaptability to strong traditions of American life. The U.S. cooking schools might claim that their mission was to bring high-class food into the supposed culinary mediocrity that was America, but they also had to do with America itself as an adventurous, inventive nation that had its own path to forge in the postwar world and that could foster its own cuisine, even if it was derived from the French. It was always important in such a context that, even as it opened itself to cultures at large from which it took some inspiration, America still saw itself in charge. Revealingly, when the film musical *It's Always Fair Weather* (1955) deals with the training of GIs in gastronomy by chronicling how one of its three heroes, the cook Angie (Michael Kidd), comes back from Europe with aspirations to haute cuisine, it is pretension of this sort that he will abandon by film's end when he realizes he has to be who he is—a good old American hash slinger at home in upstate New York.

The emergence of the two CIAs is coincidental, then, but not totally so. Both were inspired by mediations of the global and the domestic necessitated by postwar geopolitics, and it is indeed clear that America saw both the international front and the *home* front as sites for national self-promotion. Domestic affluence and domestic technological achievement were themselves presented as virtues that radiated with an aura of American accomplishment. Perfection in the perfect kitchen was indeed a confirmation of America's vital role in the world.[3]

In her own way, Julia Child labored between internationalism and domesticity, between global intrigue and the comforts of the kitchen. From work as a data collector for the OSS during the war, she moved in the postwar period into a position as an overseas diplomat's wife, this in a period when U.S. diplomacy itself was often a form of information gathering and propagandizing. Social life in postwar over-

Julia Child's last visit to the CIA.

Photograph courtesy Culinary Institute of America.

seas diplomatic circles was rarely innocent and was often overcharged with hidden agendas, acts of seduction, languages of double meaning, maneuvers, and jockeying for position. More generally, to the extent that status in the postwar period overall was supposed to be tied to appearance—how you came off to others, how they saw you—one's social performance in so many social circles of the 1950s became indistinguishable from an act of disguise, a covert operation, even a tactic of deception. For example, every good host or hostess had to have a set of strategies and even subterfuges at hand to beguile the guests and make them feel they were intimately in her or his orbit and being singled out for special and privileged attention.[4]

As a narrative act, the sort of cooking Julia Child would come to stand for can bear a resemblance to spy stories, especially those that entered the public imagination in 1962 (the year of the three pilot shows of *The French Chef* at WGBH in Boston) with the first of the James Bond films, *Dr. No*. Like the derring-do tales in which Agent 007 was caught up, the culinary narrative, especially when it deals with bringing exotic objects back from the world at large and into a contained space back home, is often about a mission with a deadline, one in which an intrepid hero embarks on his or her task in a race against time while benefiting from carefully honed techniques and specialized gadgets and gizmos. Child's forays into French cuisine can be compared to the work of the espionage agent who ventures into foreign territory and brings back important secrets to unveil to those at home. It seems appropriate that the structuralist thinkers of the 1960s (more about them later) turned to both spy tales and cuisine for examples of pure narrative whose stages and steps, and logics of transformation, could easily be mapped. These are fundamental tales of heroism, pure epics of modern accomplishment.[5]

As an icon of cinema in the 1960s, James Bond, of course, had his own investment in practices of culinary distinction. Ian Fleming's snobbery plus a new U.K. internationalism brought about by jet travel were embodied in Bond in seemingly erudite knowledge of tobacco, coffee (still an exotic drink in the 1960s), and rarefied foodstuffs.[6] Thus, where episodes of *The French Chef* from its debut in 1963 on gave some attention to the proper wines to serve with various meals, so too would the film of *From Russia with Love* (1963): on the Orient Express, Bond realizes that his supposed helper, Donovan Grant, is an enemy agent and not a true Englishman when Grant orders red wine with fish! (For what it's worth, when I saw the film as an adolescent in 1963, I took that piece of culinary pedagogy as a key bit of worldly wisdom to be stored up for later, adult years.)[7] Bond was about a cosmopolitanism that could master high cultures of the world and yet remain fully virile, fully a Cold War national subject. In like fashion, the Bond parody *Our Man Flint* (1966) had its debonair spy realizing that a poison dart bore traces of bouillabaisse and setting off on a tour of Marseille to find the restaurant that had made the dish according to the precise combination of ingredients that lingered on the dart. Just as that film was my first introduction to the French dish, many Middle Americans no doubt had first learned of bouillabaisse's existence three years earlier when Julia

Child cooked it on her show. These works of popular culture entertained but they also taught about being (or imagining being) a cosmopolitan of the 1960s. Their action heroes and heroines mediated foreign and domestic cultures by mastering equally a dandified European style and a go-getter American pragmatism that manifests itself as an insistently American valorization of direct action, a no-nonsense investment in confronting tasks and doing what it takes to get them done, including entering bodily into the fray.[8]

In this respect, more than just transmitting another culture's systems of knowledge by, for instance, *recounting* what one has learned on one's foray into foreign territory, Child's "mission" was to *embody* that knowledge, to thereby take it over by corporealizing it. Certainly, *Mastering the Art of French Cooking* is a big, wordy book rich in discourse about things French, and, likewise, *The French Chef* certainly is a talky show. Yet both are also very much about the visceral rendition of action—French cooking as something you not only talk about but *do*, and do in highly embodied, physicalized manner, because you've fully internalized its ways and means. The gerund *Mastering* that finally was chosen for the title of *Mastering the Art of French Cooking* can seem apt in this respect, for one of the book's goals is to take possession of a foreign tradition so that it can be conveyed to citizens of one's own country back home.

"Mastering" here means not simply learning abstract, foreign lore—especially if "learning" is understood to mean a merely intellective process—but incarnating it, making it part and parcel of one's own being and, by teaching it, getting others to share energetically in the act of embodiment. Hence, the title that was finally chosen for the television show, *The French Chef*, is similarly appropriate because it implied that even this rambunctious, new American woman (and her audience) could not merely emulate but *be* the role. Child herself emphasized how the title of her show referred to a generalizable activity that would not be limited to one identity—say, the professional Frenchman in the kitchen. Like a secret agent slipping into a new identity, anyone could train to be a "French chef." As she put it in a letter to WGBH when she was first militating for the station to settle on *The French Chef* as the title for her series, "It makes no difference what sex the chef is—as everyone who is a professional cook, even a cat, is a chef."[9]

As with the book that preceded it, *The French Chef* TV show had to do, then, with international relations, mastery of foreign lore, and the revelation of secrets to a domestic audience. What the medium of television added to the mix was its making the possibility of revelation all the more widely available to multitudes of ordinary citizens. Now, to say this—to link spying and television in emphasizing the moment of public revelation—might seem paradoxical. After all, where spying can seem to be about obscurity, shadow realms of the hidden and the surreptitious, television is often a site of openness and making visible. It is evident that one of the powers of TV in the 1950s and 1960s was that it made privacy and secret moments public. There might be little obscurity, little that would remain undercover, in such a realm.[10]

The 1960s are, for instance, notably the moment of that great example of televisual voyeurism, *Candid Camera*, where the assumption is that no behavior potentially remains unwatched, undetected. Such public rendering of private peccadilloes might appear the opposite of spying's need for the surreptitious, the hidden, the obscure. Spying, it might seem, relies on invisibility, whereas television is a medium of generalized visibility. As Lynn Spigel notes in her classic study, *Make Room for* TV, postwar television was often caught up in mythologies of openness and expansive witnessing as, for instance, in the notion of television as a window onto the world—not unlike the sliding glass doors, bay windows, and open-to-the-kitchen living rooms of suburbia in the 1950s and 1960s that meant everyone potentially was in circulation with everyone else.[11] As in the famous story of the near-disaster on *The French Chef* of the potato pancake (Child flipped it up from her skillet, missed catching it in one piece on its descent, and then saved the situation by cobbling it back together and advising the audience that since they were alone in the kitchen, they could do whatever they wanted), TV was a medium of *mock* privacy in which the camera caught the little details of everyday life and made them available to the watchful eyes of others. TV here was the medium of revelation, indeed.[12]

Yet one might note that spying also frequently requires instances of openness and of revelation all its own. There needs to be exposure as well as concealment, and many such moments of unveiling occurred with the help of television. At the very least, as a series of crises in international diplomacy in the early 1960s demonstrated, it was in the moment of public presentation of seemingly private secrets—the moment of unveiling of the perfidy of others—that espionage often discovered its raison d'être—for instance, John F. Kennedy's presenting of evidence of missile silos in Cuba on American television or, conversely, the Russians presenting evidence of U-2 flights over the Soviet Union through their capture of the pilot Francis Gary Powers. Spying finds one narrative endpoint in the exposure of knowledge. Spying endlessly is a hidden activity but one with a public side. You need to find out the secrets of other countries, but you also need to make them manifest and evident back home. You need to publicize what you've found out on your journey into foreign territory.

One irony of the cooking show, though, especially in the case of *The French Chef*—as concerned as it was with instruction in an elegant, exotic cuisine whose mastery was supposed to signal tastefulness and impart social distinction—is that pedagogical success might undo itself. If everyone mastered the same recipes and thereby "democratized" them, no status could be gained in any individual's mastery. Television's democratization can also threaten to become a standardization or homogenization. If television blurs private and public, it also blurs individual and collective insofar as television is about many isolated viewers all doing the same thing at the same time. Even if one typically watches television privately (or, at most, with family), there's also a collective aspect to it insofar as so many people in many houses potentially are doing it at the same time. At the beginning of the 1960s, Jean-Paul Sartre termed this phenomenon "seriality"—the atomization of the modern masses into isolated monads that, each in its own way, are doing the same thing as everyone else but doing it in discrete (and discreet) privatized realms.[13]

Specific television series play on this paradox of a privatized viewing that is also collective, and sometimes they even pretend that their presentation to the spectator is to the individual spectator alone. That is, it is you in your individuality, in your irreducible uniqueness, who is being addressed, even as any number of other individuals are likewise being addressed. The extreme, perhaps, is that weird show of the 1950s (so well parodied on *Saturday Night Live*), *The Continental*, in which a suave Latinate gentleman seductively coos to a first-person camera; it also shows up, though, in more mundane examples, such as the successful children's program *Romper Room*, whose sign-off scene involved the hostess using a magic mirror to announce by individual names the specific children who were (supposedly) watching the show at the moment: "I see Ronny, I see Billy, I see Karen. . . ." For better or for worse, television finds you where you are. It is a public medium that uncovers each person in the privacy of the home. This is why a chummy, somewhat folksy entertainer like Julia Child could make individual viewers feel she was their friend and somewhat like them, even as she presented a cuisine that presumably many of them didn't know much about.

In such a context, the special privilege of Frenchness that Child offered up was the shared promise of the transcendence of the everyday, even if there were everyday Americanized ways to get there. But to claim such Frenchness as one factor in the success of a gourmet cooking show like *The French Chef*, we may need first to address a blunt question: was Julia Child's cuisine in fact "French"? In any act of translation, there is a question about whether the result is a transposition of the original world or a transformation of it. Did Julia Child's mastering also entail distortion and, perhaps, even betrayal?

Indeed, some food writers have made strong claims that Child's cuisine was fundamentally American, and these claims have both a negative and a positive version. The negative vision of Child as fully an American cook came in a notorious screed, *The Taste of America* (1977), by John and Karen Hess. For the Hesses, American cuisine in the twentieth century was increasingly a degradation of the perfection of taste and of quality in American cookery of earlier centuries, and Julia Child was a prime culprit in this betrayal of original American ideals. She welcomed commercial products; she introduced compromises that sacrificed taste to expediency; she pretended to a culinary intelligence that really was an ignorance (of history of foods, of proper techniques); she fell into an all-too-common contemporary American propensity to make food seductive by making it sweet; and, most damaging, she used the masquerade of Frenchness to parade blunt effect (e.g., the gussied-up plate) in the place of real subtleties of taste. For the Hesses, most modern American food was a disaster, and Child was one of the Americans who had contributed mightily to that dreadful state of affairs and was enabling it only to get worse. As the Hesses saw it, the irony of the contemporary American approach to food was that it ignored the basic high quality of American foodstuffs and opted for the ersatz offerings of either the commercial food industry or pretentious would-be chefs who looked—wrongly—to France to reinvigorate U.S. cuisine.[14]

The positive version of the ostensible Americanness of Julia Child's cuisine received eloquent expression in Betty Fussell's *Masters of American Cookery* (1983), which argued, contrary to the Hesses, that American cuisine came into its own in the postwar period and that Child was one of four masters—along with M. F. K. Fisher, Craig Claiborne, and James Beard—to have brought about a revolution in it. For Fussell, the American masters were indeed deeply American in their pioneer spirit and boldness of adventure, rejection of dogmas, egalitarian ideology, fetish for motion and speed, acceptance of self-identity as something that is always refashioned and started anew, pragmatic interest in studying cause and effect and knowing therefore both how to do and how to teach acts of doing, and sheer rambunctious energy. Fussell quotes Child's dream that an adventurous America might become the future "food capital of the world" and adds her own gloss: "If America does, Julia will be more responsible than anybody because through the newest mass media she has brought home-cooking back into the American home. That she snuck it in with a French accent is tribute to the cunning of this master showman."[15]

Perhaps the question of whether or not an American can make French cuisine with the products available in America is one that can't really be answered to everyone's satisfaction, since that would require agreement on the very terms of the question. For the Hesses, who even appeal to biology and suggest that the average American today no longer even possesses taste receptors refined enough to recognize high-quality food, there can be no compromising (and no mediating or translating) of French food in a world where everything about mainstream American cookery is a compromise and even betrayal. For

"Julia Child says it's delicious, James Beard loves it, Craig is crazy about it, but Stanley J. Tischler, Jr., hates it."

Masters of American Cookery? J. B. Handelsman, *New Yorker* cartoon, December 3, 1984. Copyright J. B. Handelsman / Condé Nast Publications; courtesy Cartoon Bank.

Fussell, Americans by nature productively indigenize other cuisines and make them resonate with an American spirit of vital experimentation and dogma-free gusto.

Perhaps what matters is not whether Child's cuisine *was* French but that she and her American fans took it to be so. Fussell's reference to Child's cooking with "a French accent" is apt, since for Americans in the 1960s longing for sophistication but also wanting its achievements to come quickly and easily, it was enticing to think that the mere taking on of an accent could alter the identity of things. This again was the context in which "gah-lick" might make a difference.[16]

Indeed, Child herself sometimes said that this or that "French" dish was simply the same as something Americans already knew but with a different name, and in this respect she sometimes appeared to be directly translating seemingly exotic food back into familiar fare, as some of the TV cooks before her had done. For example, she introduced boeuf bourguignon by saying that it was basically just good old American beef stew. Likewise, in an early episode on fruit tarts (February 1963), she explained that adding butter to a sauce would give it "that certain French taste you don't get in any other cooking," suggesting that this one ingredient had transformative powers but ones that could be accessible to any ordinary American (since butter is a readily available item).[17]

In those sectors of postwar America that imagined they could go beyond the chores of domesticity to embrace creativity in lifestyles unburdened by mere necessity, French food held out particular attractions. It matters deeply that it was *French* cuisine that Julia Child claimed to be "mastering," whatever the debate about her cuisine's actual, ultimate Frenchness. The very fact that a mysterious, even exotic, cuisine redolent of European cultural distinction could be brought down from the heights and physicalized and thereby Americanized was part of the appeal. Child offered one means to mediate French culture for a U.S. (or, at least, a status-seeking demographic within in) that wanted cultural distinction, but on its own terms.

French cooking was the special path to a merging of good taste and tasting good (to reiterate the distinction that Charlie the Tuna had trouble mastering in the same period), and it promised a panache of distinction while turning out to be democratically attainable for anyone ready to follow along. For many American women, for instance, there were stirrings of dreams of new life patterns that somehow wouldn't follow the seemingly natural presumption that woman's place was, precisely, in the kitchen, either performing domestic drudgery or finding canned shortcuts as alternatives to it. In some cases, of course, this meant leaving the kitchen altogether and turning one's back on what one saw as its complicity with a "feminine mystique" that worked to keep women from power in public. But in other cases, it perhaps meant rethinking the kitchen as something other than a site of drudgery—for instance, as an arena for experimentation in new tastes, new looks, and new pleasures. Laura Shapiro's classic study of women and cuisine in the postwar period, *Something from the Oven*, chronicles some of the ways such tensions and contradictions manifested themselves, culminating, as Shapiro wryly notes, in the simultaneous appearance within a few short days in 1963 of Betty Friedan's *The Feminine Mystique* and the first episodes of *The French Chef*.[18] If Friedan's volume is fairly unambiguous in its shocked view of training in domestic skills for middle-class women as an entrapment, it is still an open question whether the emphasis on cooking as a fine *art* in the way that Child promoted it has the easy complicity with domestic ideology that *The Feminine Mystique* attributes to more evidently alienating forms of training of women in everyday household management. One has to eat to survive, but the home cook typically doesn't *need* to cook or consume in a specifically French style to meet requirements for survival, and in that distinction lay a possible margin of liberty that questing souls might try to make something of in the 1960s.

Undertaking a long, complicated recipe, when one might have just used convenience foods to meet the family's minimal needs, could be an act of self-assertion.[19] Here was one place in which French cuisine could matter. It serves as an example of the "hedonizing technologies" that Rachel P. Maines has analyzed as so defining of the leisure culture of modernity. For Maines, "hedonizing" practices are hobby-like activities with no utility and in which one engages out of no necessity, just for the immersive fun of it all. Her neologism "hedonizing" intends to capture both how such practices are about the purposeless pursuit of personal pleasure (they are hedonistic) and how they often provide a path to that pleasure by taking realms of activity that once had utility and freeing them of all necessity. (E.g., most people do not need to hunt to survive, although once some may have, and it is now considered a sport—albeit a controversial one—rather than a utilitarian practice.) Importantly, Maines notes that many hobbies and leisure pursuits take up a lot of time, and this seems to be the case not only because hobbyists become obsessive (which they often obviously do) but because the total immersion in sheer duration becomes an escape from other, more mundane, more necessary life activities. In Maines's words, "Clearly, part of the attraction is the closing-out of ordinary daily concerns: the capacity of the hobby to fully engage the attention of the participant seems to be a critical element. . . . hobby artisans and leisure-activity enthusiasts all report that the immersion of the senses and the intellect into the activity are the main motivation for engaging in it."[20]

To a large degree, French cuisine is like this. It takes time (to make, to enjoy); it demands concentration (to make, to enjoy). And, as Maines notes, what often is consuming about intensive activities of this sort is that they offer multiple and ever expanding means by which to engage in them (especially since they often lead to the creation of commercial industries that generate new items to collect and new instructional manuals to buy). The time commitment of French cuisine can also include, for instance, the time commitment of reading fat cookbooks about it (you can't just start cooking in a French way but are pushed to read texts such as the *Larousse gastronomique*), and French cooking is all about the endless gadgets (the hand technology) you need to accumulate, train with, and then haul out and use.[21]

To the extent that French cuisine had its hedonistic elements, it did not perhaps serve as alienated labor pure and simple for the 1960s fans who partook of it. Betty Fussell's celebration of the middle-class socializing scene in that decade, and of Child's role in serving as a model for refined lifestyle, tries to catch some of the more liberatory aspects of the process:

> Julia choreographed the production, plotting the time of preparation for each stage of each dish, detailing what could be prepared ahead, what frozen, what chilled. We each felt we had Julia in our corner. . . . For a long time, I was airborne by party dynamics, propelled by a group rhythm that seemed to obey principles of flight as mysterious as they were inevitable. There was that moment of suspension during the long slow taxi down the runway, the exhilaration when the party gathered speed and took off on its own and you could undo your seat belt and move around the cabin and laugh and drink wine instead of club soda and run up to the attic to the costume trunk to bring back an armful of funny hats so that

everyone could be ridiculous and next day call up and say, "Hey, that was some party." . . . There was even a pleasure in cleaning up afterward.[22]

Fussell's lyric linguistic transports hint at another important transformation in the nature of home life in the period. To be sure, the emphasis on an aesthetics of food—in its preparation, in its presentation, and in its consumption—might have to do with a feminine mystique in which the housewife plays into her own entrapment by devoting her time to food for her family that not only tastes good but looks good (and thereby visually radiates her love for them and confirms her assumption of her domestic mission). On the other hand, though, it also could break free of feminine-mystique familialism to tap into a growing concern for a personalized, individualized lifestyle in which independent women (and men, as we'll soon see) could find joys of living for themselves. Lifestyle, here, is about consumption: a self-centered, even at times selfish, taking in of pleasures more than a selfless giving of pleasures to dear ones around the self. It's also, of course, about consumerism; the assumption that it is through the buying and consuming of commercially distributed items, even if (or especially if) rare, that the intensities of pleasure are best to be had. French food—the food of distinction, the food of cultural capital—fit well into this sense of lifestyle as something to be worked at, something to be constructed through a perfecting of a self surrounded by consumer goods that radiated elegance and exoticism. The cultivation of lifestyle here entails a valorization of self, energized by consumerism, embracing private space, reveling in plays of bold performance of social status, and finding in all of this realms of pleasure, sources of self-confidence, and sites of empowerment in one's own eyes as well as those of others.

A key text in this regard is a bestseller that came out just as Child was preparing the pilot episodes for *The French Chef*: Helen Gurley Brown's steamy *Sex and the Single Girl*. Despite its salacious title, *Sex* is only partially about sex. In fact, it is more concerned overall with women discovering a consumerist independence in which they can have a good time that entails sensuous pleasures for all parts of the body, not exclusively the erogenous zones.[23]

Sex and the Single Girl lauds a world of social achievement and social status where admiring and being admired are as important as any physical contact. (That is, the enticing image of pleasure matters as much as the carnal payoff.) For our purposes, one revelatory aspect of *Sex and the Single Girl*'s expansive, and not just sexual, image of independent lifestyle is that it includes a chapter on cookery, with an emphasis on the impression that *French* food above all cuisines is supposed to impart by means of its look, its taste, and its connotations of distinction and privilege. In Brown's words, "The better cook you are the more renowned you become as a hostess. You will collect a small coterie of devoted fans who will bay your praises to every rising moon. It's a nice sound! Cooking gourmetishly is a particularly impressive skill for a career woman."[24] You might get away with entrancing that special man through steak, but for the hip crowd of one's friends, a more sophisticated French-looking (and sounding) meal might more appropriately do the trick.

Brown imagines that, like the skill-less postwar housewife living away from her mother, the single woman has no culinary legacy that she can build on. The difference is that the single woman is cooking not to satisfy a family but, rather, to impress the coterie of friends, colleagues, and interesting men who surround her in the big, bustling city. This requires food that makes one's guests ooh! and aah! with delight: striking food, exotic food, gourmet food. To a very large degree, French food is especially the answer. But this doesn't entail having to spend lots of money or, importantly, lots of time in the kitchen. Like Peg Bracken (*The I Hate to Cook Book*) in wanting to get food out quickly—but unlike her in centering culinary attention on the sort of food (and drinks) that guests rather than family will appreciate—Brown is all about shortcuts and tricks. For example, one can simply copy the efforts of some other woman who has been successful in the kitchen (and because saving time is of the essence, Brown recommends that you don't waste precious time on the phone getting recipes; instead, you should send a note with a self-addressed, stamped envelope). With careful pre-planning, one can soon be serving vichyssoise (Brown's recipe consists of Campbell's frozen potato soup mixed with half-and-half), escalopes of veal, chateau potatoes, lobster en brochette with "devil sauce" (a mixture of ketchup, Tabasco sauce, mustard, and Worcestershire sauce), and so on.[25]

For men too, French cuisine could have special meanings as an activity of the domestic realm. Masculinity was also under pressure in the postwar decades in ways that modified its relation to cuisine and the kitchen. Suburbanization and the explosion of a service economy meant that most men could no longer easily be seen as—and could no longer easily see themselves as—pioneers boldly adventuring out into new territories, and this meant perhaps that they had to think in new ways of the home-boundedness that increasingly would be their lot. (Ironically, Betty Friedan also invoked the mythology of the vanishing frontier in explaining the condition of postwar women, who also were no longer living in conditions that permitted them to be free spirits of open adventure: "The women who went west with the wagon trains also shared the pioneering purpose. Now the American frontiers are of the mind, and of the spirit. . . . Why should women accept this picture of a half-life, instead of a share in the whole of human destiny? Why should women try to make housework 'something more,' instead of moving on the frontiers of their own time, as American women moved beside their husbands on the old frontier?")[26]

There were, of course, denials at even the suggestion that things were changing for the American man. No-nonsense pulp action novels such Mickey Spillane's bestselling Mike Hammer series portrayed the city as a festering cesspool whose dangers necessitated the intercession of a macho man who was fast and furious ("My gun is quick") and who didn't need legal niceties to make his own law in the urban jungle ("I, the jury"). While Mike Hammer predictably spends very little time on lifestyle, he does enumerate his meals, which tend to consist of steak and potatoes accompanied by beer: unambiguously manly fare. (Conversely, when on a 1968 episode of *Dragnet*, "The Big High," detective Bill Gannon [Harry Morgan] devotes time to a barbecue recipe that he explains to partner Joe Friday [Jack Webb] is so good that Julia Child would be delighted to have him come on her show to present it, the would-be gastronome cop is clearly being mocked for his culinary pretentions. Gannon is seen as silly for wasting his time on a fastidious and fussy recipe that seems irrelevant to the tough cop job at hand—so much so that the barbecue sauce disquisition appears only at the episode's beginning to then drop out and never be heard of again as the cops have to deal with the sad story of a child neglected by drugged-out parents.)

Such versions of masculinity as Mike Hammer's were so sure of themselves that the men who embodied them felt they had no need to resort to performance to impress others and no need to refine their social skills in domestic venues such as the kitchen. For instance, in like fashion to Spillane's rendering of Mike Hammer, the film *Bullitt* (1968) used as one proof of its eponymous hero's total coolness the fact that, when he went to a supermarket to stock up, he simply shoveled a bunch of frozen dinners into his cart. Bullitt didn't seem to have anything to prove, so he could treat food as mere biological necessity (and he treated his girlfriend [Jacqueline Bissett] in much the same way).[27]

But it was getting harder perhaps to pull off this masculine performance, and change was in the air. For our purposes, the most curious image of masculinity in this respect might be that of the playboy man, encapsulated in the magazine of the same name, which started publication in 1953. On the one hand, *Playboy* intended to brook no challenge to the notion of man as virile conqueror. On the other hand, *Playboy*'s image of ideal masculinity was one precisely that revolved around consumerism and consumption, homebody lifestyle, bodily pampering, leisure time, fashion and finery, and so on, in ways that, if one didn't know better, might resemble a very *un*-heterosexual way to be a man. Here was a world of men who lounged around in pajamas and silk robes, who discussed colognes and fragrances, who gave attention to interior decoration, who read books and liked the world of ideas—who, in short, appreciated the world aesthetically and not only actively. Not for the playboy was life about going out into the frontier. As Hugh Hefner put it in his introduction to the first issue of *Playboy*, men of his ilk were not interested in "thrashing through thorny thickets or splashing about in fast flowing streams. We don't mind telling you in advance —we plan spending most of our time inside. WE like our apartment . . . We enjoy mixing up cocktails and an hors d'oeuvre or two."[28]

Whereas (as a long-running witticism would have it) men enthusiastically say they read *Playboy* for the articles when in reality they're really looking at the pictures, it is perhaps as accurate to reverse things and suggest that, for many men of the postwar decades, it might have been the presence of the nudie pictures that allowed them to read the articles, many of which addressed lifestyle issues in ways that could have appeared effeminate without the alibi of a commodification of naked women to affirm the heterosexuality of it all.

Not merely did the playboy man have no compunction about staying at home, but he enjoyed being in his kitchen, especially if he could make that part of a carefully staged activity of seduction, a performance of his home space for others (for example, the women who, he hoped, would be key components of his domestic life, as long as they didn't think about marriage and about settling in). As Bill Osgerby outlines, central to the bachelor pad's design in the 1950s was an openness of each area to the next. While he prepared wonderful concoctions for his guests (or female special guest), the playboy man could be watched doing his thing in the kitchen (and the distance from kitchen to couch to bed was designed to be minimal and easily traversed when the seductive spectacle of drinks and food preparation successfully worked its spell). In the playboy mythology, the function of the pad's open design was the opposite of that of the suburban home, where the open-floor layout was supposed largely to be about caring for others—about the need for the homemaker-wife to be able to know everything that was going on in the house and remedy any potential problems (which isn't to say that women in the home weren't also expected to be performing roles for the scrutiny of others around them). The playboy was playing to his guests rather than just looking out for them. Even his culinary accomplishments were not so much about giving his guests sustenance as about impressing them with a mastery that combined high culture sophistication with manly prowess.

In like fashion, *Esquire*, which also saw itself as an arbiter of men's taste (but without *Playboy*'s emphasis on nudie photography), called for men to enter into the stereotypically feminine realm of distinctive entertaining with its *Esquire Party Book*, which went through multiple editions in the 1960s. With dynamic graphics (including oh-so-'60s pop cartoons by the celebrated illustrator Seymour Chwast), the *Es-*

quire Party Book offered the impression of a world in which one had endlessly to throw social gatherings (page 1 bears the title "Parties around the Clock") and do so in a variety of forms, from the big buffet bash to the intimate affair (literally intimate and literally an affair, as one might have to think about the enticing food to serve at a midnight amorous rendezvous, as a section titled "Let the Lady Beware" advises). The *Party Book* calls for the new, hip host to challenge convention when possible—"today," we're told, "whole new courses have been dropped from the menu (the thud you have just heard was either the fish or the soup dropping)"—and take advantage of a bold, new culinary world: "While the food may be simpler, it's possibly better than ever, for a narrow clique of gourmets has broadened to include the wide new population of competent cooks and appreciative eaters. . . . Air-freight puts coastal crab and limestone lettuce on *any* dinner table with flavor-preserving speed. Belgian endive and Norwegian shrimp cross the ocean as casually as the transcontinental travelers who demand them. And self-education about wine and cheese and honest bread, which used to concern only the idle rich, has become small-talk on the commuter train."[29] That such new gourmet possibilities actually manifest themselves in the book's recipes in such items as liver and chestnuts wrapped in bacon, the ubiquitous postwar offering of Irish coffee, sherry-flamed scallops, and Trader Vic's Bongo Bongo Soup is only a testament to what in the period was considered sexy, cutting-edge party food for a certain class of entertainers.

Struggling to assert an identity, the playboy man needed performance, and culinary arts served as part of this. As Joanne Hollows outlines, *Playboy* magazine devoted regular columns to food preparation but of a very specific sort. They had to be about food in a way that was connected not to necessity but to leisure and luxury.[30] The playboy didn't worry about budget and didn't see food as domestic obligation. Food, in *Playboy*, was associated with travel, with sexual pleasure, with connoisseurship and expertise. As Hollows notes, *Playboy*'s food and wine editor, Thomas Mario, pushed for a cuisine that was refined and that stood out from ordinary domestic fare but also stood out, necessarily, from those sorts of refined cuisine that were thought to be too ornamental, frilly, and feminine. Here, French cuisine fit the bill as an exotic, alluring cuisine but one that required rational planning, that necessitated expert knowledge, that often required gadgets and gizmos, and that, if it certainly had its feminine side ("Real men don't eat quiche," as was claimed in the 1980s), also could easily be rendered as heartily masculine (any real man could eat—and have no problem making—a boeuf bourguignon). As Hollows puts it, "*Playboy*'s cookery columns often favor foods that are both 'exotic'—and hence novel—and, at the same time, 'authentic'—hence, traditional. In this way, the *Playboy* reader is directed toward novel 'foreign,' and sometimes regional, traditions . . . There is a heavy dependence on a French culinary tradition as the legitimate culinary tradition in Mario's work."[31]

For an America given over, in popular stereotype, to what the pop sociologist Vance Packard at the end of the 1950s had termed "status seeking," the aesthetic lifestyle that French food seemed to tap into was highly seductive, and Julia Child was one of the cultural mediators who made the faraway fantasy of good taste seem easily in reach for men and women. Child herself loved that men watched her Frenchified show, and she wanted more men to take over in the kitchen. As she wrote back to a male fan of the first season of her show, "It's good to know there are some enthusiastic men at the stove these days; men always have more daring and imagination than women—even if I do say so."[32] It was not so much that, in some sort of ode to metrosexuality before its time, Child thought that cooking might make macho men more sensitive but that, quite the contrary, she felt that women often had too great a tendency to dabble in the kitchen, to not take cooking seriously, to not respect it as the investment in deep pleasure that it could be. (To call someone a "housewife" was the worst insult she could come up with, short of blatant obscenity.) Women, she felt, showed a lack of commitment, of rigor, and of interest in the pleasures of food and its preparation. Men, in contrast, would in her view approach cookery with professionalism and honest engagement. Her investment in a techno-savvy masculinity as a propitious path to aesthetic sophistication in tasteful foreign cuisine is not that far from Thomas Mario of *Playboy*, whose pedagogy of culinary activity, as Hollows explains, was often about extensive pre-planning and preparation of meals (thereby both reiterating that this was cuisine that one could take time to do and appealing to a masculine interest in rationalized, rather than intuitive, procedure) and provided a lot of background history and lore about food and wine (thus, playing into a cult and culture of expert knowledge for the sophisticated man).

The American mythologizing of what it imagined Frenchness to be also entailed a mythologizing of the notion of America. That is, France meant certain things to America because America needed those things, and that says something about America too. In an interesting article on U.S. appropriations of French culture in the 1950s, Dina Smith treats the film *Sabrina* as a key text in its image of the girl-woman of the 1950s as a (semi-)orphaned waif who has culture on her side but requires strong Americans (Bill Holden, Humphrey Bogart) to give her a place in the new U.S.-driven world order.[33] Sabrina goes to France to study the culinary arts at the Cordon Bleu (where, of course, Julia Child also went); this gives Sabrina distinction, but it doesn't give her a go-getter purpose of existence. It's a two-way process. France, Smith suggests, needs the U.S. to complete her, but France has something from which the U.S. benefits. The gendering here is deliberate. Smith's point is that France is often represented at this cultural moment as a vulnerable, feminized subject who can't make it in the new geopolitical context on culture and charm alone. (Likewise, in her important essay on the history of the American reception of French culture, Alice Yeager Kaplan notes that postwar texts often spoke about English females as "women" but about French females as "girls").[34] On the other hand, as Smith notes, there's also a suggestion in these representations that a potentially bullish and brutish U.S. needs its emphasis on go-getter accomplishment at whatever cost to be tempered by the refinement that Old World European sophistication can offer it. Thus, in *Sabrina*, Bogart plays a no-nonsense, no-time-for-pleasure industrialist who must learn to open his heart to romance—to European sentiment, in other words, and all that it symbolizes of grace, sophistication, and artistry.

The mediation of Europe for Americans (and vice-versa) is a recurrent trope in American popular culture, and it is one that is often directly rendered in the body and being of select Americans who incarnate, it is assumed, the best of both traditions. In some instances, as in *Sabrina*, the mediation is spread across several bodies (Bogart, Hepburn), each of which stands for particular values in the equation and each of which needs the other for completion. In like fashion, we might reiterate how there was a certain cultural division of labor between Jack and Jackie in the White House, rambunctious energy on the masculine side and refined high culture and awareness of the arts on the feminine side. (This division would receive comic treatment in one sketch on Vaughn Meader's wildly popular comedy album *The First Family* in the early 1960s. At the reception line for a White House gala, Jackie knows each of the cultured European guests—such as Pablo Casals—and is able to chat fluently in each foreign language about art and society. Jack remains silent until he finally asks in exasperation, "Why do we always have to invite your friends?")[35]

Yet another embodiment of the American mediation of America and France was a virtually schizophrenic one in which the same body could be French in some moments and American in others. In particular, I'm thinking of *The Patty Duke Show*, whose run on TV (1963–66) overlaps that of *The French Chef*. On *The Patty Duke Show*, the single body is split into two (Patty, the American for whom "a hot dog makes her lose control," and Cathy, nominally Scottish but French-identified, who "adores a minuet, the Ballet Russe, and Crêpes Suzette"), with narratives of mediation generated about the ability of each cousin to teach the other and to learn from the other and thereby enable a rapprochement. Of course, the point was also that one actress played both characters. If Patty Duke offered the split or multiplied body, she also hinted at a hybrid body that combined in one single person facets of European high culture and elements of go-getter, rambunctious Americanness.

In these terms, we might say, Julia Child represents a New Frontier inflection of the U.S. encounter with French distinction now updated for the energetic 1960s. This new woman is no gamine, no orphan-like wisp of a woman who needs to be rescued. She is, instead, a strong, action-oriented figure who strides confidently toward her American destiny (the classmates in Child's class at the Cordon Bleu, in contrast to Sabrina's, were all former American soldiers studying abroad on the GI Bill, and Child was one of the gang even as she surpassed them in talent and accomplishment). Child offers in her own selfhood the mediation of *Sabrina*'s two cultures. She is the American "tough guy" and the European sophisticate rolled up into one. Child offers up a hybrid being that combines several cultural identities, sometimes in awkward fashion, as if the yoking together of European refinement and big-boned American boisterousness, of the French feminine gamine with the hard-hitting Yankee go-getter, issued in an eccentric composite.

As a composite of American rationalism and French fine art, Child was an apt hybrid mediator of the cultures. Within this hybridity, she offered a very specific take on French cuisine for Americans. Specifically, she was not just about preparing dishes that were French in content; she was about offering a complex culinary experience that involved specific ingredients prepared in specific ways, presented in specific ways, consumed in specific ways, and, although this initially might not seem at the same level of importance, talked about in specific ways. (As one of Gertrude Stein's witticisms would have it, the French talk about talking about food.) More than ingredients alone, it was all of this that made a dish "French."

One of Child's talents was to give attention to each and every step in cooking and suggest the particular ways they could be handled in a French-like manner, and then to talk about all of this in effusive fashion. French cooking in America, as noted, could mean doing things only in a literal French way or, conversely, trying to find parallels, if not direct equivalents, in the American context. Thus, to take just one example from the realm of ingredients, use shallots when you can, but settle for scallions (or green onions, to translate them into American familiarity even more) if need be. Or, even better, push your grocer to start carrying shallots so they become part of the American scene. Legendarily, many food purveyors found that any rare ingredient mentioned in an episode of *The French Chef* led to an influx of customers the very next day asking for that item and pressuring for it to be made regularly available. In the words of one fan letter from Oklahoma in the mid-1960s: "Through your efforts, our stores are now stocking leeks and fresh mushrooms, something unheard of 3 months ago."[36]

Conversely, however, it was not necessarily the case that just using French or French-like ingredients or French-like techniques made a meal French. The full experience required a Frenchness in all stages of the process, from planning and shopping through the prepping and cooking and into the activity of pleasurable consumption. Each of these phases had to be enjoyed—and enjoyed, moreover, in often lingering, languorous fashion. For example, a French meal is not to be consumed quickly and without unfolding waves of pleasure. Even when made with authentic French ingredients, the meal would lose something of its Frenchness in that hurried manner of consumption. To take a fanciful example, whereas a New York hot dog bought from a street cart can seem to taste best (at least in my experience) when wolfed down as one hastens to one's next appointment (and it's a great consumption in that context), that hurried eating would betray a French meal, whose effects have to be experienced in slow duration. (Conversely, the New York hot dog might itself be betrayed if one took too much time with it and gave it too much attention.) It is noteworthy that in a show on lobsters from the 1970s, Child begins by saying that she will talk in the episode as much about *the ways to eat* lobsters as to how to prepare them: for her, the work of production is wasted if it leads to indifferent, un-reflected, and therefore inadequate (in terms of taste and pleasure) consumption.

Child's own philosophy of French food eschews all implications of a firm break between the stages of preparation and consumption. Her conception of culinary quality is more generally and more forcefully about the interweaving of all the elements that make a meal seem distinctively French. For example, where the notion of stages might imply a single, forward-moving chronology—and no doubt, there *is* an emphatically progressive temporality to the cooking show where you've got to get from one step to the next and deal with the task at hand—it was necessary in French cuisine, Child emphasized, to think at the beginning of the end. Knowing how the food ultimately would be served and consumed was integral to how it was to be prepared, and the legendary degree to which she (and her husband, Paul) painstak-ingly, methodically, and minutely prepared each moment of the show in advance was about controlling the process but it was also about assuming that the ends were contained in the means and had to be envisioned together. And the ends were literally manifested in the means in those many moments along the way in the kitchen where

Child tasted dishes as she prepared them and they cooked away to their conclusion. There was simple good culinary sense here—taste your dishes as you make them—but there was also the deeper implication that each stage of your preparation already contained in it adumbration of the results: French cooking especially was an organic narrative in which present and future results melded together even as it offered distinct stages or phases.

Similarly, discourse about food would come not only at the end in the appreciative dialogue between host and guest about the qualities of what they had just consumed (or were right then consuming) but should run through the culinary process from beginning to end. *The French Chef* was in fact a very talky show, with Child and her crew pushing themselves to fill up each moment of air time with chatter. No doubt, this had to do with broadcast television's fear of dead time, but it also fit a conception of French food as something that should be explained, evaluated, commented on at each and every instant. Indeed, as Priscilla Parkhurst Ferguson notes, it is the very extent to which French food is surrounded from start to finish with text and talk that helps make it seem special (because it is worthy of so much attention): "Nowhere is culinary self-consciousness more finely tuned than in France. . . . A key element sustaining this acute consciousness of the culinary self has to do with the stories the French tell about food. . . . Although every cuisine relies on texts to carry food from its originary place into cultural space, cuisine in France is carried, and reinforced, by an especially far-reaching discourse about food. The sheer number and variety of stories, along with the cultural narrative to which they link, testify to the privileged position that cuisine occupies in singling out things French."[37]

And in Julia Child's case, it matters that the explanatory discourse that accompanies her cuisine from start to finish is itself accompanied from start to finish by the clear and emphatic expression of deep, visceral pleasure at what is being done and what is being said. In other words, the discourse is one of explanation, but it is also one of pleasure. The stages of French cuisine are linked by logic but also by the sheer enthusiasm and engagement they inspire at each and every moment. One can enjoy the act of consumption, but one should no less enjoy the acts of planning and preparation, and one should enjoy them, moreover, in anticipation of the end result (in cooking for guests, a "French chef" is using the imagination of how they ultimately will respond as itself an "ingredient" in the preparation) and as pleasurable activities in their own right.[38]

Such pedagogies of French cuisine resonated with an American hunger for the impression of cultural uplift that this cuisine seemed to promise. As Fussell, who was strongly influenced in her cooking by Julia Child, puts it in her culinary memoir of the 1960s: "To cook French, eat French, drink French . . . was to become versant in the civilized tongues of Europe as opposed to America's barbaric yawp."[39] But it is also the case that French cuisine was particularly seductive not only because of the status it imparted but also because it was easy, especially as Child translated it, to encapsulate in a pedagogy. On the one hand, French cuisine revolves around a highly codified set of manual and material practices by which recipes are brought to fruition. These practices can be articulated, verbalized, and taught. On the other hand, French cuisine not only has to do with the making of the dishes but is also about the sheer amount of discourse that surrounds culinary activity, and this makes it directly verbal in an eminently teachable manner. That those who are interested in French food, from its producers to its consumers, love to talk about it, and that this outpouring of discourse seems of a piece with a broader intellectualizing trend in French life, which refuses the distinction between manual practice and intellection, no doubt can mean that French food is often approached through conversation that easily can take on a lecturing tone. Again, to quote Fussell, "When an [American] hostess [in the 1960s] set forth a salmis de faisan, she supplied footnotes on what a salmis was. Presenting a poulet chaud-froid, she held a seminar to explain how each layer of white sauce was chilled before the next; and how the whole was decorated with medallions of chicken and topped with truffle cutouts before it was shellacked with layers of clear aspic."[40] French food was an education, and Child was one of the best of educators.

While it is common to suppose that the modern mythologizing of French cuisine started in the postwar period—Craig Claiborne once famously quipped that the gourmet revolution in American food began on June 17, 1947, when Pan Am introduced an affordable around-the-world flight and made the globe accessible to Middle America—the contemporary American romance with French food actually had earlier manifestations (with the even longer history of the romance going back to colonial times). The year 1941, for example, saw both the opening of the posh (and exclusive) Le Pavillon restaurant in New York and, as important, the premier issues of a new (and exclusive) food journal, *Gourmet*. Despite—or perhaps because of—the deprivations of the war years, *Gourmet* would have great appeal through its depiction of the fantasy of a good life centered on fine food. Postwar travel could give a sense of real possibility to the fantasy—the great French meal was now something one *could* hope to attain at some point—while the wartime *Gourmet* had cloaked the fantasy as much in nostalgia as in the promise of things to come, if or when the war ended. "France" in wartime became for America the memory of an experience—"We'll always have Paris," in the famous line from *Casablanca*—that Americans felt it important to cherish and possess, even though many had never actually been to the country. In a series of sketches that he published in *Gourmet* and then collected into the wistful and whimsical book *Clémentine in the Kitchen*, the Francophile Samuel Chamberlain mediated the dreams of a Frenchness lost to a harsh history with the resilience of an America that could offer propitious new territory for the reinstatement of that dream. Forced (by the onset of war) from a job assignment in France that brought him into contact with the wonders of French cuisine, especially through his wonderful cook Clémentine, Chamberlain's fictional counterpart Phineas Beck discovers a way to bring Clémentine back to the U.S. and re-create a bit of Frenchness there (at least until Clémentine meets and marries a Canadian—that country serving then as the final mediation of Francophone and North American ways of life).[41]

What the postwar period did was to claim to democratize the mythology and make it seem potentially in reach rather than just an object of wistful nostalgia. For instance, from the peripatetic culinary celebration hinted at in its title through the course of its narrative, Ernest Hemingway's posthumous *A Moveable Feast*, published one year after *The French Chef* started its run, offered a wistful account of the joys of

Paris for the so-called Lost Generation of Americans abroad. For all of its recognition of difficult physical conditions (the setting is Paris in a rude winter) and budgetary constraints for the struggling American writer overseas, the book is able to render Paris as the ultimate romantic city, materially tough but bountiful in emotional and cultural and culinary rewards.[42] The fantasy of Paris as something we always have with us (à la *Casablanca*), as a feast that moves with you wherever you go in life, as a force so transcendent that you can be a "French chef" even if you're neither French nor professionally a chef, and so on, perhaps even shows up in a slip of the tongue that Julia Child makes in one episode when she recommends a French utensil to purchase and advises to search it out "if you're ever . . . when you're in Paris the next time," as if the everyday viewer of her show has Paris as a recurrent destination and has made visits there commonplace. The image is of Americans who are going to go to Paris someday but in some way already know the city well enough from representations of it that they've always already been there, if only in familiar fantasy.

Of course, the spread of the mythology through books and films and television shows didn't necessarily mean a democratization of actual access to French cuisine for many Americans back in the home country. Through the beginning of the 1960s, for instance, French restaurants were still often quite costly and came with all sorts of protocols for admission. At best, the fancy-schmancy French dining venues that had sprouted up in big cities might from time to time expand beyond their original privileged customer base to become the destination for tourists or prom dates who wanted to splurge on one seemingly special night out (and yet often were made to feel inadequate in the process by maître d's whose job seemed to be that of exuding snobbery).

I've already alluded to myriad ways in which Child helped to mitigate the snootiness and stuffiness of high French cuisine. For instance, she insisted on the manner in which seemingly haute dishes could be translated back into more common American fare; she suggested that Frenchness was often a mere accent (the perkiness of garlic, for instance); she asserted that French food should be approached with enjoyment (in the crafting and consuming of it) rather than slavish reverence; and, importantly, she demonstrated that French cuisine could be cooked in the space of the home, and not only in the hushed sanctum of the snooty restaurant.

In this respect, it matters that Child embodied not just any version of French cooking but a very specific, historically rooted approach to that cuisine. Thus, as Nathalie Jordi argues in a study of different historical stages in the U.S. appropriation of French cuisine, Child offered a version of such cuisine as based in rules, rationalized procedures, controlled combination of a basic set of fundamental elements, perfection of technique, and so on (which is not at all to say that any of this should be performed without fun).[43] Jordi clarifies Child's moment in the U.S. mediation of fine French cuisine by its contrast to other periods that had their own particular ways to approaching the assimilation of Frenchness. For example, Child can be contrasted with the later efforts of Alice Waters, who substituted for regular, rationalized technique and fixed, fundamental elements a fascination with improvisation, site-specific ingredients, intuition, and sentiment. (Jordi quotes Waters talking about preparing to cook by placing a few sprigs of rosemary on her kitchen counter, wandering about the room in search of ineffable inspiration, and then whipping up a meal from her feelings of the moment. This is quite different from Child's intensive preplanning for each episode, from her assemblage and display of the basic elements to be transformed into the dish of the episode, to the step-by-step pedagogy by which she talked the viewer through that act of transformation.)

In many ways, Child's approach to cuisine offers a canonic investment in classical practices of French food preparation, even as she allows for the modifications that come necessarily from the context of the American supermarket and the American kitchen. Thus, in *Haute Cuisine*, Amy Trubek notes how *Mastering the Art of French Cooking* belongs to that "tradition in French cookbooks [in which] the first pages begin with basic definitions for fundamental culinary practices, thus providing a road map for engaging the system."[44] In this respect, Child endlessly talked about successful cuisine as based on the application of codified rules to a precisely delimited set of basic food components. (This, again, is not to say that the exercise was dry and far from enjoyable; it's also not to say that there couldn't be room for some [controlled] degree of improvisation and making do, especially when accidents occurred and one had to adapt to changed conditions).

French cooking was particularly teachable—and particularly worth teaching—because it was about codifiable structures that moved from simple to complex in calculable, communicable fashion. As Child put it in her original letter to WGBH TV (April 26, 1962) to propose a series on French cooking, "As I conceive of cooking, and as my French colleagues have tried to illustrate it in our book, the whole business boils down to a series of themes and variations in which one learns the basic techniques, then varies the ingredient. . . . [For example,] once you have learned the coq au vin [one of her pilot topics], you can make any similar type of stew, whether it be beef, lamb or lobster." The word "stew" is worth remarking on here since it resonates an Americanness and reminds us of the extent to which Child saw her role as one of cultural mediator. Not everyone would actually think of coq au vin as a stew—although, pretty much, that's what it is—but by assimilating it to a stew, Child is translating a hoity-toity sounding and seeming French dish into the American vernacular and thereby bringing it closer to home.

This act of translation or mediation is enabled by the fact that, since French cuisine is fundamentally about perfection of technique as much as, or even more than, perfection of ingredients, its procedures can be applied with highly salutary results to foodstuffs that one would not find in a French context. In other words, by learning the logic of (French) technique, one gains skills that can serve for other cuisines. As Child says, "As these [French] methods are basic to all types of cooking, one will be a better cook in Spanish, Russian or Italian if one has had French training. Thus the emphasis of each program would be on the hows and whys." What Child found valuable in French cuisine was not necessarily a list of ingredients or famous dishes—although she was also deeply invested in a love of specific French offerings—but the seriousness of purpose and rightness of reason in the preparation of those dishes, a purpose and reason that could be emulated and transmitted. As she put it in her proposal to WGBH, "Because the French have treated cooking as a serious profession as well as an art, they are far more precise about their methods than any other national group." Indeed, if one came to understand that cooking was fundamentally

My coq au vin, made for friends during a research trip to the Julia
Child Papers at the Schlesinger Library, Radcliffe, Cambridge, Mass.
Photograph courtesy Charles Acland.

about a logic—how to build complex wholes in predictable fashion
from basic ingredients—one could eventually cook fully on one's own:
"By mastering the fundamentals you are beginning to divorce yourself
from slavish dependence on recipes and you are on the way to becoming a real cook." Far from constraining the creative work of cooking
within fixed limits, then, this structural approach to distinctive French
cuisine actually contained a generative resilience out of which other
cuisines—"Spanish, Russian, or Italian," as she put it—could be extrap-
olated and perfected too, along with the original French foundations.

I've just referred to this philosophy of cooking as "structural." Without pushing the comparison too far I hope, I suggest that Child's brand of French cooking bears a similarity to the structuralism that, in the historical moment of the 1960s, was coming (notoriously perhaps) to dominate the French human sciences and that it was the structural aspect of each that was part of the appeal to Americans. Three years after Child burst onto the American television scene (and one year after she won an Emmy—the first for public broadcasting—which confirmed how great her appeal was), Johns Hopkins University hosted the quickly legendary (in academic circles, at least) and vastly influential Languages of Criticism and the Sciences of Man conference, which introduced French structuralist thought to the U.S. with some of the first visits to the country by Michel Foucault, Jacques Derrida, Jacques Lacan, and Roland Barthes, among others. A structuralist frame of mind soon came to seduce many American scholars in the humanities, who found attractive the idea that basic codes, patterns, and narratives could be articulated within the realm of culture.[45] In promotional material she wrote in the 1970s to accompany episodes of the color version of *The French Chef*, Child herself resembles nothing so much as a structuralist in implying that seemingly quite disparate human practices are actually alike in being structured according to fundamental patterns that can undergo controlled variation. Here, suggesting that the mastery of French cooking could also aid in the mastery of the French language, Child proposed a pedagogy based on basic structures that build progressively in calculable fashion: "As you already know what they are talking about—food, its enjoyment and its preparation—you are concentrating on only one specialized vocabulary which you are continually reinforcing by repetition, and enlarging by variation." Concentrating, reinforcing by repetition, enlarging by variation: these processes could apply as well to cooking as to language acquisition and imply an overall philosophy of human praxis as a set of skills used to manipulate and transform the things of the world.

Notably, a number of the figures associated with structuralism used the method to engage with the analysis of the symbolics of food—for example, A. J. Greimas, Roland Barthes (who in 1964 referred to the general, codified generation of meanings in society as a "*cuisine des sens* [kitchen of meanings]"), and, most famously, Claude Lévi-Strauss, for whom human culture was defined by the transformation of the "raw" into the "cooked." But here, I suggest a more abstract affinity between culinary preparation of the sort Child advocated and structuralist thought: both have to do with an understanding of human praxis as the controlled application of transformational procedures to a fixed set of elements that issue in logical and predictable results. This is what structuralism termed a "combinatory" (the controlled and calculable combination of new patterns that a structure can generate), and it is what manifests itself in Child's philosophy of cuisine as the sense both that specific practices enacted on specific basic ingredients lead necessarily—unless accidents occur—to specific results and that controlled variations in either ingredients or methods can generate new food permutations. Structuralists were fond of contending that signification emerges from difference—from the difference of any one particular articulation of elements from another—and in the same fashion, rationalization in French gastronomy is about procedure, variation, and structured difference. As Child puts it in the episode "Four-in-One Chicken" (on how to derive four different recipes from one chicken), a foodstuff that you can work variations on is like a basic black dress that you can dress up or down for this or that occasion (thus, necklace on or necklace off, depending on the situation).

Perhaps no episode of *The French Chef* makes this as explicit as one on coq au vin, or chicken fricassee, from the later, color seasons. The episode opens with Child displaying side-by-side preparations of chicken dishes with white wine sauce and red wine sauce (a contrast underscored by the employment of color), then proceeds through her demonstration of the ways in which variation leads to two very different dishes and can generate other possibilities. As she explains, not only is wine a variant; so is the meat on which one centers the preparation. Chicken in red wine sauce can rationally be transformed into, say, beef in red wine sauce. (In similar fashion, in an early episode, she explained how adding sugar would transform a quiche shell into a pie crust.) Coq au vin, importantly, was one of the three recipes Child presented in her earliest *French Chef* pilots for WGBH. In the script for the coq au vin pilot, she asserted, "Once you have seen how to do this dish, you can do a Boeuf Bourguignon—beef stew in red wine—or any other kind of brown meat stew." It would seem that the very resilience and adaptability of the basic recipe led her to return to it as a staple of French cuisine.

I'd argue that this "structuralism" of classic, codified French cuisine is both a source of the attraction of this brand of cooking in itself and a reason it would have resonated so well in the American context. It is a reason similar to the one that made structuralism in the human sciences so seductive for American academics. Specifically, the idea of rationalized procedure, controlled variation, codifiable transformation, and so on may characterize a certain kind of Frenchness (as, for instance, in a Cartesian rationalism that lingers in structuralism), but it also can sum up an America that is often seduced by calculation, logic, and controlled experiment—faith in techno-logics and science.

Americans love to do things, and they love to imagine that by following variant paths to a calculated result, they have asserted their freedom (the 1950s and 1960s found extreme and perfect manifestation of this in the fad for paint-by-numbers: you become an artist by filling out a pre-set pattern). In like fashion, Child fed into pragmatic American attitudes by emphasizing, with no small degree of Yankee ingenuity, the endlessly expansive versatility of cooking methods done with reason and logic. To take just one example, as she reminded viewers of her "Introducing Charlotte Malakoff" episode, the sponge cake batter that formed the basis of ladyfingers resembled other sponge cakes she had demonstrated on previous shows, and this repetition had the salutary function of emphasizing the multifarious uses of the cake in a variety of dishes. She thereby was indicating that the lessons of any segment from this case of episodic television were not isolated and self-contained but constituted an ongoing archive, a lore of cooking. The serial nature of television (each episode builds on others) and the structurally expansive nature of French cuisine (each recipe builds on or forms variants of a basic set of operations) worked together to bring promising resilience and freshness to American cookery. Here, French cooking became not a static list of classic dishes but a set of techniques that had open-ended reach.

I don't mean to imply that Child's approach to cooking was nothing but rationalist in pure structuralist fashion. It is obvious, for instance, that she had a strong belief in the irreducible gustatory quality of particular comestibles in ways that make her cuisine substantive more than merely structural. In other words, it is not just any play of differences that produces value in her cuisine; it is the differential combination of substances that themselves already have strong, associative values. This is why, for instance, the pre-credit sequence of many episodes began with Child cheerfully belting out the name of the primary ingredient or the finished dish she would be presenting. Substance did matter, and its virtues were to be extolled. You can't make a great dish from any old ingredients.

That Child's version of French cooking is—unlike, say, Alice Waters's —about planning, codes and codification, structured transformation, logical permutation, controlled combination, and so on is not to say that there isn't room within her culinary practices for the unplanned, the unexpected, the accidental. She even did an episode on "Improvisation" (episode 90), although for her that meant making sure you always had a set of staples in your kitchen that could form the basis of spur-of-the-moment meals. Such staples included "rice, spaghetti, potatoes, instant potato mix, cheese, cream, milk, garlic, carrots, onions, spices, canned ham, and tomatoes"; one also had to be willing to use instant potato mix, because it could generate many dishes. One had to know some culinary generative rules (so that one could, for example, "transform yesterday's roast into a first-class stew, or ragoût," as she put it). And one had to have done a lot of general pre-planning for such an eventuality—for example, the good cook kept a file of recipes so that she or he had something to go by when "improvising." In other words, one could improvise if—and only if—one had a lot of foundational apparatus in place and had done a lot of rational preparing for it.

Child's gambit, then, was to mediate or balance control and creativity, norm and inventiveness, and rigor and pleasure. Again, her own embodiment worked to this end by combining physical force with sophistication, gravity of purpose with flamboyant performance, humor with seriousness of intent, and awkwardness with confidence in the final results.

Child's kitchen set provided an apposite locale for such mediation, as it itself offered a balancing act: the kitchen is part of a larger world and yet can constitute a world unto itself. It gives us life (or lifestyle) but in only some of its aspects. This is both its connection to the larger world and its offer of a special time within it. French food done in an American way and for American appetites has a special American role to play in its offer of something anodyne—boeuf bourguignon, after all, is just beef stew—and yet transcending the everyday with a promise of status, pleasure, and gustatory transport. This was a promise that Middle America took to heart when Child's show burst on the television scene in 1963.

4 The Beginnings of *The French Chef*

Early in her study of the ways three U.S. gastronomes—M. F. K. Fisher, Julia Child, and Alice Waters—brought French cuisine centrally into American life, Joan Reardon notes that how French cuisine achieved an elevated status in its specifically U.S. reception is "a story that never diminishes in the telling."[1] Indeed, some key parts of that story that center specifically on how Child moved from successful cookbook writing to celebrity television performance with *The French Chef* have been chronicled several times—most compellingly by Laura Shapiro, Child's best biographer.[2] And Child herself offered an account of her creation of the *French Chef* television series in the introduction to the cookbook of the same name.[3] Here I want to tell the story anew, building with gratitude on accounts such as Shapiro's and adding important new material from archival findings (e.g., from papers archived at WGBH and from the PBS holdings at the University of Maryland) that helps us understand just what it meant for a French-connoted pedagogy of cuisine to be introduced into the medium of educational television. Understandably, most of the accounts of Child's role on *The French Chef* have been avowedly biographical and thereby focus on Child's singular contribution. At the same time, it is important for cultural analysis to understand the broader contexts that offered a welcoming space for her brand of cooking through television performance: to take just one example, whatever qualities she presented were ones that clearly met the needs of public television as it searched for a balance between seductive entertainment, cultural uplift, and hardnosed pedagogy. Child's success story is also that of educational television, and the two need to be told together. Toward that end, I start in this chapter with the briefest of summaries of Child's life up to the 1960s to set the scene for her emergence in that decade as a television icon; the next three chapters chronicle how she worked with educational channel WGBH to develop her series and how its impact resonated tellingly through the culture at large.

Julia Child (née McWilliams) was born in 1912 into a family from the business elite of Pasadena, California. Child seemed destined to remain part of a world of pampered privilege, and she followed tradition by going to her mother's college, Smith, where she majored in history not because she had any special interest in the subject but for something to declare as her field of study while, basically, she had a good time, a key goal in that period for many society women who went to college with money behind them. As Child described herself at that time, she was a "kind of Southern California butterfly, a golf player and tennis person who acted in Junior League plays."[4] To the extent that she thought much about a career, she imagined she might want to be a writer, an occupation that was perfect for socialites because it resembled real work, but not too much. In fact, for most women of Child's class demographic, the destiny that everything was pushing them toward was marriage and then a life of easy socializing, with perhaps some progressive reform work thrown in on the side.

Nonetheless, as her biographers assert, Child was restless and seemed to be looking for some cause to give purpose to what she saw as her party-girl life. America's entry into the Second World War appears to have galvanized her and given her a new sense of commitment. Eventually, she got a position as a data collector and analyst for the OSS, the espionage agency of the U.S. government, and was sent to Ceylon (now Sri Lanka) to be the point person for information that agents had collected in the field and needed sent back to Washington. In Ceylon, she met—and quickly fell in love with—another OSS worker, Paul Child, whose artistic talent had led him to be assigned to tasks in visual design, such as cartography. Paul Child, a genuine globetrotter, had had a rich and exciting past—tempestuous affairs, exotic careers, foreign adventures, and so on—and he combined worldliness with a suavity that could almost make him seem dandyish, if not effete. (In one of his rare on-camera appearances in an episode of *The French Chef*, "Ham Dinner in Half an Hour," he is dressed nattily and exudes a sophistication that is most noticeable in his accent, which seemed patrician to such a degree that Julia Child evidently initially thought he was English).

When Julia was posted to China, and Paul could follow her there after a separation, he realized how important she was to him, and their romance intensified. They agreed to see each other after the war, and in 1946 they were married. Paul remained in government service and obtained a position in the postwar U.S. Information Agency (USIA). To the great luck of the Childs, his first posting was to Paris, where he was put in charge of exhibitions of U.S. culture to the local population.

Driving from the harbor where they had landed in France, Julia and Paul stopped at a classic restaurant he had known and, according to a story Julia would recount again and again, she had an epiphany as she ate her first great French meal. (The biopic *Julie and Julia* opens with the Childs going to the restaurant for this rapturous repast.) Child had already taken classes in Beverly Hills just after the war in anticipation of her housewifely duties in her marriage to Paul, but she decided now that cooking would be her passion—her life's work, indeed. With Paul's encouragement, she enrolled in a program for Americans at the renowned Cordon Bleu cooking school in Paris. She turned out to be the only woman in classes filled with former soldiers studying on the GI Bill and quickly she realized she had a love for cuisine that led her to spend her free hours in culinary research and hands-on experimentation in ways that made her outstrip her classmates in both commitment and, eventually, talent.

At a diplomatic party, Child met Simone Beck (known affectionately as "Simca"), an elegant and confident French woman who was part of the Cercle des Gourmettes, a circle of women devoted to gastronomy, who, with another food aficionado, Louise Bertholle, had written the short cookbook *What's Cooking in France* to introduce English-speakers to French cuisine. She hoped to build on it in a longer, more comprehensive volume. Child and Beck hit it off, and Child became a member of the Cercle.[5] Soon, the three women were offering classes in French cooking for other Americans in Paris, and Child joined her two new friends as a collaborator on the cookbook project. Beck and

Bertholle provided their experience as actual French cooks, and Child worked to make the recipes useable for American audiences.

At first titled *French Home Cooking*, then *French Cooking in the American Kitchen*, the volume grew in ambition as the three women worked on it (although, in the end, Bertholle did much less on it than Beck and Child). Child in particular wanted the book to mediate several potentially conflicting goals. It should present the classics of French bourgeois cuisine and try to reproduce their wondrous flavors as much as possible, yet it should also provide recipes that an average American cook could master—without many of the special tools available in France, such as mortars and pestles, which were not common in the U.S., and without some of the ingredients, such as shallots, which were relatively unknown in America in the 1950s. The labor, especially on Child's part, turned out to be immense, especially as Paul was successively assigned to new USIA posts in Marseille (where Julia, at least, could work on regional dishes such as bouillabaisse) and then Plittersdorf, Germany. These moves necessitated voluminous correspondence between Child and her collaborators (this was, after all, an age before e-mail). There would also be a posting to Norway, where Child hated much of the food available. At the same time that these assignments took her away from her collaborators, they pushed her to think about how to make accomplished French food in compromised contexts, where authentic ingredients might not always be available. This would be useful for thinking about the tradeoffs that would be inevitable in the making of French cuisine in America.

In similar fashion, before Paul was posted to Germany, Julia was able to employ a sojourn back in the U.S. as a research trip in which she studied American supermarkets and their products with an eye to understanding just what a would-be cook would have to work with if he or she wanted to make French classics but in the American context. Child importantly did not dismiss the American culinary environment out of hand. True, a lot about its prefabricated, ersatz products dismayed her, but she also saw some advantages to the American way. For instance, there were certain gadgets (mixers and blenders, for instance) that she welcomed as shortcuts for those phases of cooking that were not always ennobled by being done at length. Likewise, certain packaged, instant products, she felt, maintained—or, at least, approximated—the taste of local, natural foodstuffs (what the French valorize as the *terroir*, regional and authentic food of the land) and could be accepted into the methods of Americanized French cooking. For example, she had such a fondness for instant potato mixes that she included them as one way to make French-style potatoes in an episode of *The French Chef*. In addition, Child liked that one could pick one's own items in the American supermarket rather than have them chosen by the merchant, a typical and traditional practice in small shops in France, where a sense often existed of the store as an inner sanctum into which one was invited cautiously and from which items were dispensed mysteriously and seemingly at the inscrutable will of the merchant.

No doubt, there was much that was dismaying to Child about the mass-production and standardization of food in postwar America, but she was also clearly enthralled by the seeming bounty of choices that a burgeoning consumer culture provided and that was being put on display in ever bigger stores and supermarkets. For example, in one episode of *The French Chef* on vegetables in general, one can see traces of Child's sense of the potential empowerment that the American way of shopping could entail. When she introduced a recipe for duxelles, a preparation of chopped mushrooms sautéed and mixed with cream and stuffed into hollowed mushroom caps, she advised the American viewer to take time to take advantage of the richness of supermarket offerings in order to select the best and biggest mushrooms (because larger mushrooms provided more room for stuffing).

Just as the supermarket allowed American shoppers to make their own choices, Child would show appreciation of the ways that, for some recipes, the American method of packaging certain foodstuffs turned out to be more useful than the typical French way. In particular, for the paella episode of *The French Chef* (admittedly an atypical episode, since it was not about an indigenously French dish), Child lauded the fact that, unlike poultry purveyors in France—who tended to sell whole chickens only—American supermarkets made cut-up parts available and often in packages devoted to just one part alone. This meant that one could buy just legs or thighs, which are more useful in making paella than the rest of the chicken. Child might be insistently French-like for certain recipes, as when, for example, she recommended parsley over celery for a chicken stuffing because the French typically would use parsley, but she also liked it when American markets made available tastes that the French might not have known very well. For example, in her notes for an early *French Chef* episode on Hollandaise sauce, she particularly recommended using it on broccoli because, as she put it, broccoli is a "delicious vegetable the French don't grow, or didn't when we lived there. Plenty in Italy. Typically French attitude: they don't grow it so it doesn't exist or if it does, not to be bothered with." Child liked broccoli a lot and that was enough for her to override the lack of interest in it in the classic French tradition.

In the foreword to *Mastering the Art of French Cooking*, Child and her co-authors write (although it is likely that the sentiment came mostly from Child herself) that the book could have been titled, "French Cooking from the American Supermarket." In an interview with the military newspaper *Stars and Stripes* (which was reprinted in part in *Gastronomica*), Child clarifies how the meeting up of two national traditions in the best cases isn't so much about compromise or betrayal as it is about amplification or even, in some cases, improvement. She asserts that in the realm of gastronomy America had lately been picking up the mantle of French cuisine from a France that itself was not maintaining the tradition and that was sacrificing quality to expediency. The very fact of forward-looking American pragmatic optimism and ingenuity would enable the U.S. to do what France was no longer diligent about.

Indeed, Child never saw herself as "anti-American" in culinary matters, and her *Stars and Stripes* interview is very much about her acknowledging comparative advantages that the go-getter American way of life might bring to classic French cuisine. In fact, she had stinging things to say about some of the ways the French regarded home cooking in particular. She showed herself, for example, not averse to criticizing some French practices or attitudes that she thought detracted from the ultimate goal of making dishes that tasted good and that were pleasurable to prepare and to consume. She felt, for instance, that in their homes average French people were no less lazy than homebody Americans at their culinary worst. It would seem that, for her, France had its own strong share of the housewifely attitude toward cooking that she so disdained, and this was all the more damning to the indigenous traditions of ambitious French cuisine. Thus, while Child asserted strongly in the *Stars and Stripes* interview that it was in France that one truly learned "what really good food tastes like," she then cautioned that this tended to be true only in the professional setting of restaurants. The fact that French restaurants were so good led ironically to a situation in which French citizens did not feel they needed to put effort into cooking at home. In her words: "I don't think you've got good cooking in the homes [in France] anymore. [French housewives] can do a little bit, but they usually—when they're going to have anyone for dinner—they either take them out or they go to the charcuterie and get something." But this meant that the average French person was doubly unable to promote good French cooking. On the one hand, he or she couldn't really judge the quality of what was being served in the restaurants, since, as Child put it, "If you don't cook well yourself, you're not a very good judge of what restaurant food is like." On the other hand, it was obvious that if one didn't cook well, home meals would suffer too. Home cooking was marred in France by the fact that, as Child put it, "the pleasure of cooking is not a middle-class hobby the way it is in the United States."[6]

As Child's collaboration with her French friends progressed, Louise Bertholle turned out to be a lackluster participant, and Child and Simca Beck ended up doing most of the work. (For the second volume of *Mastering the Art of French Cooking*, they bought out any claims by Bertholle to authorship, and therefore to profits, in the project.) Child took recipes that were part of Beck's background and sense of tried-and-true tradition—and therefore done often by intuition rather than according to rote written instruction—and tested them with American methods and ingredients. (The posting to Plittersdorf at least had the advantage that American food was available in the military base's commissary, so Child could work with them and see how to adapt them to French recipes.) She then studied variants, tried each of them out at length, and wrote up detailed instructions for the best versions in ways that tried to take no assumption for granted. Child wanted the novice to be able to follow through on all of a recipe's steps in ways that guaranteed results, and this meant explaining everything. She would often cite the (perhaps apocryphal) anecdote of a would-be American home cook, a man, who upon reading an instruction in some cookbook to "toss the salad" put the salad bowl on one side of the room and threw the leaves of lettuce at it, simultaneously wondering why this should be done but taking the recipe at its word. When they were first dating, Paul Child had introduced Julia to one of his intellectual passions, general semantics, with its concern for precision in words, and she took away from this the need for instructions that were clear and literal and not subject to misinterpretation.

The fastidiousness with which Child approached the book—and the ambition that this encouraged in her (and Beck) to imagine that they could be, and should be, writing a definitive presentation of French cooking for the American audience—meant that the volume grew longer and longer with no immediate end in sight. Early in the process, the publisher, Ives Washburn, declared the book too ambitious and unusual, and Child felt free to try to place the manuscript elsewhere. With what seemed like a bit of luck at the time, a pen pal of hers in Cambridge, Massachusetts, Avis DeVoto, had connections with Houghton Mifflin. DeVoto proposed it there, and the book-in-progress was quickly awarded a new contract. But, unexpectedly, Houghton Mifflin rejected the manuscript as too long when it finally came in (as one solution, Child proposed transforming it into a multivolume series), and then rejected even a condensed version that Child subsequently agreed to do to salvage the project. Luckily, though, DeVoto was also working as a scout for Alfred A. Knopf, and that publishing house soon asked to look at it. Alfred Knopf himself had little initial enthusiasm for the project, but one of his editors, William Koshland, loved it and handed it to another editor, Judith Jones, who had a special interest in things French and turned out to love the manuscript too. Knopf signed up the volume, and Child eventually accepted a title that Judith Jones had come up with: *Mastering the Art of French Cooking*.

Knopf's acquisition of the book, and the start of the production process for it, coincided with Paul Child's decision to retire from foreign service and the move of the couple back to Cambridge, Massachusetts, where they had friends (including Avis DeVoto) and where the Boston Brahmin cultural scene suited the two Europhiles quite well.

Mastering the Art of French Cooking came out in 1961 and received a rapturous review by Craig Claiborne in the *New York Times*.[7] However, real success came only later, when it was picked as a Book-of-the-Month Club alternate selection. Word of mouth began to mount after (as a crowning achievement) Child made the cover of *Time* magazine in November 1966 and, especially, when the visual medium of television intervened to make Child a vibrant, visible celebrity in American popular culture.[8]

Early on, in fact, Child had begun to realize that, if the projected volume eventually garnered popular success, she or her co-authors might need to anticipate invitations to conduct cooking demos and that these might even include *television* appearances (this despite the fact that she and Paul did not own a TV set and had little regular viewing experience of the medium). Child's trip back to the U.S. had shown her the extent to which television was becoming a primary source of news and information in everyday American life. (Back in France, she was fascinated, for instance, by letters from U.S. friends that recounted television's power in current-affairs broadcasts such as the McCarthy hearings.)[9] She had begun to think that her cookbook was going to turn out to be a modern classic, and she was already astute enough about publicity to know that television might play a key role in its promotion.

For their first appearance on the medium, Child and Beck were invited to a live airing of the *Today Show*, for which they had been told appropriate appliances for cooking an omelet would be available. However, when they arrived at the studio, they discovered that only a simple hotplate was on hand, and that it had trouble coming up to the requisite temperature. Ultimately, the hot plate did warm up sufficiently (like a Hollywood good-luck narrative, this happened, according to anecdote, with just minutes to go before show time), and Beck performed the task of making the omelet. An essential lesson had been learned: cooking on television, in Child's experience, would always be about the potential for things to go wrong and about the consequent need, therefore, both to do as much advance planning as possible to hold contingency and accident at bay and to train oneself to shrug off the accidents and contingencies that inevitably would still creep in and needed to be turned into lessons that one could learn from.

A little while after the *Today Show* incident, an acquaintance of the Childs' from the USIA, Beatrice Braude, who had been black- or gray-listed under McCarthyism, was working at the local educational broadcasting station WGBH. She suggested to the host of one of the station's literary shows, *I've Been Reading*, that he invite Child on TV to talk about *Mastering the Art of French Cooking*. Here, the telling of the tale can seem as caught up in myth or legend as that of the last-minute *Today Show* omelet, although the narrative in this case is almost the converse of the earlier one. *I've Been Reading* centered on authors who came in to talk about their books. The hosted conversation generally concentrated on literary and literate exchange, with no visual aids. Child, however, showed up with her own tools and ingredients and once again made an omelet (or, at least, in one version of the story demonstrated how to separate eggs and beat the whites into fluffy mountains), but this time did so in confident, pre-planned control of the situation. Virtually overnight, fan mail praising her appearance on the program came to the station. (The standard accounts have it that twenty-seven such letters showed up, which symbolized a large degree of viewer response for WGBH at that time.) This relative success led the administration at WGBH to encourage Child to develop a series of her own for which three pilot episodes would be shot.

The letter that Child wrote to WGBH on April 26, 1962, to set out her proposal for the series (now in the Julia Child Papers at the Schlesinger Library) is a research treasure trove. It is there that she spells out, in clear and concise fashion, her thoughts on food pedagogy in general; on the possible specificity of such a pedagogy *for television*; on her precise sense of what she wanted to do in her own show; and on the special value of French cuisine for all of this. Child summed up her philosophy of culinary pedagogy with a simplicity and directness that could serve as a credo for her method overall: " 'How to make cooking make sense' is an approach which has always interested me, and I would like to expound on it publicly." Cooking instruction was not just about a top-down listing of techniques dogmatically presented and slavishly followed. Instead, the steps in cooking fused together into an overall logic, an overall purpose, and this could be explicated; this could be made to "make sense." Furthermore, it was a natural extension of her own mastery of cookery and of her generosity of spirit that she should want it to be made available to others by being expounded in the public realm.

As Child announced, "I think we could make an interesting, adult series of half-hour TV programs on French cooking addressed to an intelligent, reasonably sophisticated audience which likes good food and cooking." From the start, Child had a sense of the format and length for the show and of its content. (Significantly, she wrote about programs "on French cooking," not, say, "in French cooking," so that the concern is not just to teach cooking techniques but to introduce an entire cuisine in both the means of preparation and the consumption of it. As she said, the show was not just for would-be cooks but for those who enjoyed "good food," as well as the making of it.) Child also knew the sort of audience she wanted to reach: intelligent, interesting, and adult.

It is interesting to see that Child made no reference to gender. In fact, from the start, and throughout her career, she felt that more men should be cooking in the home and she even, as noted in the previous chapter, maintained that they would add a rigor and seriousness and depth of engagement that "housewives" lacked. At the same time, it is worth noting that the emphasis on "adult" didn't anticipate something that happened once *The French Chef* got going and that ended up delighting Child. After the show took off, she started hearing that children were watching it and were sometimes asking to join in the family's cooking at home. For Child, ultimately, "adult" was an attitude, a purposeful commitment to the kitchen that she admired, no matter the age of the would-be cook.

In addition to her sense of what she wanted in the content of the programs—namely, instruction in a logic whose whys and hows would be carefully explained to viewers—Child had precise thoughts about the style, look, and structure of the show overall. As she summed it up, "As I conceive of the programs, they would be informal, easy, conversational, yet timed to the minute." (Here, we see that blend in Child of the

."Oh, Sharon's fine! She's watching Educational Television."

Children's Television? Cartoon by Bil Keane, November 3, 1968; courtesy Jeff Keane.

desire for the casual along with recognition that pre-planning and temporal organization were essential.)

In a suggestion that was not taken up, Child proposed a temporal breakdown for the half-hour shows in which the recipe preparation would conclude four or five minutes before the end, allowing those remaining moments to be "devoted to a significant book on cooking or wine, an interesting piece of equipment, or a special product." Such a coda to the show would certainly have been in keeping with that emphasis that Child had announced on "good food and cooking" in all its aspects. *The French Chef*, in her original conception for the series, was to be not just a cooking show but a general introduction to a culinary world in which recipes and their enactment would be just one part.

Even the recipe of the day would not be presented through a set of steps jumped into dogmatically. Instead, the steps would be introduced with a two- to three-minute prologue that "would discuss the recipe to be demonstrated and its significance in the art of learning how to be a cook." Ultimately, this suggestion was taken up, and actual episodes do begin with richly pedagogical explanations of recipes, recounting their origins, elucidating their ingredients and each one's specific contribution, and clarifying the wondrous benefits to be had by executing them (benefits that equally could include the tastiness or visual impact of the final culinary result or the learning that accrued from specific tasks one would engage in to bring that particular recipe to fruition and that made one a good cook overall).

Just as she wanted a coda that would touch on general things going on in the culinary world, Child asserted that she saw "no reason why, on occasion, we could not have a guest performer, such as a well-known cooking personality like James Beard or Joseph Donan [a master chef who was a student of Escoffier], a practicing chef, a pastry cook, or a wine expert." In fact, in her introduction to the fortieth-anniversary edition of *Mastering the Art of French Cooking*, Child even went as far as to suggest that one motivation for the title *The French Chef* was that, as she put it, "I always hoped we would have some real French chefs on the show." In other words, she was not necessarily imagining herself as *the* French chef of the series; instead, she saw herself more modestly, as a facilitator of both the cuisine and the chefs who would demonstrate how to make it.

Of course, the idea of visitors from the cooking world is something that Child famously (or infamously, depending on one's sense of the success of the venture) would return to in the shows she starred in after *The French Chef*, some of which even had the guest appearance as their central conceit (e.g., *Cooking with Master Chefs: Hosted by Julia Child* [1993–94] and *In Julia's Kitchen with Master Chefs* [1994–96]). Likewise, as I'll return to later, during the color seasons of *The French Chef* in the 1970s, segments were filmed in France and these often included moments in which this or that local food expert was pictured teaching Child some indigenous culinary technique or showing off some wonderful example of French foodstuffs. But through the seasons of *The French Chef*, with few exceptions, Child would be alone, offering up her own performance as the source of spectatorial delight and instruction.

What made *The French Chef* as it aired so powerful in its appeal was its concentration on Child, with the immensity of her personality, face to face with her insistent kitchen mission. Thus, instead of using the epilogue, as she originally proposed, to move into general culinary commentary in the last few minutes, the coda took, as it turned out, the far better approach of centering on Child sitting down to table with the recipe she had just completed, beginning to taste it, and summing up what she had accomplished over the course of the episode. In other words, the epilogue went back over the dish at hand rather than moving more generally into broader areas of culinary lore. And it likewise turned out to be far better to have just Child alone than to break up her presentations with visits by invitees. (There are very rare exceptions; for instance, each of the installments of the three-part "Dinner Show" ended with guests in the dining room being entertained by Julia and Paul, who was on wine duty.) For all of her modesty, Child also came to understand that people loved seeing her perform, and she learned to accept and even to obviously relish that role.

It quickly became apparent that one of Child's talents was her ability both to move a recipe forward and, at each stage of the trajectory, to provide contextualization that she could elaborate on through anecdotes, history, general explanation, and so on. That is, there were two movements always in her demonstrations: a narrative one that followed the recipe through its steps from beginning to conclusion, and a conceptual one that situated each step in its contexts and saturated it with broader understanding. Given all that went on in Child's demonstration of a recipe, any coda and any guest visits that distracted from her presence would appear to be unnecessary and undesirable.

In terms of what she was offering to do on her first series, Child's proposal letter to WGBH reveals a certain astuteness about how television works and presents clear ideas about how to adopt a performance style appropriate to the medium. She demonstrates, for instance, an effective grasp of television's particular temporality, perceptively discussing how the difference between the real time of cooking and the televisual time of the half-hour slot needs to be adjusted through preplanning and through dishes prepared to various degrees of doneness so that temporal shortcuts could be taken. "As most recipes take more than 5 minutes to do," she wrote, "we cannot take up time for long stewings, sautéings, etc. I would therefore bring to the studio any precooking necessary, so a dish would be on hand in various stages as necessary.... For instance ... if meat is to be stewed, we'd start the stew before the camera and put it into the oven; a ready-stewed batch would be removed from the oven so the recipe could be completed without delay." Today, such shortcuts seem logical and eminently commonsensical, but Child was working her ideas out from scratch, and it is striking how quickly she understood the role of time compression on television (even if, in the actual filming of *French Chef* episodes, she didn't always do as well in keeping track of the time racing by).

A young filmmaker at WGBH, Russell Morash, who had been the producer of a show called *Science Reporter*, was assigned to produce and direct the pilot episodes, and another member of the WGBH staff, Ruth Lockwood, joined as associate producer. Morash went to WGBH with a degree in theater arts from Boston University. After graduating from college, he had sent out his résumé to all of the local television stations, and WGBH asked him to come in. As he tells it, most of their young candidates from Boston University had degrees in communications, and the channel's administrators thought that, with his background in theater, Morash could make special contributions in the area of scripting and dialogue, staging of action, and eliciting effective performances from the people on camera. Morash had no training in television before he went to WGBH, but he was told he could pick up the technique in no time, and that turned out to be true (especially since budget limits and constrained working conditions meant that one didn't need to learn much more than the simplest filming techniques).[10]

Lockwood had been a volunteer at WGBH and seems to have been interested in the station's mandate to develop cultural programming in the Boston area and use television for aesthetic uplift. Like Child, Lockwood was also a graduate of Smith College (class of 1933), and she bonded with Child over food as a path to cultural distinction. Indeed, by the mid-1960s, Child would be copying the recipes and notes she was sending to Simca Beck for the second volume of *Mastering the Art of French Cooking* to give to Lockwood. As the associate producer for *The French Chef*, Lockwood concentrated her efforts on the content of the show. Were recipes getting done as they should? Had there been any errors along the way in the explanations? Morash's job, by contrast, was essentially to film that content; his role was to let Child perform and capture her actions to the most effective televisual ends possible. Lockwood would remain on Child's production team over the years of her various series (and, indeed, would become one of her confidants and advisers on myriad issues, not all of them televisual), and Morash would be a recurrent director of choice for Child's shows, although other directors also worked with her over the years from series to series.

In 1961, before the pilot episodes of *The French Chef* could be shot, catastrophe struck: a fire broke out at WGBH and burned down the facilities. Over the next year, the staff scrambled to locate venues from which to air its various shows and found that many businesses and institutions in the Boston area were more than willing to help (e.g., the universities lent space when they could). For *The French Chef*, it was discovered that the Boston Gas Company had a demonstration kitchen in its plant that could be borrowed for the pilots. Child decided to center the pilots on decidedly classic bourgeois French fare—soufflé, omelet, and coq au vin—and all three were shot in one week in June 1962. Paul Child worked as unflaggingly as Julia in both the pre-planning and shooting stages. During pre-planning, he helped his spouse establish her routine and mapped out a sequential breakdown of what should transpire during each episode; during shoots, he helped signal instructions to her, and, when the camera was close up on her, he might furtively whisk things off or onto the set for the next full shot. Fastidious to the point, perhaps, of obsessiveness, Paul worked out instructions not only for Julia but also for himself. For example, one script includes notes Paul wrote for himself, such as *"When Julia discusses copper vs. other bowls*: Remove aluminum plates w./3 unbroken eggs still on it. *Also: move in stool* for egg-beating, and get piano stool out of the way."

The first pilot aired on July 26, 1962, and more fan mail came in to the station. Child wrote to WGBH in August to say how much she had enjoyed the experience and hoped it would continue: "I love doing the show and thoroughly enjoyed working with Russ and Ruth Lockwood. It has also been a good lesson to me in how complicated the medium is, requiring much more from the performer than just cooking. If we do go on with show, I know how much I have to learn, particularly about pace, smoothness, and talk." WGBH agreed to a full season of twenty-six episodes, and *The French Chef* soon went into regular production for a debut in 1963. An ad in the Boston newspapers framed the series this way: "PULL UP A SPOON, GIRLS, and Try French Gourmet Cooking. Easy practical different. Julia Child founder of the Ecole des Gourmandes in Paris shows you the simple secrets of deliciously rich beef bourguignon . . . luscious French chocolate cake . . . superb sauces . . . soufflés that never fall or fail . . . even how to lift vegetables out of the mundane into the subtly delectable. There's much much more. See for yourself. Mondays 8 PM repeated Wednesdays 3 PM."

This notice contains a number of revealing aspects. For example, despite the eventual success of the series across the gender divide, WGBH's original publicity for the show framed it as one for the "girls." At the same time, however, the show was being aired in the evening, considered as much a time for men as for women. The 3 P.M. repeat would place the rerun of the show in a stereotypically women's time of the day, but even here the data are somewhat contradictory: while the reference to "girls" may have indicated some marginalization of the show in terms of genre, the fact that the show would air at two different times suggests that WGBH was granting it some importance. Re-broadcasting it required maintaining the tapes from the first airing and not erasing them right away (as sometimes happened at budget-strapped stations, especially with regard to stereotypically women's fare).

Quickly, indeed, WGBH seemed to commit to *The French Chef* and did what it could to promote the show in a big way. Indeed, the publicity effort was so taken to heart at WGBH that when *Newsday* ran an article on *The French Chef* (in 1968) that attributed its success to Child's charisma alone and contended that the show worked its charm without being advertised or promoted, Helen Peters, the public relations director at WGBH, wrote in protest: "That's an ouch! You see, we here at WGBH organized the national promotion of our series The French Chef, and we did it without any money to speak of, a bare $50 per program. . . . We have had a number of things going for us, of course, and not least is the splendid talent of Mrs. Child. But we also had more than 100 dedicated publicity/promotion people in our sister public television stations across the country who worked very very hard to make the most of the material we provided."[11]

WGBH's promotional campaign for *The French Chef* involved getting as much information about the content of *individual* episodes to the public as possible. In other words, not just the series overall but the offerings in each episode were made to stand front and center in the publicity. For instance, for each episode, WGBH drew up a press release that described the purpose and overall steps of the featured recipe; even more, the station soon arranged a deal with the *Boston Globe* to run an evening's recipe in that morning newspaper so that viewers could have a printed copy and thereby follow along with Child's pedagogy. Child also eventually began a series of short writings titled "From the Pen of The French Chef," each of which was sent to various newspapers (where they sometimes did receive syndication), and each of which could also be made available to fans who wrote to WGBH or to the other public channels nationwide that soon started to carry the show. The "From the Pen" writings sometimes summarized recipes that had aired on the show or offered stand-alone recipes not connected to any episode of the series. For example, "From the Pen" no. 10, "In Brine or Wine, Lobster's Divine," simply chronicles ways to poach lobster. As often, however, the pieces offered broader culinary musings in which Child reflected on this or that topic of personal fascination in ways that diverged fully from any specific content on *The French Chef*. One "From the Pen," for example, was all about a trip to England and her discovery that not all English food was as bad as legend had it (although an awful lot was).

Likewise, the station made mimeographs of each recipe and sent them out to viewers who asked for them after an episode aired. WGBH limited the number of recipes that would be sent to any one viewer who wrote in, however; there seems to have been some concern that, because many of the *French Chef* recipes were simplified versions of ones that had appeared in *Mastering the Art of French Cooking*, the show might take away from the book. Indeed, Child and the makers of *The French Chef* walked a delicate tightrope in relation to *Mastering the Art of French Cooking*. Some of this had to do with the fact that Child was only one of three authors listed for the published volume and legally could not claim the show's recipes as hers alone. Each episode of *The French Chef* would thus carry a voiceover announcement at the end that Child was "co-author of the book *Mastering the Art of French Cooking*." Eventually, though, this notice dropped away as Child's rights to the show were renegotiated with her co-authors to allow her to claim the recipes on the series as her own. Explicit mention of her as a *co*-author returned, however, when Child and Beck wrote the follow-up volume to *Mastering* and the need arose again to clarify that a number of Child's televisual demonstrations took inspiration from recipes in the jointly written book.

In 1965, WGBH even offered copies, signed by Child, of the first volume of *Mastering* as a Christmas gift for purchase by staff and close friends of the station. Other public stations also used the book as a premium gift in pledge drives. (KQED in San Francisco reported selling 1,100 copies this way in the first year or so of *The French Chef*.) But the idea of a cookbook that would derive directly from the television show and that would have an identity relatively independent of *Mastering the Art of French Cooking* also appears to have been bandied about at the time. This eventually resulted in *The French Chef Cookbook*, written solely by Child, which was released in 1968 and was a big seller, although nowhere near the numbers of *Mastering*.

The *French Chef* book is directly linked to the show in offering the same recipes that appeared on the series and in the same order, but it is primarily just a collection of recipes with minimal humor, drama, and emphasis on performance of self. Instead, the book tells viewers in fairly matter-of-fact ways how to make the various dishes that aired on the series, and it serves thereby as a concise record of techniques or as an aide-mémoire to the content of the lessons imparted in the show's episodes. For instance, whereas the televised version of episode 46, "Elegance with Eggs," had Child dramatically pushing eggs out of sight in a whimsical rejection of their commonplace—and therefore boring —utilization as a breakfast staple, the book version simply announced that the French "do not eat eggs for breakfast" and then offered egg recipes for other times of the day.

In the 1970s, as Child wound down the taping of the color seasons of *The French Chef*, she produced a second cookbook connected (but to a lesser degree than *The French Chef Cookbook*) to the specific content of the TV series. *From Julia Child's Kitchen* came out in 1975 and became one of her biggest sellers and most revered volumes. While some of the recipes in the volume derived from the show, they are not presented in the order they aired on *The French Chef* (as they were in the earlier cookbook), and the book more generally is a compendium of cooking hints, personal reflections, anecdotes, and explanation of foodstuffs by genre in ways that parallel the expansive chattiness in the television show but are in no way a transcription of it. Using some of the material from the series to build what Child herself termed a "rambling" volume, *From Julia Child's Kitchen* is only vaguely a literary translation of the television series.[12] The earlier *French Chef Cookbook* is thus, in a way, the only official tie-in to the *French Chef* television series.[13]

Yet, for the most part, like other stations in the burgeoning public television world, WGBH got most of its income from donations by viewers and from corporate underwriting rather than from direct sales of tie-ins and ancillary products. One important aspect of the story of *The French Chef* has indeed to do with the attitude of its makers to commercial sponsorship. When WGBH decided to pick up the show after the pilot episodes succeeded, it committed to carrying it through the first season, whether or not it had a sponsor. As Bob Larsen, an administrator at WGBH, wrote to Child at the beginning of 1963, if no sponsorship came through, the station would still "go ahead with the series as a low budget station undertaking." But negotiations in fact were already under way with S&H Green Stamps and that company soon decided to underwrite the first season. For episodes 14–67, Safeway also came in as a sponsor and was eventually joined by Hills Brothers Coffee, which, as the show's notoriety began to spread, started emphatically to announce its affiliation with *The French Chef* in its press releases: "As you will hear Julia Child sign off at the end of each program . . . we also say to you 'Bon Appetit.' And we naturally hope that you'll head for the *Hills*."[14] The Polaroid Corporation joined in 1965 after one of its executives met a WGBH officer at a party, and that company became the primary sponsor of the show through the end of its first run and into its second iteration as a color program in the 1970s. In fact, in the 1970s, Polaroid tried to bow out as a sponsor when its executives decided to commit the company's funds to launching a new camera. The public outcry was so great, however, that Polaroid was shamed into remaining a sponsor and did so until *The French Chef* ended as a series.

Although educational television series such as *The French Chef* generally relied on corporate funding to underwrite some of their costs, Child was insistent that she never be seen as giving an endorsement to any particular company or branded product. Many businesses wanted to get in on the success of *The French Chef*. For example, as early as the end of the 1963 season (the first season, in other words), the owner of a kitchen supply store tried to launch a "French Chef skillet" and was sent a cease-and-desist letter by WGBH. (Ruth Lockwood told Child that the station was going to "see if we cannot dissuade him in a friendly way from being a conniving bastard.")[15] More amusing in its quaintness was the request by a playwright and theater director for permission to have Julia Child's voice come over the radio in a scene of his play about a woman whose husband was threatening to leave because all she cooked were boiled hotdogs. The writer's idea was that Child would be heard offering a recipe for hotdogs done in a new, exciting fashion, and this would rescue the housewife's marriage. The playwright explained that he was prepared to use an impersonator but would love it if Julia Child herself could tape the voiceover. Unfortunately, there is no record in the archives of any reply to this request.

To obscure commercial provenances, brand and company names were systematically covered with masking tape on products that Child used on the show. (A rare exception is in the "Queen of Sheba Cake" episode, where the brand name of the rum is visible. Was this an error? Or was it decided that rum was still an exotic item so off Americans' radar that it didn't matter if it was named?) Even items as commonplace and as inexpensive as salt and baking powder were not identifiable by manufacturer (although Child sometimes read from packages' instructions or ingredients lists in ways that kept little secret).

Gifts sent to the show by businesses initially were refused. For example, when early in the run of the series Child was sent an Osterizer blender ostensibly for personal use, but clearly in the hope that she would use it on the air, Ruth Lockwood stepped in to decline it in the name of WGBH. (As she wrote, "I handle all [Child's] business affairs.")[16] At the same time, many firms were sending products that

No branding here!

were useful to the show, and it clearly was tempting for a series at a cash-strapped educational station to use the freebies. Indeed, Child hoped that some company would donate an electric blender to be used on the show ("either Osterizer [first choice] or General Electric. *Not* Waring"),[17] so long as the company did not expect the brand name to be mentioned in return. In fact, Child had thought from the start that companies associated with food and cooking should be approached for donations of equipment and supplies. In her original proposal letter to wGBH, for instance, she had suggested that gas and electric companies would be logical sponsors for the show. Indeed, when wGBH decided to commit to the series and build a set for it (delayed, as noted, by the fire at the studio), Child tried to push Morash to get General Electric to provide *three* stoves to the program: one for on-camera shooting, one for rehearsal, and one for her to practice on at home. After all, she reasoned, her own preference was to cook with gas, but if the show went with electric stoves, this would provide free publicity to a manufacturer of electric appliances such as General Electric, which should be more than willing to help out. "It will mean a great deal to electricity," she wrote to Morash. "The least they can do is to provide their chef with something to practice on, and at home. . . . I can and will cook on electricity." (Ultimately, though, there was no such donation.)

To clarify just what was permissible and not in terms of accepting gifts for a noncommercial station, Ruth Lockwood contacted the lawyers at WGBH's law firm, Covington and Burling. Federal Communications Commission Regulation 73.621(d) specifically asserted, "Noncommercial educational stations are not permitted to have program sponsorship," although underwriting was allowed. Commercial items, the decree clarified, could be used and even identified visually, as long as they were "reasonably related to the broadcasts." After studying the regulation, Covington and Burling decreed that it was OK to accept gifts and to have them appear on the air as long as "no oral reference is made to the gift, the brand name or the manufacturer, and great care is exercised to ensure that the camera does not give undue emphasis to the trademark."[18]

Of course, as a show about activities in the contemporary kitchen, *The French Chef* was selling an experience of consumer-centered modernity, even if it hawked no specific brands or tie-ins. It talked about special ingredients that would make one's cuisine distinctive (some of them relatively unfamiliar and even exotic to the average American); it lauded the virtues of gizmos and gadgets, some of them seductively unique in look and function; and it promoted an acquisitive encounter with another culture whose way of being one could approximate through things, if not by making an actual trip to the place.[19]

In short, *The French Chef* sold a lifestyle centered on the kitchen as a site of taste, culture, and fun. It succeeded in large part in that task because Julia Child—and her creative team—managed to create a show that combined an impression of authenticity (to the point of incorporating error and the constant risk of setbacks) with a great deal of planning and behind-the-scenes effort. We've looked now at how the *French Chef* came into being; building on that history, the next chapter examines in detail how its episodes were put together and produced day-by-day over the course of the series.

5 Prepping *The French Chef*

While the pilots for *The French Chef* were being prepared in 1962, the administrators at WGBH were feeling dissatisfied with the show's title and assumed that some other name for it could be found. As late as May 1962—a month, that is, before the shooting of the pilots—they were still scrambling for a new name for the series. Here, a note that Paul Child wrote to Julia about a phone message he had taken for her from WGBH while she was out is enlightening and amusing. Paul reports that Bob Larsen, the program manager at WGBH, had called to say it was becoming urgent to fix on a title, which should be one with appeal; not more than three words in length; and something that signaled the French connection. As Paul explains in his note for Julia, he has done some brainstorming and has written down a series of suggestions, some of which are strange or comical enough to suggest, perhaps, that he was not fully behind the request to rename the show and was being sardonic about the process: Cuisine Mastery, Gourmet Kitchen, Kitchen Maitrise, Cuisine at Home, Kitchen à la Française, Kitchen Française, Cuisinavision, French Food chez Vous, Savoir Faire, Cooking chez Vous, Kitchen Pleasure, Gourmet Pleasures, French Cuisine at Home, The Chef at Home, Table d'Hote, Cuisine Secrets, Cuisine Magic, The Gourmet Arts.

Paul and Julia clearly wanted to maintain the original title, and after the pilots aired under the name *The French Chef* and fan letters came in applauding the series, they pushed for WGBH to retain the title. On December 18, Julia Child wrote to Larsen to insist, "Paul and I have been doing some thinking about the title for the cooking show. We are both very much in favor of keeping the present one: The French Chef. It is short, to the point, dignified, glamorous, and appeals to men as well as women. It says what we want to say. Something like 'Looking at Cooking,' or variations, sounds cheesy, little-womanish, cute, amateurish. [Note, again, Child's desire to not limit the appeal of the series to women, since she felt they wouldn't approach cooking with enough rigor and commitment.] Everyone who is interested in cooking knows what a chef is, and longs to see what a chef does. . . . I hope you will reconsider and approve."[1] Larsen relented and on Christmas evening sent a note to WGBH's administrators and to personnel connected with the show, such as Ruth Lockwood and Russell Morash, that declared: "After having racked our collective brains for weeks to find a good alternative title for [T]he French Chef we have decided that a good alternative title does not seem to be available. And since both Julia and Paul Child are extremely fond of the original title, I have capitulated. Let us call it: *THE FRENCH CHEF now and forever!*"[2]

Over the years of its first, black-and-white manifestation, *The French Chef* was produced at three different locations. Since the fire at WGBH in 1961 had scotched the possibility of in-house production, the pilot episodes were shot, as noted, at Boston Gas Company. When the show was picked up as a regular series, Cambridge Gas and Electric Company lent its demonstration kitchen (Boston Gas's was temporary only and had since been dismantled), and that locale served for several years. In 1965 a kitchen set constructed for use within the new, post-fire WGBH building, and built especially for *The French Chef*, was finally ready, and Child's series moved in there to remain through the color version of the show in the 1970s, when the set was overhauled to give it an even newer look. The WGBH set was massive (whereas Russell Morash estimates that the space Child worked in at Cambridge Gas and Electric probably was no deeper than eight feet from kitchen counter to back wall), yet it was not a fixed, permanent set. It was made instead to be dismantled and then stored after each day's shooting so that the studio space could be used for other programs.

For the seasons at Cambridge Gas and Electric, a WGBH bus would take the technical equipment (including the bulky cameras) to the locale, and Julia and Paul Child would drive over on their own with the food for the day and any kitchen tools or appliances that Child needed specifically for the episodes being shot. Early on, Child had devised a list of items she wanted present at every episode, no matter the topic, and she used this as a checklist in preparing for the shoots. For instance, she always took with her a work apron, work towels, three clean additional aprons, three clean blouses, a toiletries bag, lipstick, gum, a zipper bag with cigarettes in it (until she gave up smoking), matches, masking tape, Magic Markers, a ruler, scissors, a stopwatch (important for keeping track of the timing of the show from segment to segment), safety pins, rubber bands, and three copies of the Ecole des Trois Gourmandes badge, which Paul had designed in honor of the cooking classes she had run with Simca Beck and Louisette Bertholle, and which she insisted on wearing in every episode over the course of every season of *The French Chef.* There was also a list of kitchen tools and appliances that Child wanted at every shoot and that simply were kept waiting for her at the set: a contingent of saucepans, frying pans, casserole and baking dishes, bowls, molds, blender and mixer, rolling pins, wire whisks, spatulas, and so on, all specified in precise detail—for example, a nine-and-a-half by two-and-a-half inch frying pan in stainless steel with a cast aluminum bottom should be available for cooking chicken. For individual episodes, Child also came up with lists of special items she needed to bring. A handwritten note for the day she shot the episodes "Elegance with Eggs" and "Apple Charlotte" side by side reminds her to bring egg dishes, egg cocottes, egg stands, muffin tins, her French omelet pan, charlotte molds, a masher, an orange juicer, and so on. In somewhat edited form, the list of such items was also sent out by WGBH (and later by other stations that picked up the series) to local cookery stores that could then ensure they had the items on hand for the many fans who would come in after an episode and ask for gadgets and utensils whose virtues Child had extolled. (The kitchen gadgets store Williams-Sonoma of San Francisco was less than a decade old when *The French Chef* debuted. It got a major boost in sales this way, which helped it mightily on its path to becoming a nationwide chain.)

When they arrived at Cambridge Gas and Electric, everybody on the *French Chef* team carried equipment into the building, which, with the large cameras, was not the easiest thing to do, especially as the set was on the second floor. The freight elevator turned out to not be convenient, and *The French Chef* team ended up using the fire escape (which often was dangerously icy in the winter) to lug the material to the kitchen set. (The freight elevator posed additional problems of its own. A bell rang when it reached each floor and sometimes was audible during live shoots of *French Chef* episodes. Legend has it that during one such interruption while a shoot was in progress, Child claimed that a repairman was at the door, thus playing into the conceit that this was a real kitchen in her home, not just a set.)

Child seems to have loved the new set at wgbh when she moved onto it in 1965, and one can sense a new confidence and enthusiasm in her in the episodes from 1965 on. Certainly, she became more playful and daring, and perhaps the grandeur of the new set contributed to her increasing—and increasingly dynamic—sense of the potential for vivid kitchen drama. In a promo filmed at the end of 1964 in which Child shows off the new set to spectators, her pleasure is evident at every moment. As she put it at the end of the promo, "I just love cooking in this kitchen." This was a space she could really move around in.

Through 1964, wgbh's assistant general manager, David Ives, had been negotiating with Boston Edison for donations of equipment, and the company ultimately came through with a bounty of gadgets and gizmos for the new kitchen. The set, as Child explained in the promo for it, included working double ovens, a rotisserie, an extra large refrigerator and separate freezer, double sinks, a tap that produced immediate boiling water, a seven-burner stove, and a lot of counter space. The set was distinguished by a French country visual style created by wgbh's set designer Francis Mahard (who later won an Emmy for the set design of *Frontline*), with chestnut paneling throughout (showing quaint scenes of French cookery) and carefully placed rustic items such as pitchers, decorative plates, earthenware jugs and jars (all of which Mahard had found in antique stores in Boston) on the back counters and hung up on the walls. To the left of the kitchen (from the viewer's point of view), and acceded to by a door at the back of the set, was a dining-room set (at Boston Gas, the dining room had been to the right). Windows on the back wall opened onto what was supposed to be a garden, indicated by a solid background (blue in the color episodes) standing in for sky with tree branches, creating the impression of a pastoral locale (in the plans for one episode, Child was to throw scraps out the window as if feeding farm animals). Most important, especially in light of the earlier discussion (in chapter 2) of the cooking shows that preceded *The French Chef* and often opted for a lateral setup in which the cook stood in front of or beside a table or counter and was filmed straight-on by the camera so that everything seemed flat and frontal, the new set for *The French Chef* centered on a counter that was divided into three to four sections, each of which was on rollers and angled at the end so that, when they were put together, they formed a sort of semicircle. The rollers added a few inches to the counters' height, but that was more than OK, since Child's own height required everything to be higher. This modular construction allowed mobility (the counter could be set up in different positions from episode to episode), while the angled look gave more variety to the visual content. Child could move and turn in different directions, as could the cameras that were following her. The new *French Chef* set clearly played into Child's energetic sensibility and virtually restless possession of the space of the kitchen. The new set opened up the work of the kitchen and dynamized it in a manner that probably had not been evident in cooking television before, where instructors either budged very little or moved only laterally behind a straight counter or displaced themselves fully only when moving into a new fixed position for an interposed sketch or for a commercial plug away from the kitchen set.[3]

In passing, it is worth noting that the rolling, modular counters for the in-house set were soon lent to another WGBH cooking show, *Joyce Chen Cooks*. That program debuted in 1966, with Ruth Lockwood as producer, and introduced the talents of Chen, a celebrated chef in Cambridge whose restaurant evidently was among the few in the area that Child seemed particularly to like going to. For Chen's show, which focused on Chinese cooking, the French images on the front of the counters were covered with Asian designs, and the set was re-configured into a kind of minimalist space whose backgrounds were bathed in darkness and dotted with curtains, lacquer patterns, and Asian pottery. (Chen used lifts to bring her up to the right level to use the counters, which had been designed specifically for Child.)

Kitchen spaciousness

However, one need only watch a few episodes of *Joyce Chen Cooks* (available in the WGBH archives) to see that, even after borrowing part of Julia Child's kitchen—and a part of it, moreover, that could specifically encourage the dynamic possession of space if the cook moved around—Chen did not have the same vibrant, kinetic presence that viewers saw in Child and that would flourish on the dynamized set for *The French Chef*. Some of the difference may have had to do with Chen's playing into an image of the Asian woman as modest and unassuming. Toward the end of an episode on sweet-and-sour pork, she explained that it was bad for an Asian to show off about his or her accomplishments but then conspiratorially told viewers in a mock whisper, "Between you and me, it [the sweet-and-sour pork] is really good, really wonderful." It also simply may be the case that Chen didn't have the breadth of personality and dynamism that made Child take so well to television, and that made television take so well to her. We see the same sort of setup overall, with two women talking to us from behind an angled counter, but Child's performance conveys a brisk energy that is absent from Chen's more subdued presentation. For one,

Chen doesn't move around very much and comes off much more as the calm, possessed talking-head version of the pedagogue. That the same central elements of the set were used in the two shows to such divergent results gives us yet another way to witness the difference that Julia Child made.

One particular benefit of moving *The French Chef* into the WGBH building became apparent in the mid-1960s. It was decided to open tapings of the show to studio audiences, who would pay for the privilege and thereby provide a new revenue source for the station. It was much easier to manage this at WGBH than at the tight space of the temporary locales. For each taping, 100–150 paying guests would come to one of the episodes being shot that day, at 4 P.M. or 8 P.M. Significantly, the later taping was termed an "evening performance," as if to give it the patina of the special event, the culturally enriching evening out on the town. Admission was $5 (not a small amount at that time). Often, the audiences were composed of special groups. There were frequent visits by women's clubs, and on one occasion students from the Harvard School of Business attended. Staff members specifically were not allowed to go to the tapings so as to avoid the impression of favoritism. Interestingly, in another confirmation that *The French Chef* was always being thought about in terms of its ability to bring in male viewers, when the idea of allowing audiences in was first broached, the WGBH administrator David Ives suggested (in a memo dated 1965) that this would have specific and special attraction for men: "Mrs. Child's mail shows a very substantial number of men among her fans— and those husbands who don't really care about cooking itself would be intrigued by the intricacies of studio production."[4]

Typically, the tapings before live audiences would begin with Paul coming out and talking to the crowd, less to warm them up than, actually, to cool them down by explaining the fundamental ground rule that there could be *no* audience reaction during the taping. After each shoot, Child would meet with the audience. As an internal memo explains, "For ten minutes—no more—Julia will answer questions and will then flee the audience so as not to get trapped."[5]

Laura Shapiro notes that Child had always enjoyed cooking with an audience (even family and friends could serve as such for meals cooked

Audience participation. Courtesy WGBH Educational Foundation.

at home), and her pedagogy took much of its force from her awareness of the reader (in the case of the cookbooks) or the viewer (in the case of the TV series). Maybe the acceptance of a studio audience came from the same impulse. Child wanted not just to cook but also to show off cooking and to talk about it. Through the run of *The French Chef*, in fact, she showed that she was eager to participate in charity events when that specifically entailed doing cooking demos before live audiences. As she put it in an audio promo for a demo at San Francisco's Tour of Dining Decors in 1965, "I so much look forward to meeting you, and talking with you. Cooking on the TV is great fun—I love it—and I think television is a marvelous teaching medium. But I don't meet anyone—except the camera. I miss live people that I can talk to, and who can talk back—so we can exchange ideas."[6]

The use of live audiences for *The French Chef* seems to have dropped away for a while in mid-1966. Specifically, Ives appears to have felt that, if everyday viewers were able to see the set, they would realize that Child was not being filmed in her home and that this would somehow diminish the sense of folksy intimacy she was establishing with them.

The culmination of Ives's concerns came when the financial offices at WGBH proposed to televise one of the station's membership pledge drives from the *French Chef* set. Ives demurred and explained, "The fact that Julia will not do any more live programs for a while has not been publicized and I do not intend to announce it. I hope the audience will simply go along in the belief that Julia is still right there doing what she always has been doing."[7] Ives hoped that, by keeping audiences away from the set, the illusion of an actual domestic origination for the show would be maintained. Nonetheless, the practice of taping in front of audiences returned and persisted into the 1970s.

Whether in the early days at Cambridge Electric or the later ones on the studio set, Julia Child tended to follow a work pattern that combined extensive at-home preparation with the on-set live shoots. For the earliest seasons of *The French Chef*, the Childs and the crew adhered to a schedule in which they shot four episodes per week over a four-day period—two days each of rehearsal and shooting of two episodes, then two more days each of rehearsal and shooting of an additional two episodes. Sometimes, depending on the difficulty of a recipe and which dish was more or less inviting to make earlier or later in the day, the two episodes might be shot in reverse order to that in which they would air. For instance, a show about cream puffs was shot before the same day's soufflé, even though the soufflé recipe was to air before the cream puffs.

On the days they were not on the set, the Childs worked at home on the steps of the dishes Julia would be preparing before the cameras. On one typical day at home, for example, she sautéed a chicken, made braised onions with cream sauce, cooked a soufflé, made rice, and baked two cakes, most of which she then did again on-set the next days in the shooting of four episodes that presented those recipes. Throughout the home prep, she and Paul worked out the timing, which would then be recorded on cards that could be flashed at her from an off-camera position during the shoot. There would also be cards that were simple reminders of the successive actions to be undertaken in a recipe. The archived folder for a veal-and-rice dinner, for instance, includes cards with instructions such as sauté rice, add stock, bridge veal [make the transition from rice prep to veal prep], sauté. Likewise, for some episodes, especially those with multiple dishes or variants of a primary dish, Julia and Paul, along with Ruth Lockwood, might devise nicknames that would go on cards and help her distinguish items. In her preface to the *French Chef* cookbook, Child recounts that, for a show in which she was to make three brioches, it had been decided to think about them as the three bears; this then led to cards that said things like "Punch Pa" or "Slash Mother."

In passing, it is worth noting that, during the shoots, cards also would be written up from moment to moment to handle unforeseen occurrences. These might include instructions about demeanor (such as "stop gasping"), about errors that needed to be corrected, or about things Child was forgetting to do. The cards helped Child manage her actions, but they also brought a roughness of their own. Endlessly throughout the episodes of *The French Chef*, one can spot Child reading an off-screen card, absorbing its instructions, mulling over her options (to speed up an explanation, for instance, or drop some variant step), and sometimes thereby losing her train of thought and stumbling over her next moments.

In the prep work, Paul Child even found occasions to use his design skills, which once he had hoped to parlay into a professional art career. For example, he drew detailed layouts of the kitchen counter and the items that would be on it from Child's point of view that she could use during a taping to find things as the cameras rolled.

Likewise, Paul diagramed the body parts of various animals, such as the cuts of meat on a cow. One can see the pride in Julia Child's face when, in an episode on tripe in the 1970s, she outlined the parts of a cow's stomach with a complex diagram and then added that it had been created by her husband. My favorite among Paul's drawings is a delightful rendition of male and female lobsters with the symbol for their sex next to each one.

Beyond planning for how each episode should unfold and how best to fit a recipe into the time constraints of half-hour television lay even more extensive research by Julia into French recipes and how best to do them to get the highest quality and taste. Here, Child relied on research methods she had honed in preparing *Mastering the Art of French Cooking*. For any dish, she would look up its recipe in all the classic French

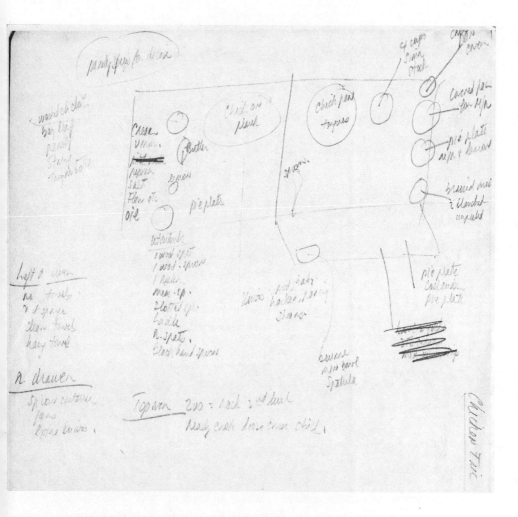

Paul Child's pre-planning. Courtesy Julia Child Foundation.

cookbooks and note the similarities and differences. Were there, for instance, disparities in cooking time, in ingredients, in order, in method, and so on? When variations existed, she tried to figure out the logic behind the differences. Why did one expert recommend this way and not another? And she would attempt to determine whether any compromises or combinations of recipes were possible. Was there in any

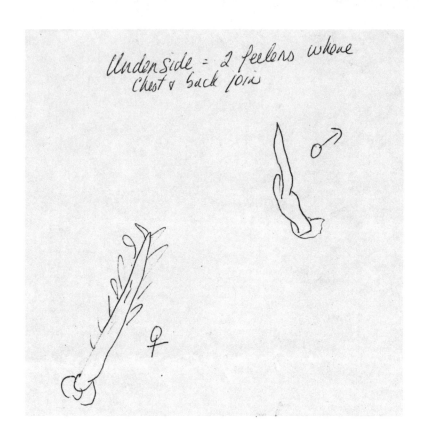

The sex lives of lobsters. Courtesy Julia Child Foundation.

particular case an Ur-version for which all the individual recipes were simply compatible variants? All through this process of collation, combination, and distinction, Child not only would be studying the variant recipes; she would also be testing them through experiments that often extended over many days. Child came to the set without a shot-by-shot, word-by-word script for the entire episode, but she did have detailed lesson plans that were still very much a script of sorts. With that, and with all sorts of preparatory research and rehearsal behind her, she could jump into the live shoots with trust in her own professionalism and, as important, in that of her production team and crew.

The idea was to turn the cameras on, let her start talking and acting, and then follow her from beginning to end.

On the days Child was not on the set, she shopped and visited the beauty parlor, as an invoice for two episodes shot on October 14, 1965 ("Saddle of Lamb" and "Soupe au Pistou") shows. Child submitted a request to be reimbursed $60 for groceries (which included vermouth and frozen spinach) and $7 or so for taxi travel between the two days of episode shooting to go to her hairdresser and from there to her butcher (Jack Savenor, who became famous in Cambridge as Child's meat purveyor).[8] For what it's worth, the production budget for each episode was $255. Camera and lighting costs were $40 each; the mobile unit cost $125; recording cost $50.

With the Childs' concern for perfection, manifested as a push to preplan everything, the original four-episode-per-week routine actually entailed a seven-day-a-week work schedule. Over the years, the four-episodes-per-week schedule proved relentless. When enough episodes had built up to create a block of reruns, the number of episodes shot each week dropped, and rehearsal days came to combine the at-home blocking of the action, the shopping, and the visit to the hairdresser, leaving a little more time for rest and for research into the background of the recipes.

A handwritten schedule (undated but obviously from the period in which there was a live audience) offers a breakdown for a typical day of shooting. Both of the episodes to be shot were to be set up by 1:30 P.M. Sound checks would then be done, and Child would rest for fifteen minutes. Then a forty-five-minute on-set "walk-through" of the first episode to be shot that day would be done. For the walk-through, Child actually cooked the recipes she would be making during the taping; she didn't just pretend to go through the cooking motions. This meant that for any topic, several examples or versions of a dish might be necessary, especially if she planned to show it at several stages of its preparation, and especially if any of this was to be presented out of order. For example, to offer a shot of a completed dish at the very beginning of an episode meant having a finished version there from the start. For an episode on beef tongue, she ended up requiring eight tongues on the set: for the walk-through she needed an uncooked tongue, a cooked but

L'ECOLE DES TROIS GOURMANDES

MASTERING THE ART OF FRENCH COOKING

Paris

SIMONE BECK FISCHBACHER &
LOUISETTE BERTHOLLE-REMION
23 Bd.d' Argenson, Neuilly (Seine)
Maillot 74-78

Cambridge

JULIA CHILD
103 *Irving Street, Cambridge* 38
Massachusetts
(617) 876-1072

October 16, 1965

TO: Ruth Lockwood, Producer, The French Chef, WGBH-TV, Boston 02134

FROM: Julia Child

SUBJECT: Expenses in connection with the following French Chef Shows
         #110 Saddle of Lamb
         #116 Sooupe au Pistou
         Production Date: Oct. 14, 1965

#1	Vegetables and eggs	8.75
#2	2 saddles, endive, misc. veg.	20.24
#3	Chick. broth, o.oil, cream	7.33
#4	Froze. spinach	.75
#5	2 saddles, misc. veg.	20.09
Misc. list		
	Taxi, Tues home from studio	1.80
	Taxi, Wed. to hairdresser	2.10
	Taxi, Wed. hairdresser to	
	butcher	3.10
	Vermouth	2.40
	Stamps, fan mail	5.00

      Balancue due $72.81

Food - Misc.   72 81
Talent - 100.00
172.81

I hereby certify that this is a full and true statement

Julia Child

Submitted: Dec
RJL

Cooking costs. Courtesy Julia Child Foundation.

unpeeled tongue, a cooked and peeled tongue, and a plated braised tongue, and then another full set for the actual shoot.

The walk-through was often more like an exercise in blocking than a simple rehearsal. Child went through the stages of cooking while the director and cameramen worked on the best angles to cover the action. When necessary, Julia and Paul Child and the crew stopped to mull over alternative ways to do things (culinarily and televisually), which is why the walk-throughs were necessarily longer than the half-hour live shoots (but not much more; it was far better to just let Child do her routine from beginning to end and then discuss how best to film it). While some of the crew also used the walk-through time to set up the lighting and cabling, it was particularly important for the camera-man who was working the close-up camera to participate in the walk-throughs. He would be capturing the most detailed and, in a way, most specialized aspects of the food preparation in the live shoot. As Russell Morash explains, the close-up cameraman often came to the show without the sort of culinary knowledge that would enable him to know where and what to shoot; the walk-through let him see how Child would be proceeding and understand what her culinary jargon meant for the action.

At the same time, the walk-throughs generally didn't take more than the allotted forty-five minutes, and a variety of factors lay behind this. For one thing, Paul and Julia had already pre-planned the unfolding of the episode to such a degree of exactitude that, once she got to the set, Child could simply jump into action (and follow the time and instruc-tion cards when necessary). Once she got going, her energetic momen-tum meant that any interruption (say, to try different blocking) might throw her off her demonstrative game. Likewise, the director and his crew had a general sense of how the cooking show would unfold and preferred to make many of their editing decisions during the live shoot. In any case, the relatively low budget didn't permit lengthy rehearsals. (Some bias may also have been at work here in that the male crew may not have wanted to spend a lot of time on a cooking show, which was considered a lowly genre of educational television). Morash proudly asserts in an e-mail to me that the walk-throughs never went beyond their allotted time, and overtime was never required. As he describes the role of the technical crew in relation to the walk-through and the shoot itself, "We came to each session with only a rough outline in my mind of how the program would move along. We rehearsed very little because it took so long to set the camera and light the scene; we never got cameras until late morning. Once cameras were finally ready, we shot the program live on tape with only a minimum of rehearsal. But keep in mind we got very good at anticipating where she was going next, so it became routine." Both because the walk-throughs were preparatory sessions and because there was *no* post-production editing of the material that was shot (thus, having footage from the walk-throughs would have been irrelevant), the cameras didn't film the walk-throughs, and there was no visual record of what had happened in these moments. At best, during the walk-throughs, the cameras simply presented live, unrecorded feed to the director, who might take note of what worked and what didn't so he could use that information when the actual recording of the program began. In fact, it seems that the director and technical crew did not always participate fully in the walk-through— which often was more an occasion for the Childs and Ruth Lockwood to ensure that the culinary aspects of the show worked and were ready to be filmed. As Morash notes, he and his crew were busy setting things up, and the walk-through was less for them than for Child to have one last chance to work through her routine before the actual shoot began. For all of the Childs' detailed pre-planning, there was a desire—especially by Morash and his technical crew—to just get the shoot going and then capture its unfolding as spontaneously, but also as expertly, as possible. Early on, in a 1963 memo, Lockwood had momentarily voiced regret that the show had no shot-by-shot shooting script. In her words, "We wouldn't lose many of the close-ups that we often wish the camera had gotten." But too much scripting at a shot-to-shot level would not have matched Child's propensity for boundless, restless action of a sort that couldn't be fully scripted in advance. And, as Morash points out (and as the problems that came with the cue cards confirm), too much planning might have derailed Child. One of her greatest talents was simply talking things out to her own contentment while going about her kitchen business. Detailed scripting also would not have fit in with the ethos of the (male) technical crew, whose professional practice in the case of a live, one-take shoot of a low-budget nonfiction show in a somewhat lowly genre likely would have entailed just jumping in and filming with the faith that one was trained well enough to know how to capture the action.

After the walk-through, Child took a half-hour break, and then the shoot took place. Because the food was being prepared in real time and transformed in real time, there generally could be only one take of any moment in the cooking process (it would be hard to start over once she started doing things to ingredients), and everything had to transpire chronologically. Overall, Child would soldier on through her errors and fumbles, even in cases where the problem revolved around physical discomfort, if not outright injury. For example, in an early episode on vegetables, one can see Child choking on a string bean she has tasted and one can feel her evident suffering at the impairment, which lasts through much of the episode. Likewise, in an episode on omelets, she forgets that a skillet has just come out of the oven and grabs it with her bare hands, shrieking for an instant but going on through the pain. In fact, retakes were done only when something failed completely and there was no way to fix it on-camera. For example, a soufflé fell just as Child was transporting it to the dining room and made all her banter about serving it meaningless, so the scene was stopped, and another soufflé was cooked up on the spot. In another episode, an early one, Child moved too quickly through her recipe and ended up in the dining room with too many minutes for her wrap-up chat. In this case, the episode was taped again from the beginning, but she still came up short. This incident was one key factor in Child's decision to conduct carefully timed rehearsals and then to have either Lockwood or Paul Child hold up timing cards as the actual shoot unfolded.

Generally, it was considered too expensive to start any action over (and some actions obviously couldn't be restarted—namely, any culinary act that had already transformed an ingredient beyond its beginning state). It was also next to impossible to edit the early videotapes, which would have had to be spliced with Scotch tape, which clearly was not desirable for a show whose videotapes were often hand delivered from one station to another in the educational television network. At best, the on-set team sometimes had ways to compensate, without interrupting the shoot, for those mistakes that came from Child's frequent slips of the tongue and errors of statement. In particular, Lockwood and Paul Child watched closely as each shoot transpired, looking out for the culinary content of the show and trying to keep it clear and on track. When either observer spotted a verbal mistake, an off-screen card would be flashed to Child so she could correct what she had said. For instance, when Child confuses the amount of almond extract in "Introducing Charlotte Malakoff" (see Chapter 1), one clearly can spot her looking off-camera in response to a signal and absorbing the corrective message on a card just before rectifying her erroneous instruction. (Conversely, when three minutes before the end of the episode she says that "the buttered paper was not molded," when she evidently means "the molded paper was not buttered," the verbal slip is not corrected. Either no one spotted it or it was decided there was no time to correct or it was deemed inconsequential enough not to need rectification.)

After shooting the first episode of the day, Child spent ten minutes filming a promo for the next episode and, as noted, in the years after 1965 when the show was shot at the WGBH studio, she spent another ten minutes talking to the studio audience. She then got the set ready for the next episode and took a half-hour break before the process started again at 6:50 P.M. Cleanup began at 9:35, and Child often arrived home quite late and ready for a nightcap.

Legend has it that the crew used the lunch break to devour the culinary results of Child's morning efforts, and the Child archives have a delightful cartoon that shows a bunch of chubby men walking past a visitor to WGBH who is being told by a tour guide that this is the crew of *The French Chef.* But Russ Morash claims that many members of the crew found what Child was making too exotic and strange and they preferred to bring downscale grinder sandwiches almost as a reassertion of their working-class identity. In fact, when the show moved to the WGBH studio in 1965, it took on a group of (female) volunteers who helped with prep (cutting vegetables and so on) and cleanup. They, not the crew, were given the day's cooking as a reward. Eventually, these volunteers came to matter very much to Child, and she trusted them to try out her upcoming recipes in their own homes to make sure her lessons could be reproduced by average cooks in a variety of kitchens.[9]

Let us look a bit more at the production process as it transpired concretely in the actual shoot of *The French Chef*. As a first step, we can consider how all of the prep work Paul and Julia Child did back at home helped to prepare filming at the studio. Paul's and Julia's at-home planning and timed blocking typically led to scene breakdowns for each episode, most of which are saved in the Julia Child papers at the Schlesinger Library at Radcliffe College. These clarify the relation between the written plan and what showed up on the screen when Child engaged in her performances. For example, it is interesting to note that Child ranged between two seemingly opposed scripting methods for the opening segment of each episode. The opening, a sort of pre-credit sequence in which Child triumphantly announced the ingredient or dish of the day, clearly mattered to her a great deal. It was the only part of her half-hour patter that she actually committed to memory and did not just improvise as the cameras rolled. It was also where she provided the most humor, the most historical background, and the greatest context for what she was doing. Strikingly, then, Child either typed out this part of the show verbatim in all its detail *or* left blank space open at the top of the script and waited until the walk-through to choose the language for the opening, which she then wrote out in detail at the very last minute. (For many scripts, the blank space turned out to be too small, and the lines she wrote and then committed to memory sometimes continue to the back of the script's pages). She described the latter option to Lockwood in a memo at the conclusion of the first season of *The French Chef*: "You will note on the scripts I have not always given anything for the opening shots—takes so much time to think of those that I thought it better just to do the scripts and get them finished."[10] In other words, she scripted the opening sequence but did so either way in advance or under the inspiration of being on the set in the moments just before the shoot. In either case, Child evidently thought of the introduction to each episode as a thing apart—something whose precise wording, for better or worse, would set the tone of the episode and therefore needed special care.

In passing, it might be worth noting that pre-credit sequences were frequent in film and television of the 1960s. They served as a kind of teaser, a jam-packed invitation into the narrative world proper of the show or film. Think, for instance, of the television series *The FBI*, in which a violent crime was committed before the credits, and the rest of the episode was devoted to tracking down and punishing the perpetrators. Such segments served as a quick seduction into the narrative world to follow, and it is revealing that Child so readily and quickly adopted the format. Child's show was a bit of nonfiction instructional television, yet she clearly saw the dramatic and entertainment potential that could be brought to the cooking show genre by a whiz-bang opening. Thus, while the earliest episodes had just a few moments of pre-credit patter, as *The French Chef* developed, and as Child came to understand how she could use her performance style to capture and captivate the spectator, her openings became more elaborate and more about staging a dramatic effect and articulating the promise of exciting things to come. To take just one example, the color episode "Coq au Vin, alias Chicken Fricassee" begins pre-credit with Child dramatically taking the lids off two side-by-side dishes (chicken in red wine, chicken in white wine), then banging the lids together as if to boldly announce the theme of the cooking session as the credits roll. (Amusingly, she also splattered herself with sauce and had to begin the post-credit body of the show by apologizing for her messiness and mopping herself off the best she could.)

Even though the episodes began with emphatic, demarcated pre-credit sequences, the immediate moments *after* the credits of *The French Chef* were also generally explanatory of things to come rather than actual enactments of the cooking itself: Pre-credit Child announced and dramatized a topic in thrilling fashion; post-credit Child then spent a few minutes providing a more measured introduction before moving into the narrative of food preparation proper. In other words, just as the pre-credit sequence was about announcing a future (here is a first, tantalizing glimpse of what Child is going to be doing today on *The French Chef*: "We're doing brioche! Today on *The French Chef!*"), the immediate post-credit moment was also future-oriented but in a more soberly pedagogical way (we now learn in greater detail what food is going to be prepared during the remainder of the episode and why it matters and what its history is). In the first moments after the credits, Child might provide history, lore, and an overview of the foodstuff and its variants. Between these two sequences (pre- and immediate post-credit), the action that went on behind the credits was frequently dealt with telegraphically in the scripts, which might say something like, "Fuss about," to indicate that Child simply had to pass time getting this or that utensil ready while the opening credits rolled. In several episodes, under the credits' musical theme, one can hear her mumbling to the production team. In the episode "To Roast a Chicken," she can be seen behind the credit titles dancing a light jig. Credits, in other words, were something to get out of the way so that one could get down to real talk and real cooking. Certainly, there were times where she used the credits for visually engaging action that could carry interest in and of itself—for instance, a lumbering lobster she had introduced just before the credits and who continued his slow movements into the credit sequence. But it was evidently important to the on-set team not to have anything important transpire during the credits, as all felt that this was merely a passage to get through and not to be regarded as an instructional moment. In this respect, it is noteworthy perhaps that the script for an episode on roast suckling pig (1966) indicates that, during the credits, "J. CONTINUE DOING SOMETHING USEFUL AND REAL, LIKE BRUSHING PIG'S TEETH, AND CONTINUE WITH IT ON INTO INTRODUCTION," but that in the episode as filmed the credit image simply holds on the inert pig and has her doing nothing with it. Child explains the tooth brushing once the credits have ended and her real instruction has resumed.

After the pre- and post-credit preliminaries were out of the way, the narrative enactment of the food preparation could begin in earnest. The typewritten breakdown for episode 46, "Elegance with Eggs," which was shot on a Tuesday, offers a typical example of the format Child honed for her "scripts" for *The French Chef*. The page is divided into four vertical columns. On the far left is the suggested timing for each segment. The next column is devoted to the main themes (in this case, eggs "en cocotte," followed by molded eggs, shirred eggs, omelets, and serving suggestions) and the main actions for each segment (cooking in the oven, under a broiler, in a pan); The third column contains a summary of the patter and a more detailed breakdown of actions for each segment. Finally, the far-right column is devoted to what were termed "setups"—that is, the utensils and pans and foodstuffs needed for each segment.

As noted, Child worked out the wording of the pre-credit sequence of *French Chef* episodes in detail. The "Elegance with Eggs" script spells out the shtick of its pre-credit opening and shows how Child was thinking about the ways to give something as seemingly ordinary as eggs an "elegance" that would come from dramatic effect. As the camera focused on a platter of standard egg dishes, her voice buoyantly announced, "Boiled eggs, fried eggs, poached eggs, scrambled eggs. These are breakfast eggs. [The last line is handwritten into the script]. We're doing eggs, but we aren't doing any of these today on *The French Chef*." As she was saying the last line, she was to take the platter and dump the eggs on it into the garbage. Then the opening credits would come up ("Fuss about"). Once the credits were over, the patter of the beginning would be picked up again and expanded on: "Welcome to the FC [*French Chef*]. I'm JC [Julia Child]. The egg, you know, can be your best friend—if you give it the right break. I'm not talking about eggs for breakfast, but eggs for Brunch, eggs for Lunch, Eggs as appetizers, for company, Eggs for Elegance." This introductory material is indicated as running about a minute or so from pre-credit to post-credit. For what it's worth, the actual filmed version ended up keeping most of the dialogue from this script but eliminated the action of the breakfast eggs being thrown out. Instead, they are simply removed off-camera. Perhaps it was decided that the image of eggs going into the garbage would look too wasteful and be criticized by viewers.

With the all-important annunciatory opening sequences out of the way, the remainder of the script, given over to the actual work of making the recipes, could be more telegraphic and present actions through curt, concise instructions. For instance, the action of one segment from "Elegance with Eggs" is handled by the commands to "Discuss filled omelettes, while bringing over mushrooms, etc. Make omelettes, fill, cover with mushrooms, cover with sauce, sprinkle cheese and butter. TO OVEN. BROWN TOP OF OMELET." Other scripts, in

NUTES	I. CARDS & TITLES	ACTION and talk	SET UPS
	OPENING SHOT	EGG SET UP ON PLATTER	

Oeuf a la Coque, Oeuf a la Poêle;
Oeuf Poche sur Canape, Oeuf Brouillé .
Boiled eggs, Fried eggs, Poached eggs,
Scrambled eggs. *They are breakfast eggs -*
We're doing eggs today, but we aren't
doing any of these ~~bnnmfmnhmnmnmnmmmmhmfnimm~~
today on The French Chef
    DUMP EGGS AND PLATTER INTO WASTE BASKET

CREDITS   Fuss about. HANDFUL OF EGGS

INTRODUCTION   Welcome to the FC. I'm JC.
    The egg, you know, can be your best friend --
if you give it the right break.
    I'm not talking about eggs for breakfast,
but eggs for Brunch, ~~fnmninnmning~~ eggs for Lunch,
    Eggs as appetizers, for company
    Eggs for Elegance

L
(4:30)   COCOTTE   Take L'OEUF EN COCOTTE, for instance -- eggs   2 rectangle
                4:30   baked in little ramekins -- fireproof dishes,   ~~dhsha~~ pan,
                       like these (SHOW EACH DISH)   simm. water
       plain; cream;   1 per person as appetizer, 2 as main course. buttered cocottes
       ham; tomato   ~~fighndnphnnngnmnhhnnnmmmm~~ Butter ramekin,   buttered muff.
                       break in egg, set in hot water to set bottom.   tin
       why pan water   Add cream and chopped herbs   Tomato sauce
                           Add chopped ham or chicken livers   Chopped ham
       Muffin Tins   Add tomato sauce   * Molded eggs
       Molded in tins Use muffin tins, make molded eggs like these,
                           substitute for poached eggs, and easier.   Ready eggs in
.80   OVEN & BACK   Heavy butter in tin so will unmold   oven; very
30   375 8 min   TAKE TINS TO SIDE OF AUX. STOVE. REMOVE   little water
          ~~fnmnfmmfnihmnmhnhd~~ READY MADE FROM OVEN ~~nnmnhhmsmnmnhpmm~~ in pans; oven
                                                                           off.
                       SHOW COCOTTES
          MOLDED EGGS SHOW MOLDED EGGS & REMOVE WITH KNIFE   Table knife (for
            Other sauces   ARRANGE WITH SPINACH, etc.   removing eggs)
5:30   Benedictine   Viroflay & Florentine   Serv. dish with 2
(5:00) Viroflay   n pieces toast
10:00   *30 sec egg?*   ready spinach
10:30 SHIRRED EGGS   Show metal shirred egg dish, other   ready cheese sauce
            Lower l. burner high   dishes, simmer plaque   fluted mushrooms(2
fnmfifi Pot holders   Butter in metal dish, break in egg,   Simmer placque
(2:30)   add more butter & heat to film   other shirred dish
13:00 TO BROILER   Show one with cream and cheese   Ready with cheese
                       BROILER: Finish eggs   to~~simmmm~~ shirr
4:30 CLEAR FOR OMELETTES SHOW EGGS, and clear up for omelettes   J. broiler pan,
                                                                         correct hight
5:00 OMELETTES   for quick broil
            Front left burner high
            7"bottom, long handle
            sloping sides
            Scrumb, heat, oil, *Sau*
15:30 MAKE 1st Omelette
16:00 ~~fmmmmmmmmmm~~
(2:30)

contrast, provided more detailed indications of the timing an action should involve. For example, for episode 89, "French Veal Stew," one sequence comes with the following indications of the timing of the pedagogy and the actions associated with it:

3:15 WATER IN
TO COOK TOP
on high heat
simmer 2–3 minutes
called "blanching"
3:50 SCUM TALK
why veal scum
TO SINK
4:35 DRAIN

In other words, the instructions here—for Child, for in-studio helpers such as Paul Child and Ruth Lockwood, and perhaps for the director in the control booth (who, during the shoot, actually was more likely to be following the action on the monitors than consulting a verbally jampacked script breakdown with multiple columns)—were indicating that Child should start by putting veal chunks into a pot to simmer. While that was under way, she would talk for forty-five seconds about why the simmering caused scum to rise to the surface, then, to end the action, she would go to the sink and drain the cooked meat.

Of course, in addition to the opening sequences and then the narrative actions that constituted the body of preparation of the dishes of the day, there would be a concluding sequence in which Child summed up the work of the session and presented the final dishes (in, as noted, a separate dining room). Again, as with the opening sequences that spoke of the immediate future (in which the announced dish was to be brought to fruition), the closing moments addressed and anticipated a future, but one that had to do with consumption (how should this completed dish be eaten, and with which accompaniments? with what wine?) rather than production (how will this dish be prepared?). Here, the typed scripts were generally telegraphic or abbreviated and left lots of room for Child to improvise in relation to the amount of time left before the final credits had to roll. For example, in "Elegance with

Eggs," the end moments of presenting the dish are simply summarized as "Filled Omelet, Salad, Bread, White Wine," leaving it up to Child to decide the language to explain that. No doubt, this had to do with Child's considering precise wording for the finale less important than that for the opening, where she would be establishing the tone of the episode about to unfold. But it may also have had to do with the live, no-retakes, half-hour format of the show. Specifically, by leaving the ending relatively unscripted, Child was giving herself the room to expand or contract her patter as the show neared its conclusion and as it became clear just how much or how little time was left. Thus, in the script for "Elegance with Eggs," Child is expected to be in the dining room by minute twenty-six-and-a-half, which is about two minutes before an episode's average ending time. After that time marker, there is little detail other than the indication "20 seconds" (to the show's signoff), followed by a few handwritten concluding remarks by Child: "Here are just a few of the hundreds of ways of cooking and serving eggs. All it takes is this, and a little imagination." Evidently, Child was to get to the dining room two minutes before the end of the show and start her concluding chatter, and exactly twenty seconds before signoff, someone would signal to her to begin the final wrap-up. What she did between getting to the dining room and signing off was up to her and couldn't or shouldn't be planned in advance. It was better, then, to keep the business of the last minutes somewhat elastic and adjustable to the time available.

In its shooting style, *The French Chef* used several electronic cameras that were always on and with the director calling for cuts back and forth between them (so that only one camera was actually producing video feed at any one moment). This was typical of many television shows of the period that were filmed in real time to capture actions, such as pedagogical demonstration, that needed to be shown chronologically from beginning to end. In other words, cutting was done live on the set by switching from one camera to another. Such multicamera shooting could be used for fictional and nonfictional series alike.[11] But simultaneous multicamera filming was not the only method available at the time. For example, the visually striking *The Twilight Zone*, which achieved much of its creepiness from complicated visual interplays of clarity and darkness, was filmed with a single camera, with the lighting set up anew for each shot. This method would give *The Twilight Zone* a look that was somewhat cinematic in a film noir style (predictably, some of its directors and cameramen had worked on noir films), as each shot would be lit according to its own dramatic needs (brightness here, shadows there). In contrast, multicamera shooting required even lighting (since all cameras were looking at the same set) and worked well for sitcoms (where even brightness matched the seeming cheerfulness of the subject matter), along with programs with a more instructive nature (where the even brightness conveyed the clarity of the educational mission).[12] Unlike that of, say, *The Twilight Zone*, which was about the construction of fantasy situations, multicamera shooting was particularly useful to shows whose actions needed to be filmed live in an everyday world and with respect for chronological unfolding.

Such was the case of the cooking show, where there could be some cheating with time but where, essentially, an action once begun needed to be followed to its conclusion. Obviously, for example, it would not be effective to begin the cooking of a dish and then have to wait while cameras and lights were jockeyed into place for a new visual setup— better to cut between cameras as the action unfolded uninterrupted than to interrupt it for new camera setups. Uninterrupted chronological shooting was particularly appropriate, as noted, to Child's style of cooking and instructing, because once she got started and the words came pouring out, any disruption in the flow would take her off-course and create problems.

In its multicamera mode, *The French Chef* employed two cameras, with the director giving instructions to cut back and forth between them as the filming transpired. Generally, the first camera was devoted to views of the overall scene and to full-body shots, while the second was available to catch details, partial views, and close-ups. While either camera was shooting, the other could be jockeyed into a new position, or its lens could be changed to put a different focus on the action. (Lens changes were more typical for the second, detail-oriented camera, which was used for a variety of shots from a variety of distances. It was better not to change lenses on the first camera and instead have it always ready to capture longer views of the scene.)

Even though the multicamera method was typical of much television production at the time and had to do primarily with a perceived need for visual diversity (but also, as a legacy from the days of live transmission, to have more than one camera around in case a bulb blew out), it was a system that seems particularly appropriate for a cooking show, especially one as driven by personality as *The French Chef*. The content of the cooking show, after all, has to do with a human agent interacting by means of tools (utensils, appliances, and so on) with foodstuffs that will undergo dramatic transformations. It thus seems logical to have a shooting style that can, in real time and respecting chronology, alternate full-body images of the cook in all her or his evident personality and closer shots of human-driven technique acting on the foodstuffs as they undergo transformation into the dish of the day. Two-camera set-ups are ideal, then, for the cooking demonstration, and in any case, the low budgets and low reputation of the genre overall generally meant that no more than two cameras would have been made available to a kitchen show. (One exception is James Beard's shows from the 1940s, which had three cameras. With so little programming coming out of the studios in those early days, his station, WNBT, could afford to dedicate all of its cameras to one show. In any case, the third camera tended to be used most to film non-culinary action at the periphery of Beard's kitchen activity. For instance, the third camera filmed the titles and credits and was used for cutaways to the guests that came into Beard's kitchen world. For Beard's in-kitchen cooking demonstrations themselves, the standard two-camera method of long shot and close-up was still the dominant style, and the third camera rarely participated in that activity.)

An episode of *Chef Milani* shot in Los Angeles in 1957, and now in the archives at UCLA, shows that the two-camera method became so conventional to such programs that it could be a subject of parody. While Chef Milani was away on vacation, a comic, Robert Ali, substituted for him, pretending to be a French chef and humorously directing the cameramen to cut from one view to another. In one case, he instructs that a close-up of one of his concoctions should not be taken because "it looks pretty bad right now." In another, he pointedly turns from one angle to another and strikes an impressive pose "for the benefit of the camera" as a cut from one camera to the other follows him in this action.

A randomly chosen episode from 2008 of *Everyday Italian*, Giada de Laurentiis's series on the Food Network, suggests that, in matching the functionality of two-camera shooting to the specifics of the cooking demonstration as a combination of hand work and full body activity, much remains of the basic conventions from the earliest years of the TV cooking show. Except for a few moments that go out of the kitchen—for example, a prologue in which, in one extended shot, de Laurentiis lounges in a comfy chair and explains how her philosophy of food fits within her philosophy of lifestyle, or a montage in which de Laurentiis shops at a farmer's market—the episode is composed primarily of cooking sequences made up, like many shows from the 1950s and *The French Chef* in its early years, of alternating close-ups of food and hand techniques with medium-range shots of de Laurentiis talking to the camera as she cooks. Yet there is one striking difference. Many of the full shots of de Laurentiis are framed from the chest up, disconnecting the image of her upper body from her hands, which go out of the frame so we don't see what they're doing at the cutting board or wherever. (In contrast, it is rare to have a full shot of Child that does not include her hands and the actions in which they are engaged.) The predictable effect is to focus attention on the shapely de Laurentiis as a striking, even sexy figure and to render her as having visual interest independent of the pragmatic task of food preparation. If, as I've suggested, one difference that Child brought to the cooking show on television was that she made her visual embodiment and the concrete rendition of her personality key to the pleasure and pedagogy of the show, more recent shows, especially those that revolve around sexy women in the kitchen, take the next step by making body and personality assume so much importance that the cooking starts to become irrelevant. From the anonymous hands of the *Knox On-Camera Recipes* discussed in chapter 1 to the full-body shots of Julia Child with her hands going about their business to the chesty shots of de Laurentiis or Nigella Lawson or Rachael Ray (and so on), in which the hand work is pushed off-frame, very different notions of women's relation to domesticity and to lifestyle are bandied about.

Throughout the history of the cooking show, two-camera shooting has enabled a certain degree of openness and variability in filming. While one camera is following the action, the director can get the second camera ready to capture something new in the action. The two-camera setup thus provides a bit of breathing space, so to speak, in that one camera can pick up a current bit of action and stay with it while the other camera is being moved into position for the next bit, or the scene can cut from the cook to something else, such as a close-up of a dish, to allow the cook a moment, if needed, off-camera. Thus, the script for "New Year's Party," episode 37 of *The French Chef*, contains the comment, "Camera switch to table set up to give pause if needed," the idea being that, because the episode is as much about how the dishes should look to guests as about how to prepare them, a shot of the food on display could be an opportunity for Child to take a breather or for the other camera to catch up on some action for which it needs to be jockeyed into place.

One might think that the ability to cut back and forth between two cameras would encourage directors to engage in a frenzy of editing, since it allows cuts to break up the action to add new visual interest to a sequence. It is indeed the case that recent cooking shows often appear over-edited, the scene seeming never to stand still and space becoming fragmented at an ever faster pulse. But with *The French Chef*, it was more common for the pace of editing to be slow. Some of this had to do with the content of the show. On the one hand, Child was clearly an enthralling on-screen presence, and it was most appropriate to capture her performance with as little interruption as possible. On the other hand, insofar as she was performing an instructional activity (the tasks of recipe preparation), a utilitarian need existed for the camera to follow through on each action from beginning to end with as little interruption as possible and with the editing keyed to the content of the instruction itself. In this functional style, cuts tended to be used less for rhythm or even visual diversity (although there would be a cut if a specific action—mixing a batter, for instance—went on for a while and the director felt a change was needed in the imagery) than to follow from one action to the next and to give emphasis, when needed, through revealing close-ups. One unwritten rule, as Morash explains, was that the cameras should never cut to a close-up that had no visible action going on in it (in other words, they did not cut to a static image) unless something Child said indicated that such a cut was necessary (if she asked the viewers to appreciate something about the look of a foodstuff, for instance).

The reasons for not cutting too often were also technical. Cutting between two long shots or between two close-ups (in other words, between cameras that were the same distance from the action but at different angles to it) could seem jarring. To take one common occurrence, Child did not always know which camera was on, and which direction she should be looking in, and a cut between two long shots of her would only make her misdirected gaze more noticeable. Sometimes, indeed, one can see Child looking at the wrong camera, and things then seem doubly awkward (the wrong angle combined with her own realization of the error). Morash contrasts this to another WGBH production, the lead-ins to the American versions of *Masterpiece Theatre* in which the host, Alistair Cooke, always knew which camera to look at and thereby permitted dramatic cuts from frontal to side views. (Steven Colbert parodies this convention in the opening credits of *The Colbert Report*, where he turns emphatically to cameras that, one after the other, capture him from a series of angles in fast cuts.)

In standard two-camera television practice, the cameras on the set fed their signals to a control booth, where the director watched monitors and made choices about which camera to film with at each moment. He relayed his instructions to a technician called a switcher, who, from the control booth, would switch electronically from one camera to the other. In other words, only one camera would actually be shooting at any one instant. In the first years of *The French Chef*, when the show had to be produced off-site, the feed from the cameras actually went out two hundred feet from the building to a Trailways bus that WGBH had converted into a mobile camera center and that had not been affected by the fire. In the bus, Morash watched the monitors and made his editing decisions. In fact, Morash was assigned to *The French Chef* in large part because he had had a lot of experience with on-location productions that involved directing camera work from the bus. One of the shows he worked on just before *The French Chef* (and continued to direct on his days off from Child's series), *Science Reporter*, involved remote shoots at the Massachusetts Institute of Technology, wherein Morash showed his expertise in directing two cameras at a remove from the action—in that case, classrooms from which the feed, again, went out to the bus some distance away.

By not actually putting the director in the immediate presence of the filmed action, this kind of setup no doubt cut him off from a larger view of the scene. The consequences of this are obvious in moments in which Child did things that would have been shown better in a full shot, but, in the actual unfurling of the shoot, the primary camera was in too close to catch it and the second camera was focused somewhere else. In such a moment, Morash had little or no indication of what he should direct the cameramen to film—and when to cut from one camera to the other—because he had no video feed of the scene overall. In the first episode of the series (on beef bourguignon), for example, as Laura Shapiro notes, Child suddenly started to use her own body to indicate the position of various cuts of meat, but neither camera caught her gesture in time. It is likely that the director was getting no visual cues of what Child was doing and didn't know to cut to the full-body view.

On the other hand, by working only from what was available on monitors and by not being visually present in front of the action itself, the director could gain concentration and thereby think of the live space before the cameras as already a televisual space to be cut up and reconstituted at will. In this respect, it is interesting to note that, at the Food Network's studio in the Chelsea district of New York City, some of the most popular cooking shows are filmed from a control booth that has minimal or *no* direct visual access to the stage set (although the director does have communication from an assistant director who is present on the set and can whisper observations back up to the control room through a headset).

In fact, in the design of the new WGBH facilities after the devastating fire of 1961, *none* of the studios was planned to have control booths visually open to the performance area, and directors seemed to prefer this arrangement. In my interview with him, Morash told me that he saw it as desirable *not* to be able to see the set, because he liked to work only from the feed on the two monitors keyed to the cameras. This pushed the director to think less about the live action than about the edited results that would show up on viewers' TV sets.

Except for some follow-up instruction to the cameraman if he wanted camera movement in any particular shot, the director's work on any shot generally was done the moment he ordered the cut that initiated it. As Morash explains, the good two-camera television director is thinking not about the current shot but about the one he is going to cut to. But if the two-camera system put pressure on a director like Morash, who had to keep making decisions whether to cut or not and risked missing an important view, it also sometimes created difficulties for Child who, as noted, was not always sure where to look and in which direction to show off her actions. According to legend, the cameramen would hang a sign on whichever camera was not currently filming the shot that, in one version of the story, said, "Julia Child is a wretch, but she won't know this if she looks into the other camera." The sign indicated to Julia that this camera was not where she should be focusing her efforts.[13] More generally, the interaction between Child, the cameramen, and the director was an ongoing learning process in which everyone had to adapt. In particular, Child learned increasingly to give verbal and physical cues when she was about to do something that might best be followed by a change of cameras. For example, she might say something like "And look at how those eggs are whipping up" to signal that a cut should be made to a close-up of the bowl in which she was beating eggs. One problem was that most cameramen predictably would have no particular background knowledge of the kitchen world and might not always know what the terms she was using meant. The director had to translate her nomenclature into non-culinary terms and do so within the few instants before the cut had to occur. Again, as noted earlier, the participation of the cameramen in the walk-throughs, when time permitted, was one way to acquaint these technicians with the equally technical world of culinary activity.

Despite the signage to tell her where to look, Child can be seen peeking at the wrong camera throughout the seasons of *The French Chef.* This frequently occurs, for instance, on the big, in-house WGBH set when she moves from a speech she's giving at the countertop away to the oven. Since Child often spent time at the counter offering general discourse on issues and items of interest, she would, it seems, become fixated on the camera that had been capturing her speech and she would consequently not realize that the cameramen were switching to the other camera for a better view of what was going to be happening at the oven. Perhaps the very spaciousness of the new set meant that there were many more places for Child to be and many more places for the cameras to be, and these didn't always coincide.

To clarify just how the two-camera system worked for a classic cooking show such as *The French Chef*, and how it revolved around complex interaction between the performer's actions and the director's cutting choices, let's again look somewhat closely at the first moments of the episode "Introducing Charlotte Malakoff," with which this study began. Notably, "Introducing Charlotte Malakoff" starts in close-up with an inverted pot surrounded by ladyfingers and with the hands picking the ladyfingers up to demonstrate their texture. In contrast, it is common (although not inevitable) in Hollywood fictional filmmaking for scenes to begin not in close-up but with what is called an establishing shot, a view taken with the camera set a bit back so that it captures (or establishes) all of the on-screen actors and the overall space in which they will be operating. Once the overall view has been set, closer and partial views can hone in on parts of the scene (what is commonly called "analytic editing" because it trades for the synthetic view provided by the establishing shot a series of partial views taken from within the overall scene), although most classical Hollywood films will cut back to the establishing shot every so often before the scene ends as if to remind the viewer of where everything and everyone in the scene are. While many cooking shows use an establishing shot (especially recent shows that focus on vivacious hosts who visually can seem to matter even more than the content of what they are cooking), *The French Chef* typically began with a close-up, called a "tease" in the industry. Perhaps the force of Child's personality combined with the familiarity that viewers would have had with the kitchen set from watching previous episodes, and with the ways the rest of any episode would open up to fuller views of Child going about her business on that set, meant that the initial shot could permit itself to open with a more constrained, close-up view (usually of either a finished dish or the key ingredient of the day). Perhaps too viewers were playing into the aforementioned suspense and slowly unfolding sense of drama to which beginning with a close-up contributed. To be sure, not all episodes started with the tight view. For example, the color shows began with establishing shots more frequently than the black-and-white episodes did, maybe because a longer view would show off more things with a diversity of colors to them (Child, the set, the food, etc., and the frequent visual shtick in which she interacted bodily with gadgets and ingredients).

When the opening shot was a typical close-up, there were still variant possibilities in the uses to which it was put. The close-up might be a static shot of the key ingredient of the day or a display of an example of the final results (the executed dish) that would emerge if the ingredient was prepared according to the recipe. Or the close-up might be an action shot of Child's hands doing something to the ingredient as she moved directly into the prep work. Most often, though, the close-up began with raw foodstuffs, as if to clarify that the primary concern was to chronicle how the ingredients—or the featured key ingredient— would be transformed from their raw state into the promised result. Since the close-up was designed to tease the viewer with glimpses of what was coming in the next half-hour, it was used especially when the action was dramatic or lively. "The Lobster Show," for example, begins with a close-up of Child's hands pulling seaweed off an enormous lobster that lumbers toward the camera, and the image combines the drama of the thrilling reveal, the shock at the enormity of the creature, and the impressiveness of the fact that this tremendous beast actually is alive and moving around.

Of course, as noted in chapter 1, the voiceover that always accompanies the close-up and cheerfully announces the theme of the day immediately lets us know that this is not just any cooking show, but Julia Child's. Yet the decision to start in close on the food and the hands that are either manipulating it or pointing out something about it immediately clarifies that this show will indeed have pedagogical content, that it will not be just about personality. The show has its utilitarian side, and the fact of that utility is functionally underscored by a utilitarian visual style that begins close to the action and keeps returning to it.

At the same time, it might be worth noting that close-ups in the filming of gourmet food often work with extremely limited depth of field, and this has effects other than just the utilitarian ones. In the case of *The French Chef*, the close-ups were often filmed not by bringing one of the cameras close to the action (since that camera then risked coming into the view of the other camera, something that does in fact happen at one moment in "Introducing Charlotte Malakoff") but by putting a telephoto lens on the close-up camera so it could catch a close shot from a bit farther away. The lens had the effect of flattening space in the close-up and making the backgrounds blurry. (Telephoto lenses give sharpness to only a limited field in the visual plane of the image from front to back.) In such cases, a technical choice could play into an aesthetic effect wherein the food was not merely emphasized in utilitarian fashion but was given affective resonances through the process. The close views in *The French Chef* are already of a piece perhaps with the more overtly sensuous visuality of celebrity cooking in later decades, where visually defined dishes stand out against fuzzy, indeterminate backgrounds. In these recent celebrations of wondrous, seductive food, a prepared dish will be displayed succulently and sharply in the foreground, with a very dramatic falling off of visual clarity as one moves further back in the frame. This is a decided aesthetic choice (since a wide-angle lens could overcome some of the blurring of the background), one that focuses attention on the food and creates an ambience of fantasy-inducing insubstantiality. (For example, as I pull a book from my cookbook shelves at random—Tom Colicchio's *Think Like a Chef*—I find on page 46 a glossy photo showing sweetbreads cooking in a skillet in sharp detail, with a background that is so out of focus that the sprig of thyme the recipe calls for appears as little more than a smear of green and brown. About two inches of the sweetbreads are in focus; the rest of the photo is ethereal, a dreaminess echoed in the foaming of butter in the pan and on the glistening sweetbreads themselves.)

No doubt, the falling off of visual clarity in the close-ups in *The French Chef* was not managed to an aesthetic degree as strong as in these later cases, but it does contribute to the televisual style of food presentation as one that simultaneously is highly functional (here is

Ethereal sweetbreads, photographed by Bill Bettencourt.

intense concentration on the food at hand and on the actions to be done to it) and highly enticing (here is food that is part of a dream—part of a soft, sinuous seduction). The close-ups in *The French Chef* are themselves expressions of an *art* of cooking.

Not that the episodes of *The French Chef* don't provide broader, more distanced overviews of the scene similar in effect to what an establishing shot offers. But they tend to do so only *after* focusing in through the initial, annunciatory close-up on the primary foodstuff and the hands that are interacting with it. Typically in Child's show, the first transition from close-up to the broad view is effected not by a cut to the second camera but by a movement of the first camera, which, having begun the close-up, pulls back to a more distant view. From the hands doing their utilitarian work to the longer view of Child, the transition is a smooth, logically connected one. Thus, "Introducing Charlotte Malakoff" starts with a slightly angled close-up shot of the Charlotte on a baking sheet, where it is surrounded by ladyfingers. After Child announces the topic of the day, the camera moves backward to provide a bodily image of Child herself and, most important, to turn the close-up into a more distanced, medium shot of the overall scene. We then view Child standing behind the counter on which the baking dish is placed as she explains that this one kind of pastry serves many different functions. Behind her the kitchen set now is visible. This broader view will effectively serve as an establishing shot to anchor all upcoming partial views and to be reverted to every so often to remind the viewer of the scene.

Up to this point in "Introducing Charlotte Malakoff," there has been *no* cutting, just camera movement. From close-up to pulled-back long view, this first shot of the episode has lasted for more than a minute, but there's been nothing static about it. Now, as Child, in medium shot, picks up a limp, horrid, commercially made ladyfinger and bends it into mushiness to show how inadequate it is, the second camera picks up the action through a cut (the first one in the episode) to a close-up, but from a different angle from the close view that the first camera used to initiate the episode. In other words, the first camera—which had started as a close-up camera—has taken on the function of providing medium shots, while the second camera (which only now is being brought into play) will become the close-up camera for most of the rest of the episode.

Squishing the failed store-bought ladyfinger is a quick, punctual activity, and the close-up shot from the second camera needs to last only a few instants to capture the action. Thus, the finality of the gesture—Child dramatically and manually making her point about ersatz ladyfingers—cues another cut, which leads back to an anchoring, instructional long view of Child at the counter facing the first camera. Child lectures for a bit on general qualities of the ladyfinger, and the only camera work that is necessary is minor reframing as her body moves slightly from the energy (and perhaps nervous edge) she is putting into her discourse. We see, then, a complex interaction and even literal interchange between the two cameras as each serves for a time to take close-ups and each has the potential to assume multiple functions in the filming of the narrative overall.

I don't want to imply any special aesthetic achievement to the opening moments of "Introducing Charlotte Malakoff" (but I also don't want to deny the inventiveness of the camera work and the cutting in keeping things going and in changing the scale in ways that are both pedagogically functional and dramatically engaging). Clearly, there has to be something fairly functional and utilitarian about the shooting style for a cooking show. The goal is not to compose beautiful images (in fact, visual style might need to efface itself to let a beauty of content—the dishes Child is preparing—show to full advantage) but to capture in all their clarity a series of actions as they unfold. That in itself was a challenge. Morash cautions that everything that was accomplished in the unfolding of an episode of *The French Chef* was done in the context of limited budgets, limited time, and limited resources. As he explained in an e-mail to me in August 2008: "wGBH, its budget, the [TV] methods and equipment of the time, the meaning of no editing, no overtime, no reliable wireless mikes, inferior cameras, no zooms, no field dollies, etc, no money except for limited underwriting. Remember, as you recall the shortcomings, these crude programs were produced four episodes a week with almost no rehearsal on bad equipment with [a] cast of one."

In fact, the opening of "Introducing Charlotte Malakoff" is particularly instructive to look at in this respect because it does show some glitches in shooting that put into relief the moments when everything did come together. A first stylistic mishap comes in the pulling back of the opening shot from close-up to the broad view of the scene. For an instant, the reframing as the camera moves back catches the operator of the other camera in its field of vision and confirms that one liability of filming in live time with little or no possibility to re-shoot is that mistakes have to be left in. It shows how much the effective use of the two-camera system required careful choreography of the cameras in relation to each other. Another error seemingly has to do with one of the two cameras not being ready to capture an action that should have been its responsibility and the other camera, placed in a less than ideal angle or distance, having to try to make do. In this case, the close-up camera is following up-close action on a baking sheet, as it should be doing, and has started to move in for an even closer view when Child, clearly unexpectedly, pulls the baking sheet away, walks to the back wall of the kitchen, and performs the sort of full-body action (in this case, a vigorous shaking of the sheet to get excess flour off it) for which a shot from the longer-view, establishing-shot camera would have been expected. However, there is no cut to that camera; instead, the close-up camera tries desperately to follow the action. Whether Child's big movement back to the sink was not anticipated or the longer-view camera was being made handy for some other angle in another spot and was therefore not ready and in the right spot to capture her action, the close-up camera does its best to keep up and follow Child's broad bodily movement by pulling back, frantically trying to keep the bustling Child in view (for a few moments it fails and shows dead space), and refocusing the lens to adjust for the new, non-close-up distance (an attempt that causes it to go out of focus for an instant).

Between ingredients on a counter and Child leaning over them and doing things to them, between the hands doing a task and the voice explaining its purpose, between the multiplicity of actions often engaged in energetically by Child (full body activity and hand work), there were multiple things to film and competing ways to film them. The editing had to do what it could to get this or that camera to a propitious spot when possible. In any case, the roughness—the mistakes and the

Momentary fuzziness

glitches—could be part of the attraction. It was exciting to see that Child and the crew could always seem to pull it off and triumph in this tense half-hour of television drama, even as things (in both the content of the show and the manner of filming it) seemed to have a somewhat caught-on-the-fly quality.

Although each episode of *The French Chef* offers a relative match between the duration of the broadcast (generally twenty-eight to twenty-nine minutes) and the live-action time spent in front of the camera, it is the case that the editing constructs the drama as much as it simply follows the action in chronological succession. It is intriguing in this respect to note that several critics and fans specifically noted the contribution that cutting between cameras made to the affective impact of *The French Chef* as a cooking demonstration. It was evident to them that the show found some of its drama through specifically televisual means. For instance, a very early local review of the show singled out the close-ups for particular praise: "Close-ups of the food cooking atop the stove and the finer points of preparation that one wants to see are brought right to the TV screen through the focusing of the TV camera on an overhead mirror."[14] Likewise, a fan (writing in 1966 from a theological school) offered a general appreciation that ended, "Let me add a note of praise for your camera men. The alternation between you as teacher and your work as model is extremely subtle and well handled."[15]

Perhaps one shouldn't assume from a few letters or reviews that this one show generally led viewers to become aware of the role of formal devices, such as editing, in the construction of the show's meanings. But it is interesting to note that, while two-camera shooting was standard for cooking demonstrations in this period in employing cutting to go back and forth between cook and close-ups on the manual manipulation of food, something about its use on *The French Chef* seemed fresh enough to be noticed by some viewers. It made the standard, utilitarian procedure seem to be something more.

While the cooking show required a relative transparency of style and restraint in the employment of formal devices so that the actions of the cook could be followed through functionally, there was nonetheless a far from complete match between the temporality of the live action and the temporality of what would appear in the broadcast. In the gap between real-time action as it unfolded on the set and the constructed flow of images in the show, narrative meanings were created that made the show more than a mere chronicle. First, as noted, there were some violations of strict chronology. Some episodes included flash-forwards. For example, a dissolve might demonstrate the transition from raw food to its final, cooked version in a mere moment and thereby provide dreamy adumbration of the end result that was sought. Such dissolves became more common in the color shows of the 1970s, where clearly there was a concern to liven things up visually.

And while the cooking show necessarily entails a forward-moving chronology in which a recipe is enacted from beginning to end, it was also the case in *The French Chef* that sheer chronology could be uprooted through flashbacks. These might be of a metaphoric sort—as when, at the end of an episode Child verbally summed up what she had done over the course of the half-hour. But there could, on rare occasion, also be literal flashbacks, as in the three successive black-and-white episodes concerned with a "Dinner Party," in which Child devoted one episode to each stage of the party (appetizer, main course, dessert) and concluded her lesson by extolling how she had done the same dishes for a party at home the previous week. This cue a direct cut to the dining room, in which Julia and Paul are seen dining with two other couples and in which the dapper Paul takes on the task of serving the appropriate wine for each course. That these flashbacks actually take place on the studio set—and not in the Childs' home—is only one more demonstration of the show's manipulation of reality for televisual dramatic effect. (As noted earlier, though, the "Dinner Party" episodes are rare not only in forming a linked sequence of several episodes but also in bringing people other than Julia Child onto the show's stage. Perhaps, then, the flashbacks make sense as a way to mark the specialness of the occasion. This is not the typical story of Child alone in her kitchen—and dining room—but a unique occurrence in which other people connect to her world.)

As a second reworking of temporality, there is quite obviously a gap between cooking time and in-studio live time in those cases where some phase of a recipe needs more than a half-hour or part of a half-hour to be done on time. Throughout her show, Child condensed cooking time into the "live" time of a half-hour demonstration by having several examples of foodstuffs at various degrees of doneness. For example, since much baking could not be done in a short time, Child would put the dish to be baked into the oven and then, often immediately, pull from another rack in the same oven a version of the dish that had already been baking and was now ready to come out and be shown off.

Even as the demonstrations unfolded in real, chronological time, Child, as noted, played on a sense of narrative anticipation, visible especially in her prologues, wherein raw passing time would be charged with supplementary, resonant drama. And as we've seen, even when the two-camera system was used to cut spatially between parts of actions while respecting chronological time so the cut didn't entail any temporal condensation, the very fact of such cutting could in the best moments add drama, suspense, visual variation, narrative flourish, and rhetorical underscoring to the chronology so that it took on more affective and engaging values than just the neutral capturing of real time's unfolding. At their best, Child and the camera style (both the editing and the camera movement) dynamize the scene and render it dramatic. When one fan wrote in after the show on artichokes (with its flamboyant pulling away of the veil from a steamy pot) to say, "Artichokes and I were complete strangers until you made the introduction," perhaps it was the content of Child's discourse that was responsible, but it is as likely that the seduction came from the entertainingly demonstrative way in which she and the camerawork led into the banter and made artichokes seem dramatically intriguing.

As a television performer, Child tried to make it seem as if her interactions with the cameras (and the crew behind them) were really about intimacy with a viewer who was vicariously experiencing the final results through the medium of the television screen. In other words, Child did not acknowledge the presence of the camera as a camera (except unintentionally when she looked at the wrong one and needed to switch her eye-line direction) and pretended instead to talk *through* the camera to the viewer. The sense of intimacy this created was one virtue that critics and fans singled out in their appreciation of the show. For example, Cleveland Amory, a critic for *TV Guide*, praised Child for being "so completely oblivious to the camera that she seems to come right through to us without any camera at all."[16]

It might seem obvious that a pedagogy that wants to transmit content to viewers as directly, as functionally, and as simply as possible would want particularly to do this by pretending the camera isn't there and that the consequential contact is with the spectator. But clearly one can cook—and talk about cooking—while making manifest the presence of cameras and crew. Think, for instance, of *Iron Chef,* where the cameramen are down in the midst of the action and interacting directly with the competing chefs by moving around them and being filmed themselves by other members of the crew. It is possible for a cooking show to respect the content of its pedagogy while acknowledging the contributions that the cameras are making to the rendition of its content in specifically televisual form. Indeed, Graham Kerr, whose aptly named *Galloping Gourmet* came to American television soon after *The French Chef,* used the entire studio set (including the audience bleachers) to move around and rendered quite manifest the whole machinery of television filming.

Of course, Child was all about creating a sense of intimacy and folksy collusion with the spectator, and for this a relative stylistic sobriety and an effacement of the mediations that came from the presence of camera and crews would appear to be preferable. Child's relative non-acknowledgement of the physical presence of the camera might be contrasted with the very different attitude toward the camera demonstrated by Keith Floyd, a famed chef for the BBC, as examined by Niki Strange in an essay on variations in the form of the genre of the TV cooking show. In Strange's analysis, Floyd distinguished himself as a TV chef not just by addressing the camera (Child does this but with the assumption that she is talking through the camera to the viewer who is spatially elsewhere than in the room with her) but by addressing it *as such*. He talked overtly to the cameraman, gave direction of the scene, and ignored the imaginary boundary between the space of the action and the space of the crew filming that action. Strange contrasts Floyd to another BBC chef, Delia Smith, who, like Julia Child perhaps, was all about constructing folksy intimacy through a chatty relationship with an imagined viewership beyond the kitchen set. As Strange puts the contrast, while "both presenters directly address the camera, Floyd actively directs it. In programme six, for example, he directs the camera-operator on some 13 occasions, with comments such as 'Follow me please, Paul . . . good close-up on that, please. . . .' His exposure of the mechanics of television . . . is subsumed to become a trait of his televised personality."[17]

Strange suggests that this playing with, and acknowledging of, the mediating role of, the apparatus of television may come more easily to—and may be more necessary for—the male presenter of cookery who thereby takes an ironic distance from the seemingly feminized position of domestic intimacy. In other words, by showing that the set is a set and not a real kitchen, the male television cook is presenting himself as someone who is not automatically and inevitably tied to the domestic realm and can take distance from it when he wants. As Strange puts it, Floyd is "framed by his role as a male adventurer, as traditionally masculine in its dynamic journey through the public sphere whereas Smith's private sphere stasis is traditionally feminine."[18] Strange's point echoes one made a few years earlier by the Australian scholar Frances Bonner, who, in an essay on representations of television cooks, also mentions Keith Floyd's flamboyance in contrast to feminine sobriety. For Bonner, in entering into a realm that may not be considered toughly masculine (until, perhaps, the efforts of later macho TV cooks such as Emeril Lagasse and Bobby Flay), the male chef has to show that he is not falling fully for the ideologies associated with the feminine-associated, intimate, folksy kitchen. Being playful and acknowledging that it is all just a lark is a means by which the male chef can show that he is not taking things too seriously, not overly identifying with a role that places him too naturally in the kitchen. In Bonner's words, "The male presenter of a cooking programme is acting contrary to his public masculine role, while a woman in the same position is acting centrally within her feminine one. . . . [A] man has to make a performance of doing the cooking."[19]

Be that as it may, I think the case of Julia Child complicates the contrast. True, there are few moments in *The French Chef* wherein the specific technologies of television themselves are acknowledged and welcomed for their role in mediating and constructing the dramas that are transpiring in front of the camera. At the same time, however, there is a clear and quite playful fascination with gadgets and gizmos that Child makes into key components of a flamboyant performance and a highly physical, even "manly," one: big swords that swoosh down to chop fish, big saws to cut through carcasses, grinding apparatuses, blowtorches (one of Child's favorite gizmos), and on and on. It could be argued, then, that in Child's case, there is a displacement from any sort of play with the camera itself to a play with tools and technology in front of the camera—that is, within the controlled space of her cooking universe. Child loved these culinary gadgets and devices, and for all her sweaty emphasis on bare hands doing their thing with gusto and fortitude, she seemed as much to enjoy the mediation that utensils and machines brought to the encounter of human bodies and foodstuffs. Thus, as she explains in the color episode "To Roast a Chicken," a rotisserie spit allows one to cook in a fashion that is both ancient (slow roasting over a fire) and fully modern (doing the roasting with an electric gadget).

Of course, as the stereotype would have it, loving gizmos and gadgets is a guy thing, and Child was crossing into a man's realm by being so

A fondness for gadgets

caught up with tools and instruments, especially ones that did violently dramatic things to the objects of their actions. Indeed, where the female cooks that Strange and Bonner deal with display culinary action on television in ways that are supposed to be natural extensions of women's domestic work for family, Child was cooking in a realm that traditionally had been thought of as masculine: French gastronomy. Fancy French cuisine was in many ways a male sanctum, and Child was entering it boldly and defiantly, making of her activity a performance that was both real and put-on.

Like other female cooks, Child downplayed the apparatus of television to foster a connection of intimacy with her viewers to whom she seemed to communicate immediately through the mediation of the camera equipment. But like male chefs, she also engaged in comedic, even flamboyant, play when she got into the kitchen, treating her role as a woman in the kitchen not as a quiet, effaced one but as a boisterous act that had a degree of carnivalesque clowning in which clear gender distinctions were toyed with.[20]

In playing like a man in the kitchen, through gadgetry and physical

"And now it's time once more for Julia Child."

action, Child was doing something to traditional masculinity, but she was also revising notions of what being feminine might mean. While I emphatically eschew the sexism that judges women in terms of conventional canons of beauty, I also think we need to eschew that sensualist approach to Child offered only a few pages into the biography by Noël Riley Fitch that, out of a need to imagine a fully eroticized version of Child, emphatically and unambiguously declares her to be "strikingly beautiful."[21] Undeniably at work in the cultural reception of Julia Child was the image of her as gangly and awkward, frumpy and even a bit freaky, not classically feminine and even somewhat masculinized— precisely the sort of character to encourage the sorts of wacky impersonations that culminated in Dan Ackroyd's famous cross-dressing imitation on *Saturday Night Live*. It makes sense perhaps that a number of the cartoons about Child that circulated in the popular press in the 1960s showed witches avidly watching her series. Maybe there was a hint of the transgressive in her performance—a gangly American woman in the male-dominated inner sanctum of haute cuisine—that made it comically logical that social outcasts such as witches could take inspiration from her pedagogy.

For what it's worth, Child was aware of—and sometimes worried about—the ways her image crossed boundaries of feminine and masculine identity. In 1973, she responded to a caricature that PBS hoped to use in promotional campaigns with the declaration, "I hope the projected drawing will not be as dreary as the rough you sent! I look like a female impersonator in it. (Woe!)" At the same time, it is clear that she relished participating in activities that played across gender stereotypes —bringing tools traditionally associated with men to the set (such as the blowtorch), costuming herself in traditionally macho-men's accoutrements (such as a fireman's hat), and reveling in every whack of big knives and even swords that she used to cut up carcasses. In her own way, she was a gender-bender, and this may also account for her unique appeal in her cultural moment.

6 The Success of *The French Chef*

I don't know why but whenever I see you it makes me feel good.
—Bobby Keddy, aged 13, fan letter to Julia Child, 1967

The twenty-seven letters that came in to WGBH after Julia Child's first appearance on one of its literary programs, and which led the station to be receptive to a series focused on her cooking, turned out to be the mere tip of the iceberg. WGBH (along with the other stations that eventually picked up *The French Chef* for broadcast in other areas) quickly discovered that each installment of the show brought in a mass of fan mail. At first, in fact, this posed a practical problem for WGBH because Child and her production team felt it was necessary to answer all letters, and some absolutely *had* to be answered because viewers had been told that they could write in for copies of recipes, which created budgetary hassles for the station as the quantity of postage stamps it needed increased dramatically. For example, when Child submitted the $66 invoice to WGBH mentioned earlier, for two shows taped in October 1965, $5 of it was for stamps to reply to fan mail. But clearly WGBH knew it had a hit on its hands, and it made the necessary allowances.

Some fan mail didn't require a personalized response. For example, requests for recipes were met simply by mailing back the required item. But many letters addressed questions to Child—why didn't this or that recipe of the fan's work? could such-and-such ingredient be substituted for the one recommended in a recipe? could Child propose a recipe for some dish that she hadn't dealt with on the show? where could one buy this or that kitchen gadget she had mentioned?—and here there was an attempt to always give some answer. Child tried to help even when the questions didn't have anything to do with home cooking. For example, viewers regularly asked about developing professional careers as chefs, opening restaurants, or finding reputable cooking classes. She gave special attention to letters that came with personal gifts (of which there were many) or culinary advice (and there were many). For instance, when one fan sent fresh thyme, Child said she would use it on the show (of course, as noted, she would never use a gift that entailed a product placement or hint of commercialism), and when another suggested heating hard-boiled eggs in water mixed with vinegar as a quick way to remove the eggshell, Child wrote back appreciatively to say that the tip seemed a good one, that she was delighted, and that she would try it out immediately.

The rare exception to Child's wish to reply to as many letters as possible came with letters that were weird or aggressive or uncomprehending. One viewer, for example, thought that the very idea of fish soup was too "way out." But there were very few of these, and even in such cases, Child sometimes attempted to enter into dialogue when she felt that the writer of a critical letter had misconceptions to correct or could be engaged in conversation. For example, when the Florida Federation of Humane Societies wrote (in 1967) to protest the use of pale veal in her cooking, she offered a reply replete with faith in democratic dialogue, "Unfortunately, that is the only kind [of veal] that is of any culinary interest, from the French cooking point of view. Feeling as you do, I suppose the only thing is to continue [fighting] against it through your organization. Thank heaven, in this free and democratic country, every citizen has the right to work for his own beliefs in just the way you are now doing."[1] For Child, flavor and the canons of French cuisine overrode any such moral issues and any compromise with gustatory quality that such moral obeisance would lead to, but still she responded to the criticism. At the same time, her response demonstrates her own generosity as a public figure in her desire to engage with critics (even if in private, she might have unkind—and even fiery —words for some of them). But letters that were just too strange or aggressive she simply collected in a folder labeled "Unusual Letters," sometimes with a note to herself or to Ruth Lockwood. For instance, when one viewer wrote to say that it had been horrifying to see a recipe that melded lobster with tomato, Child filed the missive with a note that dryly said it was "amusing."

Of the negative reaction to *The French Chef*, especially rare was criticism of an aesthetic sort. Letter writers, that is, rarely expressed the feeling that the show came up short in terms of style, drama, entertainment, or similar artistic virtues. Quite the contrary: when criticism was expressed, it tended to focus on moral or health issues. Was it right to eat this or that food? Was it sanitary to do this or that act in the process of cooking? Writers might even suggest that the very aesthetic strengths of the show were part of the problem in this respect—that is, in these cases, there was a worry that the seductive effectiveness of the show as entertainment meant that it too easily conveyed its morally or medically risky lessons.

The most typical moral critique (and it must be noted that the show did not receive a great deal of this or of the critique from a health perspective) had to do with liquor. From time to time, teetotalers, and even religious dogmatists, wrote in to complain about the wine used in recipes or recommended by Child as an accompaniment to a meal or even tasted by her as she presented her dishes. (As one writer put it, "For the good of the world may you speedily repent, turn from your evil ways, gain knowledge and wisdom and use it for the good of the world.")[2] In fact, for drinking scenes on the show, Child substituted Gravy Master, which had a similar color on black-and-white television, for wine, which would have gone to waste if decanted for the show. In one episode, she even made a toast with, as she put it in a mock French accent, estate-bottled "Gravée mastère," which led fans to ask for the brand at their liquor stores. One of her bottles of Gravy Master is enshrined in a display case inside her kitchen, which she donated for display at the Smithsonian Institution.

The other critique had to do with health or nutrition, and here Child would give serious thought to the charges and was likely to opt for one of three options in response. First, certainly, when letter writers turned out to be right in catching something that might be risky from a health

"*Sock 'em again, Julia baby!*"

Lee Lorenz, *New Yorker* Cartoon, December 23, 1967. Copyright Lee Lorenz /
Condé Nast Publications; courtesy Cartoon Bank.

perspective, she would try to amend her ways. For instance, she worked
to tone down her tendency to taste various dishes from the same spoon
and to keep wiping her hands on a single apron tied around her waist
(but in later episodes, she would refer wryly and with great emphasis
to her "impeccably clean" wiping towels as if mockingly overachiev-
ing the aura of hygiene). Second, she might defer to authority—or, at
least, what she considered authority: the canonic books of French (and
other) cuisine or various publications of the commercialized food industry. As Laura Shapiro notes, Child's relation to the big companies was complex. On the one hand, she lamented some of the shortcuts and compromises in taste that their prepared foodstuffs revolved
around. On the other hand, she tended to put virtually blind faith in the
things the companies said about the nutritional value of their foods and
the proper ways to prepare them. Thus, when a nutritionist wrote in to
say that Child was using too much water to boil vegetables, she re-

sponded, in keeping with her prioritizing of taste, that in a big pot of water, the vegetables appeared to plump up with richness of color and fullness of shape (they seemed, as she put it, to be "bursting with goodness"), but she also noted that it was the way the big companies prepared their vegetables for canning and freezing, so it must be right.

Third, and most important, Child was ready when possible to override nutritional concerns for the sake of gustatory good taste. Eating was about enjoyment, and if such enjoyment was assailed by nutritionists, something was clearly wrong with the world. Today, Child's constant recourse to butter and more butter and then again more butter to add supplemental luscious flavor to many of her dishes can make the health-conscious viewer cringe. (She even recommended serving at least one meat dish on a buttered platter!) But her liberality with butter was a direct expression of her desire to make food rich and vibrant in taste.

Child tried to answer personally the letters that most intrigued her. For instance, when one fan wrote an admiration in the form of a poem, she responded likewise in poetic fashion. But the mass of letters she received meant that soon Child couldn't handle all the replies herself, and staff members such as Lockwood helped out. (Lockwood bought a typewriter with French accents to correctly render the names of dishes, an acquisition of which she was quite proud.) In delegating some of her dealings with letter writers to colleagues and staff, Child again closely managed her image as she carefully laid out the dos and don'ts of responding to fan mail. She wanted to convey a precise and particular image and wanted it to be as controlled as possible. As she put it in a memo to the staff, "We are old-shoe, kindly, easy going, but basically efficient."[3] (This could stand likewise as a description of how she wanted to come off on her television series, as in other manifestations of her public image.) Thus, while Child spent each summer in France, away from the hustle and bustle of the *French Chef*'s shooting schedule, she instructed the staff never to say that she was on "vacation" (that, she explained, was "not professional"). She was simply "in France," with the implication that she was continuing to soak up useful lessons in the country of culinary choice. When a letter could be answered sufficiently by Lockwood—for instance, if it concerned a technical issue in the filming of the show—Child might not add a response of her own. Thus, to take just one example, it was enough for Lockwood to explain to a viewer who had wondered why Child kept wiping her hands on her black skirt that, in fact, the item was a dark apron tied around her waist, but that in black-and-white filming, it tended to blend into the equally dark outfit she wore. But sometimes, on her return from summers away, Child got back to mail to which the staff had already responded and added a more personal follow-up. For instance, when one woman wrote to ask why Child pre-baked piecrusts for quiche, the staff had simply replied, with some lack of specificity, that Child was away but that her reasons were based on careful experimentation. When she returned, Child came back to the letter to clarify that putting quiche filling into an unbaked crust tended to lead to sogginess, especially with French dough, and she cited culinary books in support of her practice.

Child received a massive amount of fan mail. Clearly, she brought out something in viewers that they felt they had to respond to. (Many writers asserted that they were writing their first fan letter, but that might be a convention of the fan-letter genre, in which one feels impelled to claim a special relation to the object of current adoration.) A basic set of themes recur in the fan mail. People liked to see food that they wanted to reach out and touch; they loved that, no matter the official topic of an episode, they learned all sorts of other useful hints along the way; they reveled in seeing a cooking instruction that was so hands-on; and they admired Child's directness, naturalness, lack of guise, and spontaneity.

An early piece of fan mail, written in response to the pilot shows, can stand as a summation of many of the things fans wanted to say about Child—and, more important, *to* Child. It is not surprising to learn that WGBH quoted it extensively in its publicity material for the series:

> Not only did I get a wonderfully refreshing new approach to the preparation and cooking of said poultry, but really and truly one of the most surprisingly entertaining half hours I have ever spent before the TV in many a moon. I love the way she projected over the camera directly to me the watcher. Loved watching her catch the frying pan as it almost went off

the counter; loved her looking for the cover of the casserole. It was fascinating to watch her hand motions which were so firm and sure with the food. And her to-do about the brandy-firing was without parallel for that rare tongue-in-cheek sort of humor the viewer longs for in this day of the over-rehearsed ad-lib.[4]

Many of the recurrent motifs of the fan mail are fully on display here: the feeling that this was a pedagogy that offered something new; the simultaneous appreciation of the show not just as a bit of instructional TV but as entertainment; the sense of intimacy in which it was felt that Child talked directly to the viewer; the acceptance of gaffes and near-disasters and of Child's resilient ability to deal with them; the admiration of her confidence, reflected in the surety of hand movements; and, of course, her sense of humor and the impression she gave that everything was spontaneous and heartfelt.

At the same time that they talked about her personality, many fan letters situated Child in relation to television itself as a medium and made suggestions regarding her relation to televisual traditions. That is, they felt she was bringing something new not just to the art of cooking but also to the medium of television on which that art was being presented. Many such assertions by the letter writers claimed her uniqueness for the medium. She was much more compelling, several fans wrote, than Dione Lucas had been, and she offered an alternative, as a number of writers asserted in direct quotation of the term, to the "vast wasteland" that television had become, as Newton Minow, chairman of the FCC, lamented in 1961.

Viewers felt that Child was offering something fresh in the often formulaic landscape of American television. Sometimes this had to do with a sense of Child as an effective, compelling teacher. Here my favorite from the fan mail is from a seven-year-old from New Jersey, who wrote that she had watched the *French Chef* lobster show and a few days later, in science class, when she had to dissect a crayfish, was the only pupil who knew both how to remove the shell without hurting the inner body and how to extract the internal organs intact. Child wrote back that this was a "good illustration of how so much knowledge is inter-related." Here, with this young fan, we see the broadness of Child's pedagogical philosophy. As in the tight structural logic of French cuisine, examined in chapter 3, where the complex is built up out of simple and codified elements and procedures, learning for Child more generally was about structured, extendable connection rather than intuition or haphazardness.

As often, fans wrote about their appreciation not just of the pedagogy but of the program's entertainment value. Letter writers compared Child to other vibrant television personalities (Lucille Ball was a recurrent point of comparison) and treated her show as if it were a gripping piece of television narrative at its best. Thus, a professor of theater at Penn State gushed in a fan letter, "Your own innate theatrical sense has made *The French Chef* the finest drama series on television."[5]

At the same time, it is amusing to note that some urbane viewers went as far as to consider the viewing experience of Child's show as a form of *modernist* art activity, more like the experimental film and video work that was coming onto the art scene in the 1960s (and increasingly being shown on public television channels) than the narrative popular culture of mainstream television. Here, Child was seen in avant-gardist terms as someone apart from the bland regularity of commercial television, someone who offered a glimpse of experimentation with the televisual form. (It might be relevant that in New York City, the center of the avant-garde, *The French Chef* aired on the educational channel WNDT just before the program *The Art of Film*. Perhaps the cooking show and the cinema appreciation program could seem to the viewer to be part of the same cultural universe, one devoted to new modes of telling and to experiment in the practical and fine arts.)

Endlessly, for instance, newspaper articles about *The French Chef* in the 1960s reported on a group of Greenwich Village bohemians who met regularly to watch the show as a bit of campy comedy.[6] In a curious, later moment, an art-teacher fan of the closed-caption version of the show that came on in the 1970s wrote to declare that watching *The French Chef* was like looking at subtitled European art films that urban sophisticates were fond of at the time. (It's worth noting, as I'll elaborate later, that *The French Chef* was the very first PBS show to be tried with closed-captioning for the hearing-impaired, so it really was experimental in its own way.) That fan wrote, "English subtitles with

English spoken language is 10 years ahead of its time. . . . [Compared to art cinema,] the context of the same thing being used on a *syndicated* TV show . . . is downright FREAKY. The artist in me loves it."[7] Most noteworthy of all, Lenny Lipton, the famed experimental filmmaking guru and author of the poem that became the hit (and, some say, druggy) song "Puff the Magic Dragon," wrote an ode to *The French Chef* in that most outré underground 1960s "newspaper," the *Berkeley Barb*, to declare that, having only recently decided to try to watch popular television to see if it was as bad as he anticipated, he felt confirmed in his suspicions, with one notable exception: The experimental feel of Child's show made it stand out from all other programs. "All the rest were totally worthless junk," he wrote. "The best program on TV, the very finest I saw, one that's absolutely good in fact, is 'The French Chef' with Julia Child. Julia Child is presently the world's greatest television personality. If I could still enjoy the show, even when I loathed the content [in reference to the black-and-white episode on lobster; he had been horrified by the on-screen killing of the crustacean], what then Marshall McLuhan?"[8]

Perhaps the eccentricity of personality that made Julia Child distinctive within television culture was taken by the avant-gardists to position her not so much as the paradigm of a pandering commercial form of television but as the model of a television performance that actually countered commercial middle-browness and hinted at other, creative possibilities for the medium. Perhaps, like Andy Warhol's long-form films that, at the same historical moment, captured mundane reality in slowly unfolding temporality (*Eat, Sleep, Couch*) and gave them a sometimes queer or outré inflection, the real-time duration of *The French Chef* offered a direct experience of time in a quotidian dimension but rendered it off-kilter through Child's performance. Perhaps there was something provocative and avant-garde about lauding a figure who seemed so much an incarnation of an unfashionable domestic realm but made it seem weird, uncanny, different. One year after *The French Chef* premiered, Susan Sontag published "Notes on Camp," one of her highly influential announcements of a new sensibility in the arts, and it could well be argued that Julia Child fed easily into the camp aesthetic. She offered a drag queen–like theatricality that seemed to mix up the genders even as she, to quote Sontag on camp, engaged in "corny flamboyant femaleness"; even at her most intimate and sincere, she seemed to be engaging in performance (life "in quotation marks," as Sontag put it); she stood for an aesthetic position that championed taste and style for the benefit of what was imagined to be an affluent culture free of the constraints of necessity; her flubs were failings from which triumph and aesthetic pleasures could be wrought (just as camp is often about the trans-valuation of bad art as good); and the very ordinariness of what she was doing (the everyday work of cooking food) lent itself to that camp reversal of values in which the banal becomes brilliant and the seemingly forgettable becomes formidable.[9]

No doubt, of course, many young people probably found the dinner-party world of *The French Chef* a bit too fuddy-duddy and would have been less inclined toward the exotic but increasingly anachronistic gastronomy of French haute cuisine than the new exoticism of brown rice, macrobiotics, and diets for a small planet that would bring about even newer food trends from the 1960s into the 1970s. In America, classic French cooking too often connoted stodgy restaurants where one went with parents for meals that were overly formal and overly shot through with rules and prissy principles of decorum. Yet it is clear that, increasingly, other versions of Frenchness could also invoke a new world of sensuous fun and cool hipness, and maybe *The French Chef* tapped into the new sensibility, at least a bit. For instance, Child's promotion of wine as the thing to drink with a good meal was certainly of a piece with new taste cultures of the moment. Thus, as George Taber shows in *Judgment of Paris*, his classic account of the rise of wine to prominence as the sophisticated drink of choice for cutting-edge trendsetters, the 1960s were a period in which wine came to symbolize the new drink of the young, as opposed to the stiff and hard drinks of their parents.[10] For instance, the proliferation of bistros and hip eateries—sometimes near college campuses but not only there—was often about Frenchness and signaled the development of a new taste culture that received its definitive statement perhaps in the founding in 1971 of Alice Waters's Chez Panisse. Here was all of hip culture to-gether: Berkeley, sexual freedom, food that appeared to respect natural origins, art-film culture, and an American-inflected Frenchness. Like so many young Americans of the middle class, Waters had participated in the study-abroad wave of the 1960s. France was the preferred destination, and the outcome frequently consisted of ebullient contact with French-accented exoticism and eroticism and new awareness of contestatory modes of social thought and action, all of it generally (and generously) bound up with paroxysm-inducing discovery of new tastes through French food. Waters would help update French cuisine for a new, seemingly liberated world.[11]

Julia Child probably didn't imagine she belonged to that world—and no doubt many participants in the '60s youth culture would have agreed—but she had qualities that spoke perhaps to the newness of the New Generation. As a young fan, for instance, wrote to Child in 1967, "My mother cannot understand how I appreciate Julia Child on one hand, and the Beatles on the other. It just goes to show that all is not lost on the young!"[12] Indeed, Child's fans could be found across the generational and political divides of the period. Traditionalists could find in her the virtues of an authenticity they saw as an alternative to the vast wasteland of formulaic junk they felt television was becoming. Mods could find in her the glimpses of a new taste culture in which sensual enjoyment and being at the cutting edge in lifestyle increasingly mattered.

Revealingly, when the *Saturday Review* published a special issue in 1967 on what it termed the new "mobilism"—Americans traveling to discover new worlds of experience—it singled out the impact of French cuisine in the opening of American attitudes. More tellingly, it offered as a centerpiece a chart titled "The Ins and Outs of a Mobile Age," and included Julia Child among the "Ins" (along with, among others, Kir, the Redgraves, Aznavour, Twiggy, St. Moritz, California, and knees).[13]

Along with the fan mail came an explosion of reviews and journalistic accounts of *The French Chef* as a new, striking phenomenon on the television landscape. Like the fan letters, the appreciations in newspapers and magazines increased exponentially as the show moved beyond its initial Boston market. The high point of this journalist interest came in 1966 when Child made the cover of *Time* magazine, her head filling up much of the frame while a batter of copper pots are being put to effective work around her, and, at the bottom, a decorated whole fish is displayed.

Significantly, with a few exceptions, the primary focus of the journalism around *The French Chef* had to do with it as a bit *of television* rather than as a case of culinary activity. That is, reviewers might comment in passing on the effectiveness of the show's cooking pedagogy, but more often they were interested in the extent to which the show provided great entertainment and of a sort that they took to be new to popular television. Insofar as most American press commentaries on *The French Chef* judged it in terms of the potential of the medium, it was talked about in a manner directly imported from common television criticism. Thus, it was evaluated (positively, in most cases) in terms of its dramatic effect and the personality of its host. Here, as with the fan mail, comparisons were made with existing examples from entertainment television and other forms of narrative popular culture. One instance of this is in a review from the *San Francisco Chronicle* early in the run of *The French Chef*: "This week, Mrs. Child was costarring with a most appetizing-looking chicken in a domestic drama titled 'Supreme de volaille a blanc.' The chicken lost and ended up poached in butter and covered in white wine sauce. . . . My neighbor Mrs. Pellachotti reads cookbooks with the same relish most people get from a good novel. With others it's less like a novel than a mystery story since they're not sure how the dish is going to turn out. In either case, 'The French Chef' is recommended."[14]

Likewise, several reviewers made the Lucille Ball comparison that fans had also offered up, while another likened Child to Gracie Allen for the malapropisms that both brought into the world on the television screen. Indeed, like the fans, the critics loved that Child made gaffes yet in a way that was endearing and still effective as pedagogy. Logically, it was often the television critic at this or that paper who was assigned to comment on the show rather than someone from the food section. One exception was Craig Claiborne, the doyen of food reviewing, whose glowing review of *Mastering the Art of French Cooking* had played no small part in that book's success and who, at the beginning of 1964, offered a profile in the *New York Times* of Child and

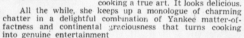

MEET JULIA CHÍLD

'French Chef' Cooks Up Humor, Suspense

By Jane Claney

SOME MONDAY NIGHT soon, if you've never considered it before, let yourself be persuaded to watch a cooking lesson—Julia Child's *"The French Chef"* at 8 on WGBH-TV, Channel 2.

You will be a reluctant viewer only once. And it won't matter at all whether you have the slightest interest in food before it reaches your plate.

This show has everything. Take a recent evening, for example, when Mrs. Child undertook the preparation of "lobster l'Americaine."

There was suspense (does she notice that the mixture in the frying pan is beginning to smoke?), excitement (she leaps backward in the nick of time after setting a match to her wine-loaded concoction), humor (pushing her glasses back up on her nose, she says casually, "well, I was just going to say you have to watch out for the flames").

And drama is definitely present as she wields her sword-size knife with obvious relish and warns all would-be gourmets to "be sure to cut off the claws first (whack! goes one) so you won't get bitten (whack! goes the other). She then attacks the still-moving remains with knife, scissors and gusto until the viewer begins to wonder if he has tuned in a scene from the French Revolution.

At just about the point where you decide never to eat lobster again, Mrs. Child pops the lobster pieces into a skillet and begins to add all the tasty trifles that make French cooking a true art. It looks delicious.

JULIA CHILD

All the while, she keeps up a monologue of charming chatter in a delightful combination of Yankee matter-of-factness and continental graciousness that turns cooking into genuine entertainment

Mrs. Child's Boston show is carried on 20 television stations throughout the country will increase to 40 stations this month, and to 85 by the end of the year.

She and her husband, a retired diplomatic official, live in Cambridge where they devote their leisure to gardening.

★

It was while living in Paris where her husband was attached to the U. S. Embassy that Mrs. Child began to study French cuisine, and with two French women set up a cooking school, which they still run In 1961 the three published a cookbook, "Mastering the Art of French Cooking."

"My biggest project right now," she says, "is trying to finish Volume 2 of our cookbook. Even though the first volume has 750 pages, we didn't touch on many aspects of French cooking—which just goes on and on, there's so much to it."

She and her co-authors in Paris test recipes until all are satisfied that they will work.

"I think," she says, "that anyone who can read and follow simple directions ought to be able to turn out a dish which is just as good as the recipe. If it doesn't turn out perfectly, it's the book's fault, not the cook's. That's the way I feel about it."

her successful television series along with an accompanying recipe of hers (for turbans of sole).[15]

A more interesting exception to the emphasis of the journalists on the televisual aspects of the show over its culinary content came in the French press, where, predictably, a number of writers seem to have wanted to decide what it meant that an American was trying to present French cuisine to her compatriots. Impressively, none of the French reviews appeared to begrudge Child her attempt. Quite the contrary: the French commentators appreciated that, even though she made mistakes (she was, after all, not French but American, so culinary perfection could perhaps not be expected of her), Child still managed to cook well. They lauded her for the attempt to bring their cuisine to Americans, and they acknowledged that her sojourn in France, with its official (Cordon Bleu) study of culinary practice, had given her some claim to legitimacy in the realm. At the same time, she was congratulated by the French for admitting that the goal wasn't perfect attainment of authentic French cuisine but an approximation that met American needs. It is tempting to see this as a backhanded compliment that targets both an inevitable falling short by Americans in a realm that is not really theirs and the concomitant insufficiency of a woman to be perfect in a domain that, for the French, was still very much the property of men.[16]

Although *The French Chef* never aired in France, the fact that the French critics felt the need to take notice suggests how far Child's reputation had spread. Within the U.S. itself, she quite simply became a star and showed that the world of educational television could go beyond dry instruction and, as important, didn't have to have current events of a consequential political sort as its subject matter. In fact, the success of *The French Chef* coincided with and, in its own way, contributed greatly to the shift that turned the educational television of the 1950s into the "public television" of the 1960s, where the concern was very much with cultural uplift, a learning of lifestyle, a turn from civic and global issues to domestic ones, and an increased leavening of instruction with entertainment.

It is a commonplace to call *The French Chef* a PBS show, but that's not exactly accurate. As a specific organization for the dissemination of educational television, PBS did not come into existence until the late 1960s, under the auspices of Lyndon Johnson's administration and after *The French Chef* had already been airing for several years nationwide. Indeed, one could reverse the causality and argue that it was *The French Chef* that helped foster and cement the idea of a national system of public television. In large part, awareness that there could and should be a national organization of television stations for the spread of *cultural* programming came from the station-by-station success of *The French Chef*, which garnered great interest in all of its markets and represented the first major breakout success for a local educational station (WGBH). It is revealing that when the Carnegie Commission, empowered in 1965 by the Johnson administration to investigate the idea of nationwide educational television, issued its report (which led in 1967 to the founding of the Corporation for Public Broadcasting), the *single* example it cited of an educational show that represented what it hoped for in the future was *The French Chef*. Child's show served as a model in the dream of an entertaining education. That may have been predictable. The Carnegie Commission's board had a strong Boston contingency—for example, James Conant of Harvard and James R. Killian, the head of the Massachusetts Institute of Technology, were members—and, importantly, it was WGBH's director, Hartford Gunn, who wrote up the first draft of the commission's proposal, and it was the Boston benefactor Ralph Lowell, chairman of the Lowell Institute, who delivered the final version to President Johnson. Rather than being the mere beneficiary of a nationwide public broadcasting system, *The French Chef*, then, stood as the pivotal success that helped construct that system.[17]

It is noteworthy that in 1966 *The French Chef* won the first Emmy for educational television. Child's win was often mentioned in the same breath as Bill Cosby's award as best dramatic actor for the commercial series *I Spy*, the first such award to an African American artist. Both awards seemed to signal a new recognition in the 1960s of television's moral and educational responsibilities.[18] On the one hand, fictional entertainment could be infused with social relevance. On the other hand, the previously staid world of educational television, with its cliché of talking heads intoning boring lessons, would itself be infused with the energy of diverting entertainment. There would still be a talking head, but in the guise of Julia Child, it would be a far-from-boring one, and she would add to her discourse wit, whimsy, and vibrant action. (At the same time, one shouldn't overestimate what that first Emmy for educational television portended. Advocates of, and figures in, educational television, including Julia Child herself, expressed no small amount of anger that *The French Chef* received its award off-camera and after the live transmission of awards given to fictional shows had ended for the night.)

In the early 1960s, there was no national system of educational television. Only local, frequently isolated stations serving specific communities existed. (Many educational television stations were based at land-grant universities and colleges in the Midwest, and they broadcast programs for students and residents around town.) In 1948, the Federal Communications Commission (FCC) had put a freeze on new licenses for television stations, and one of the provisions in lifting the freeze was that channels be set aside throughout the nation for educational stations. (A little more than one-tenth of the 2,000 or so licenses to be issued were to be reserved for what were termed noncommercial stations.) But the FCC had also allowed educational frequencies to be sold to commercial stations if there were no noncommercial takers for the slots or if a noncommercial station was in financial difficulty and had to be sold off. This meant that through the 1950s, the operation of educational stations was frequently sporadic and somewhat disorganized. Not merely were there not many so-called educational stations, but a number served only their immediate geographic area through regionally specific instructional programming. It is worth noting that at the beginning of the 1960s, there were *no* educational stations at all in such major cities as New York, Washington, and Los Angeles. Furthermore, some of the existing stations were limited by having been placed in the UHF frequencies, which not all television receivers were equipped for and which had a reputation as a lesser part of the television spectrum. (Only in 1962 would the FCC mandate that all new television receivers be equipped to receive UHF signals, and the implementation of that decree would take several more years.) Thus, to take just one example, while WGBH's centrality to the cultural life of Brahmin Boston was demonstrated by its placement at Channel 2 on the dial, KCET in Los Angeles, which started broadcasting in 1964 and to which *The French Chef* was pitched early on, was on UHF Channel 28 and didn't get the viewership numbers it might have enjoyed as a VHF station.

No national system could flourish in such a context. Individual stations sometimes formed more or less loose affiliations with other stations, usually in the same geographic area, since that made it easy to share tapes or relay transmission of programming. One fairly informal network was the Eastern Educational Network (EEN), whose flagship station was in fact WGBH in Boston, the eventual producer of *The French Chef*. EEN counted stations across New England and western New York in its structure, and these stations often shared programs simply by capturing them off the air during their transmission. When Ampex Electronics introduced a professional video-recording device at the end of the 1950s, WGBH was the first educational station to purchase one, and it used it to make copies of some of its shows for rebroadcast and for distribution to other EEN stations. Thus, shortly after the debut of *The French Chef* in Boston, the series was being aired in New Hampshire, Maine, parts of Pennsylvania, and parts of New York State, as well as in New York City (an important venue whose local educational station, WNDT—later, WNET—received its tape just seven days after the show had aired in Boston).

As noted, many individual educational stations began as instructional ventures sponsored by—and generally housed at—local institutions of higher education. Boston's WGBH had as one of its founding impulses the desire, expressed in 1946, of the Harvard president James Conant to have electronic media serve as means of transmission for a public pedagogy. A committee that Conant had created at Harvard had just issued its famous influential report "General Education in a Free Society" (also known as the "Harvard Red Book" for its vibrant cover), which called for systems of public education that would be made generally available through far-reaching modes of communication. Evidently wary of having staid Harvard itself be the owner of a mass-media outlet, Conant turned to the philanthropist Ralph Lowell, the descendant of another Harvard president, who was in charge of a bequest from an ancestor to fund public lectures for the citizens of Boston.

Lowell was administering that legacy through a consortium of academic and cultural institutions, and that structure met Conant's needs for an initiative that would not be exclusively Harvard-based, so he encouraged the consortium to consider taking on public broadcasting of a cultural and educational sort. The consortium created a committee of academic administrators called the Lowell Institute Cooperative Broadcasting Council, which eventually decided that the creation of a radio station, WGBH, which went on the air in 1951, could represent a first step in the articulation of a public pedagogy through broadcast media. (A joke has it that the call letters stood for "God Bless Harvard," but they actually stood for the Great Blue Hill, land that Harvard owned and had offered to the station.) In 1955, four years after the radio station was founded, WGBH-TV began its first television transmissions with a program of folk songs for children under the tutelage of the Nursery Training School at Tufts University.[19]

Several facts already stand out from this early history of WGBH. For example, it matters that, if the initial impetus for the station came (as it had for many other educational stations) from academe, it developed also out of a subsidiary history of educational television stations that started in philanthropic enterprise. Such stations were a twentieth-century legacy of the museums, Chautauqua lectures, and other pedagogies of popular uplift that dotted the American landscape from the nineteenth century into the moment of Progressivism. Insofar as these stations connected as much to the private elite as to academic enterprise, the goal was often as much cultural (programs of uplift in the arts) as directly civic and educational. Thus, viewing a performance on WGBH of the Boston Symphony may have involved a level of instruction—one "learned" perhaps what a particular piece of music sounded like—but the greater function was the seemingly more ineffable one of contagious proximity to the arts under the assumption that they wove their spell at an affective, rather than intellective, level. As Laurie Ouellette notes, there were several different (and sometimes overlapping) target audiences for educational use of the medium: an audience in need of practical instruction through direct educational programming such as science shows and language instruction; an audience whose interests were political and for whom educational television should provide schooling in civics and government; and an audience for whom public television was about uplifting, even spiritual exposure to—more than instruction in—fine arts and culture.[20] While in its early radio years WGBH aired extension courses for the various universities and colleges in the consortium, thereby fitting a need for direct instruction, at the same time it had its first studio in the building of the Boston Symphony to make it easier to film concerts, thereby fitting a need for less pedagogically focused cultural uplift. It's appropriate, in this respect, that that very first WGBH show used folk *songs* to reach children. There had always been a tension in educational television between flat-out pedagogy based on lectures and on dry conveyance of information by talking heads and one that leavened its lessons with aesthetic diversion and entertainment. Along with the radio stations that preceded them, the television stations in this orbit had varied definitions of their fundamental identity—were they examples of *educational* television or of *public* television?—with the distinction often coming down to the difference between a mission of instruction (such as the lessons of science or of civics) and one of spiritual or aesthetic enlightenment through a less didactic contact with culture and the arts.

On the one hand, as Ouellette shows, postwar efforts in educational television originated in large part from a Puritan conception of pedagogy in which learning, to counter the frivolities of fun morality, had to be serious and to banish traces of the "merely" entertaining. In Ouellette's formulation, "Good Television was valorized as active, redeemed by a positive association with work, self-improvement, purpose and studious concentration." This philosophy eventually resulted in programs that "minimized television's unique capacity for orality and visuality and instead came across as unadorned and slow-moving interpretations of the written-word . . . erudite, serious, complex and subdued—the exact opposite of the pleasure, fantasy, formula, and spectacle promised by commercial broadcasting."[21]

On the other hand, postwar Middle America was luxuriating in affluent commercialism and consumerism and wanted to *enjoy* the diversions that the new mass culture was offering. It was apparent to the middlebrow mediators of high culture and high knowledge that, if they wanted to spread their educational offerings widely, they had minimally to lighten them with entertainment values and maximally to turn to the very commercial forms that highbrows might have disdained as threats to culture's integrity.[22]

In fact, the idea of making education entertaining through television and the struggle to find "fun" hosts in the service of that mission were already being played out in the 1940s and 1950s, when, for instance, as Lynn Spigel confirms, the Metropolitan Museum of Art and Museum of Modern Art in New York City and the Museum of Modern Art in San Francisco were trying to put culture on television in, they hoped, a visually dynamic fashion that simultaneously would show off the content (great art) and exploit the kinetic resources of the medium to do so. As Spigel clarifies, "In seeking entertainment formats, museum officials knew that they faced stiff competition from 'hobby art' programs on commercial stations that featured 'telegenic' art teachers with audience appeal." They adopted viewer-friendly tactics such as a televisual "sense of intimacy and spontaneity" to offer programs that appeared more as "casual conversation" than as arid lessons pronounced from on high. Of course, such intimacy, spontaneity, and casualness of instruction, combined with a televisual style marked by movement and dynamic cutting, were also what *The French Chef* would be all about, and Child's series inherited the legacy of a postwar consumerist conception of learning as potentially fun and self-empowering.[23]

As Ouellette notes, the mavens of educational television frequently pushed for their programs to be more affectively engaging: "In the mid-1960s, NET attempted to reposition itself as a 'fourth network' known for quality cultural and informational programs, not pedantic lessons delivered by tweed-coated professors . . . more as superior program service than an electronic schoolroom."[24] In Julia Child, the need to educate while maintaining seriousness of final purpose and rigor of the lesson plan merged with the entertainment impulse to make learning engaging and even joyous.

For example—and here I would reiterate the analysis in chapter 5 of the typicality of two-camera filming of cooking shows—conventions that had been born of mere functionalism (if you have to film cooking, the ability to cut back and forth between the whole person and her hands is propitiously utilitarian) and of necessity (for many cooking shows, no more than two cameras were available anyway) were turned in Child's case into joyful displays of entertaining instruction. Thus, for instance, where Spigel chronicles how space was often at a premium in television production in the 1950s, with tight, cramped sets and studios—and many cooking shows of the period adapted to the physical constraints by offering restrained demonstrations in which a frontally viewed and relatively unmoving pedagogue delivered an arid lecture in which the kitchen tabletop became a sort of podium—Julia Child's show was about rendering space dynamic. The editing tried to keep pace with her breathless demonstrations, and camera movements attempted to keep her in the frame as she energetically bounced around on the kitchen set, and, in the big payoff of the finale, bounded into the dining room, where she offered the fantasy spectacle of the finished dish that she vicariously shared with the spectator.

Within the EEN network of stations, *The French Chef* was a phenomenal hit. But to reach national audiences, the program needed wider distribution, so the station turned to National Educational Television (NET), a New York-based clearing-house for nationwide distribution of educational programs. WGBH even went to the seemingly rare extreme of offering the program to NET without asking the distribution network to shoulder any of the production costs if it made *The French Chef* part of its programming. Strikingly, however—and ironic in view of the program's quick national success—NET's administrators and programmers initially decided, even with the financial incentive, to take a pass on the show, because they felt it resembled too closely the standard talking-head pedagogy of the cooking realm. As Paul K. Taff, an administrator in the NET programming division, wrote to WGBH on November 21, 1962, after he saw the pilot tapes: "We admit the talent was good (food excellent) and that she was talking about a different level of cooking, but I imagine that most stations would feel that the program was similar to the cooking shows we've all seen."[25] Clearly, however, viewers immediately saw a difference, and soon educational stations around the country were clamoring to add the hit to their screening schedules. NET came around in 1964 and accepted distribution of the show to stations in its network.

Amusingly, for each tape that went from Cambridge to NET for national distribution, WGBH had staff members who, while filling out standard forms for all shows at the station, evaluated the content to make sure it was morally pure. Predictably (but despite Child's legendary fascination with ribald and risqué humor off-camera), episodes of *The French Chef* were found to be free of obscenity, defamation, personal attack, lack of equal time to opposing points of view, unfairness, plugs for commercial products, and "drug lyrics" (this, after all, was the

1960s). Staff members also evaluated the technical quality of each tape, and here it is as amusing to discover that whoever the staff member doing this was (probably a man), he often felt impelled to comment on the quality of the dishes Child had made. Such comments included, "Julia really makes a mess—flour all over the floor but ends up w[ith] a soufflé-type cake," and "An ungodly concoction of cooked artichoke bottoms with a mushroom filling, topped with poached egg and béarnaise sauce. Nice, but all at once?"[26]

WGBH helped stations that picked up *The French Chef* with a lot of promotion and publicity. For example, for the release of the first color shows at the beginning of 1970, WGBH offered to assume some of the expenses if local stations invited the press to a French party in the show's honor. "Any station that would like to give a press party for *The French Chef* will be sent a beautiful check for Fifty Dollars which will buy all sorts of French Goodies for the hungry press. A French Bread, Cheese, and Wine Party would be lovely or perhaps Croissants and Coffee (contact WGBH)."[27] WGBH also prepared copy for local stations to use to promote the show when they gave it its first airings:

Superb French gourmet cooking is easy and practical even for the busiest housewife [again, the gendering of the target audience] when the engaging Julia Child shows how to use supermarket materials. Her clever television program "The French Chef" comes to [City] on [day, date, and time]. Discovered in Boston, a year ago, Mrs. Child has become a national celebrity as much for inimitable personality as for her skill. Things happen in Julia Child's kitchen just the way they do in anyone's home. . . . [T]he butter is misplaced, fillings drool, the lighted brandy singes her hair, she can't find her glasses . . . but she handles everything with a sense of humor and a disarming frankness. . . . It's the techniques that count, and Mrs. Child demonstrates them all in a series tailored expressly for the busy American homemaker and everyone who loves good food but has never thought there was time to prepare it.

At the same time, distribution came with a set of inviolate instructions. Episodes could not be altered (except to add a title card to acknowledge local sponsorship), and Knopf's copyright had to be acknowledged on any recipes from *Mastering the Art of French Cooking* that were published in local newspapers. Most important, if local educational stations chose to send printed recipes to viewers who asked for them, they had to do so in ways that didn't risk excerpting too much from *Mastering*. "Recipes," a WGBH information sheet instructed, "must be distributed singly and may not be stapled or bound together or in any way collected to resemble or imply a booklet. The reason is that Knopf has the publication rights, and has given [educational television] stations permission to send individual recipes on request, to promote the recipes on the air, or to give permission to newspapers to publish one recipe each week to tie in with the program being aired. If, however, a viewer writes that she [*sic*] missed the past two or three programs and would like to catch up, you may send the number requested on single sheets, as long as the several recipes are not stapled together."[28]

Each educational station had to show the episodes in the order they were filmed, and WGBH sent out lists of topics for upcoming seasons so individual stations could begin local promotional campaigns if they wished. Stations were encouraged to seek out local underwriting to help with distribution. Thus, to take just one example, WMVT in Milwaukee received support from Sentry Food Stores, a chain of Wisconsin supermarkets.

NET's distribution of *The French Chef* began in the fall of 1964 with thirteen programs, numbered 14–26 (the original episode 13 had not been saved). Five taped copies of each episode were made at WGBH's expense and were sent to local stations, which then had precise instructions about where to send them next. As an NET memo from August 1964 clarifies, each tape initially made the rounds of four stations at two-week intervals. KERA in Dallas, for example, received its copy from KCET in Los Angeles, showed the episode twice (on a Thursday evening and then in a Monday afternoon slot), and then sent the tape on to KTXT in Lubbock, Texas. At first, the grant to WGBH from Safeway enabled the station to charge no distribution fees to individual stations, yet the ever expanding number of stations that got in on *The French Chef* soon led to a $5 fee per station per episode to cover some basic costs. As a mark of how the network of distribution expanded, the first NET memo about distribution, dated August 1964, identified seventeen potential stations for the series, whereas the comparable chart for the beginning of 1968 has close to 100 stations showing *The French Chef*, with ten tapes in circulation at any one time. To make the distribution system manageable, NET tried to think about the series in terms of smaller blocks of episodes that would be distributed at staggered rates to various stations. The idea was to have no more than two stations in the network airing a particular episode at any one time. But as the length of time required for such staggering meant that some stations were taking much longer than others to go through an individual season, a problem arose. When WGBH wanted to air a new season, it found itself competing with older episodes from the previous season that were still being aired. In 1968, WGBH even had to resort to the drastic measure of withdrawing all distribution rights to *The French Chef* from NET, instituting a deliberate hiatus for all airings of the show (including the current season), and then starting over from scratch with the next season and greater synchronization of showings around the country.

Around the same period, NET was entrusted with the task of trying to formalize sales of *The French Chef* to foreign networks around the world. But, to put it bluntly, the attempts failed. Insofar as the content of *The French Chef* had to do with bringing the world to America, not taking America to the world, the show remained a resolutely U.S. experience with virtually no play elsewhere in the globe. Interestingly, in at least one case, an indigenous government appears to have shown active resistance to what it perceived as a form of cultural imperialism. In a telling memo now in the PBS archives, an administrator at NET wrote to Lockwood that South Africa, which was just developing its first television network, had decided against broadcasting shows from the U.S. because it felt it "would be swamped with Anglo-American material."

The failure to place *The French Chef* internationally was due not to lack of interest on the part of WGBH or NET or even Child herself (at least in the beginning, before she generally soured on the idea). Everyone connected with *The French Chef* wanted the right sort of distribution deal, and that didn't come easily. Financial issues certainly played into the desire for international distribution. For example, Lockwood noted in a memorandum in 1966 that many countries lacked either an *educational* network or one for which an entertainment-heavy (rather than more dryly pedagogical) cooking show would be appropriate, so the show might find rewarding sales to *commercial* networks overseas. But Child and the people at WGBH were adamant that pecuniary concerns must not lead to alteration of the show's format. Thus, when NBC offered to get distribution of *The French Chef* in Latin America, Asia, Australia, and New Zealand, WGBH was intrigued enough to send over two sample tapes (one that particularly emphasized Child's teaching method and one that focused on her ability to show preparations that could solve kitchen emergencies). But NBC, it turned out, was looking overseas to get the show on commercial networks only and wanted to sell time for commercials that would be inserted into the show. In January 1967, Dave Davis, an administrator at WGBH, informed Lockwood that he was terminating discussions with NBC because "we agreed that we really had nothing to talk about."[29]

There were also up-and-down negotiations with the BBC in England. Around the end of 1964 or the beginning of 1965, Lockwood was in touch with the BBC and sent tapes of a few select episodes. However, on February 15, 1965, Doreen Stephens, the head of the Family Programmes (Television) Division, wrote back that the BBC wouldn't be taking the show. Although she admitted that the BBC's resident on-camera cook, Fanny Craddock, didn't have Child's ease and relaxed buoyancy of presentation, Stephens nonetheless felt that the introductions and conclusions to Child's show seemed forced. "It is the only false note," she wrote in a memo now in the PBS archives, "and the only moment at which she seems the least bit nervous." (Need it be noted that, as outlined in an earlier chapter, Child admired the lead-ins and conclusions very much, and that it was these elements in particular that had won over many U.S. fans to Child's world, in no small part because of the charm and authenticity they saw in the nervousness on exhibit there?) More damaging, Stephens and others at the BBC seemed to feel that the fact of American measures, rather than kilometric European ones, combined with the Americanisms in Child's speech, meant that the show wouldn't translate well. The BBC took a pass.

On a more promising note, with the release of the color iteration of *The French Chef* at the beginning of the 1970s, the BBC would revisit its first hesitations and announce itself now more favorable to a pickup of the series. As early as 1967, when WGBH began planning the color series, the BBC had reopened the conversation. At a cocktail party in Cambridge in the late 1960s, it seems, a BBC programmer had met Child and been won over by her energy and the promise of the new version of *The French Chef*. For a sum of 1,500 pounds, the BBC offered to try six episodes, including ones on bouillabaisse, salade niçoise, omelets, and fish brochettes. It was even suggested that Child shoot episodes specifically for a U.K. viewership. As one memo put it, the idea was to have Child "plan a series of recipes with maximum impact for our English audience." But it also appears that another thought was to shoot segments, rather than full episodes, tailored to the U.K. that could be inserted into existing episodes of *The French Chef*.

Everyone seemed initially to have had high hopes for a U.K. edition of the color iteration of *The French Chef*, and a decision was made to have new promos and lead-ins to the episodes (because when the BBC first reviewed the show in the mid-1960s, it felt that the U.S. lead-ins didn't work) and for Child to use an upcoming trip to England to film the new material. It even seems that the promos were to be longer than the brief ones WGBH shot regularly for upcoming episodes, with Child announcing a following week's episode in detail. Thus, Child's papers include a script for a BBC promo during which she would make a mushroom and shallot omelet in quick fashion while offering the following comments: "Welcome to the French Chef. I'm Julia Child, your non-French French chef. You'll be seeing some of my French chef shows at [time] in the afternoon. This is to give you a sampling to see how you like them. I've done over 200, some very complicated . . . some middling . . . some fast and simple. So whether you are just starting out in the kitchen, or whether you're a pro, I hope and I think you'll always find something worth watching."[30]

In anticipation of the visit, and with her usual concern for preparation, Child wrote up a memo for the BBC about the filming and what should be expected of her. This planning document for the production sessions at the BBC is intriguing because, regardless of the eventual failure of *The French Chef* as a BBC offering, Child's musings reveal a lot about what she thought her television methods were and how she felt she came off in the medium. For example, she clarified her need for someone off-camera to flash cards at her with timing, instructions, and reminders: "I am used to working 'ad-lib,' with cue cards giving key words or phrases. I also have no time sense, so need cue-cards for each change of segment—30 seconds—40 seconds or however long it lasts. The cues give the action 'Butter in pan,' 'Slice mushroom fast,' and so forth." Likewise, she wrote: "Make-up: Usual face make-up, but 'natural,' no false eye lashes, etc. Hair 'comb out' needed, but nothing fancy— chic but natural. Must have freckle-cover for hands, otherwise brown spots are most distracting!"[31]

Ultimately, however, the BBC didn't know how to deal properly with *The French Chef*. At first, for instance, it aired episodes with the U.S. intros cut out; then it put the intros back in. Despite Child's insistence at WGBH that the show have its primary airing at night, and despite the proven success of the show in the evening slot in the U.S., the BBC clearly saw it as daytime television and aired it at 3:40 P.M., where it became associated with light fare for women. As a male British friend put it when I corrected his impression that Child had never aired in the U.K., "Well, there you go! In the late '60s I was at university without access to television (except in the odd pub) and daytime TV would have been of no interest." Furthermore, the BBC put on the show without advance publicity, with no consistency in scheduling (it showed up on random weekdays) and with constant pre-emption by other events (such as horse racing). Without a regularized broadcast, *The French Chef* came to English viewers with little context, and the few reviews of it that did appear in the English press (partly because daytime television clearly didn't merit critical attention) tended to treat it as a pedestrian cooking show that was not much different from other offerings within the genre. No one seems to have gotten Child's distinctiveness, and her show was pretty much passed over in silence (at best—or maybe, at worst—some viewers thought her demonstrative style meant that she was tipsy). Within half a year of its "debut," the BBC canceled *The French Chef*. Interestingly, the BBC tried to recoup some of its losses by conducting its own sale (to Ireland) of the series episodes it had bought, only to be told by Ruth Lockwood that Child was so annoyed by what had happened that she wanted no further effort to get the show into the U.K. market, and she refused the resale.

By this time, however, PBS was in full swing in the U.S., and *The French Chef* was one of the top-rated shows in its distribution to member stations throughout the country. By 1968, Child had wound down production of the black-and-white seasons of the series and had begun preparing for a new iteration that would be in color and, she hoped, would open up things in even greater fashion.

7 New Beginnings and the Ending to *The French Chef*

In March 1967, the manager of WGBH, Dave Davis, sent a compelling memo to his staffers to encourage programming that was in keeping with the new visually hip and politically engaged culture of the time. More people, he said, were watching television; more of them were younger; more of them had college educations and therefore needed television to be stimulating; and more of them had traveled to other countries and therefore needed television to be cosmopolitan in its content. "The visual electronic world is providing a total assault on our senses," Davis asserted, and his conclusion was dramatic. "The pressure is on for Public Television. It's probably now or never—and we don't intend to sit back and wait." He went on to suggest that WGBH programming incorporate a new, dynamic visuality that itself would call out to and captivate those spectators who were becoming habituated to the seductive styles of the moment. In this respect, he particularly lauded the announced coming of color programming as a way to create a new, engrossing look for WGBH shows: "With color, we will create a whole new approach to the presentation of the visual arts."[1]

In the previous chapter, I showed how *The French Chef* was key to WGBH's attempts to present itself as a bastion of cultural uplift. However, culture here could mean lots of different things—for instance, the highbrow world that looked back to venerable tradition (from the symphony to haute French cuisine) but also an earthy culture that sought forms of authenticity in an everyday life freed from staid conventions and snobby dogma. Boston (and Cambridge, in particular) served as one site where it could all come together. Cambridge, as the artist Barbara Westman summed up the 1960s there in a folksy book of drawings, was neither a big city like New York nor an isolated, uncosmopolitan small town like the villages of Vermont.[2]

In such a context, it might well be that Child welcomed the invitation from WGBH to liven up the show, because it perhaps met her own interests in mediating venerable French tradition and an openness to life lived in a very modern way. Like Cambridge itself which managed to be folksy, hip, and avant-garde all at once, *The French Chef* could serve as an intersection of country lore and an up-to-date and invigorating modernism marked by the new looks that were coming to influence the popular arts in the 1960s. In this respect, Child's series offered a transition from a seemingly stuffy high culture of the 1950s into the looser world of the 1960s. It matters that *The French Chef* was all about *home* cooking (to such a degree that Child said early on that she wouldn't do a bread show since, even though it's a French staple, it's something generally bought at the boulangerie rather than made at home). Even if one invited guests over for social occasions that were also intended to convey status and impression, Child's cooking was not about urbane, snobby haute cuisine. Rather, it was centered on something more homey, more hearty, and the set and decor for her show spoke of folk values. In its own way, *The French Chef* radiated a sense of local, personable folksiness that benefited from mythologies of a life lived away from the bustling metropolis. Child's universe was not totally apart from the bistro and folk clubs of Cambridge in the '60s, and it does make sense that she and WGBH, by the second half of the decade, wanted to imagine ways to use *The French Chef* to target a new youth demographic.[3]

After receiving Davis's memo (which, because she wasn't actually an employee of WGBH, was forwarded to her), Child wrote a quick note to Ruth Lockwood to declare her hope that this new direction meant that WGBH would "get out of its somewhat ladylike rut." (Like "housewife," "ladylike" was a term of strong opprobrium for Child. It connoted superficiality, amateurishness, stuffy pretension, and a concomitant inability to appreciate in earthy fashion the pleasures of life.)

As early as 1966, Child had already begun to think about upcoming seasons of *The French Chef*, and she initiated discussions with WGBH about ways to move the program in new stylistic directions. Toward the end of the year, for instance, she had discussed the possibility of new formats for the program and had called for color in anticipation of Davis's memo a few months later. Ruth Lockwood agreed with the general idea of adding something new to the show. She suggested that it might be good for some episodes to get out of the studio kitchen—even go to France, perhaps—and Child concurred. Soon after she heard Lockwood's ideas, she wrote to the WGBH administration to suggest that scenes in France could expand on the show's appeal by showing the life, people, and food of that gastronomical paradise. At the same time, Lockwood also warned that Child should not move too far from those qualities of charm, intimacy, and personality that had made the first iteration of *The French Chef* such a success. As she cautioned Child in a memo dated December 6, 1966, "Stay away from technical TV terms and just let it come from the old French Chef heart."

The original intent was to have episodes of the new *French Chef* appear in 1969, but the logistics for what became, as we'll see, an opened-up and more ambitious program meant that the new version didn't actually air until 1970. WGBH had wanted to maintain public attention to Child during the intervening years, and it proceeded first by broadcasting reruns of the black-and-white series whenever it could (and re-lending episodes of the series to other stations throughout the country). The station also encouraged and facilitated Child's appearance on various television specials so she would still have a presence in the medium. The most important of the special appearances was a half-hour color program, "The White House Red Carpet with Julia Child." Filmed at the end of 1967 and aired in 1968, the program chronicled the "back-stage" preparations that would go into hosting a dinner at the White House—in this case, for 185 guests for the prime minister of Japan (with music by Tony Bennett). Child did not cook the dinner (lamb with artichoke and asparagus); the official White House chef did, and Child served primarily as an emcee who narrated her way through the White House and interviewed various staff members.

Of the qualities Dave Davis had imagined would make *The French Chef* "pertinent" to the visual style of the 1960s, color in particular became central to the new version of the show—and to promotion of it by WGBH before the first episodes aired. As Hartford Gunn, president of WGBH, wrote to Julia Child in 1967, a few months after Davis's memo: "I cannot conceal my excitement at the prospect of *The French Chef* in color—green greens, orange oranges."[4]

The canny punning here hints at two functions color could have for a cooking show such as *The French Chef*. One would be to bring out qualities in the foods themselves and let viewers see what ingredients and their successful transformation into a final product "actually" looked like. It was an issue of realism and content, then: the role of color could be the documentary one of providing precise information about the things (in this case, the food) that passed before the camera. At the same time, color could have, we might say, a function more of form than of content. That is, color could serve—especially in the context of the 1960s and its imputed "total assault" on the senses to which Davis alluded—as a form of vibrant, seductive spectacle that reached out to viewers and awed them through its visual and visceral qualities independent of any particular content. Think, for instance, of Stanley Kubrick's film *2001: A Space Odyssey* (1968). The psychedelic explosion of images that the astronaut Dave Bowman (along with the spectator) experiences toward the film's end might be interpretable in relation to the film's concern with the development of, and transcendence of, human consciousness. But the sequence is also there just to look cool, to be an extreme funhouse spectacle: take the ultimate trip, as the advertising slogan for the film had it.

Color, it might be noted, served in much media culture of the 1960s as the mark not of realism but of fantasy, imagination, a palette of impressions imposed over reality and transforming it according to aesthetic fancies. (Significantly, when Peter Ustinov directed a film version of Melville's *Billy Budd* in 1962, he said he pointedly opted for black and white because it connoted realism better than a filmic look that captured all the colors of the world did.) For so much popular culture of the 1960s, color was seen more as something added to—or laid onto—the world than something in that world to be captured in documentary style, which was done more appropriately in black and white.[5] Think, for instance, of Andy Warhol's pop art silk screens of famous events and celebrities in which black-and-white photos from news media often were treated as a mere historical referent which then underwent aesthetic treatment by color permutations that served as so many palimpsestic layers that vibrantly floated over social history. Or think of *Yellow Submarine* (1968), in which the Blue Meanies suck the color out of life and the Beatles have to embark on their mission in the colored vehicle of the film's title to restore visual vibrancy to a stolid world. Think too of the ways that the massive turn of the television networks to color was presented as a special event ("*Combat* in Color"!) and was played on as a gripping spectacle in its own right. Evidently, the demos for the new *French Chef* that were shown to WGBH staff members and then to other stations in the PBS orbit so they could see what a color version of the show would be like started with a close-up in black and white of strawberries that suddenly went into color and blew away everyone who saw the scene.

It is worth noting that color on television sets in the 1960s seemed not like something that arose naturally from the filmed world but that derived artificially from gadgetry. The controls of the television set had to be adjusted correctly or the colors would turn incorrect or smear and flare into bright orbs of weird luminosity. Color television in the 1960s often just doesn't look right from a realist point of view, and the sheer constructedness of a studio set like the kitchen of *The French Chef* becomes all the more evident with the addition of color. (The later, postmodern *Pee-wee's Playhouse* astutely included in its pastiche embrace of a constructed pop look awareness of just how unreal studio-set television series of the 1960s appeared.)

The color episodes of *The French Chef*, then, can often seem more campy than folksy. Perhaps that strong sense of ease and intimacy on camera that fans had already found in Child was able still to compensate for the tone of artificiality that the color version of the show imparted. But it seems that any impression of naturalness that persisted through the color version of *The French Chef* fell apart in Child's next PBS show, *Dinner at Julia's* (which debuted in 1983), as the visual style came to seem so unreal as to appear garish. As Laura Shapiro says of the later show, "Julia looked grotesque, her hair frizzed and her makeup garish, dressed up in caftans and evening pajamas, or rigged out for a barbecue in jeans, a vest, and a purple ten-gallon hat. . . . She looked as if she were a cardboard replica of herself, deployed to lend the symbolic presence of Julia Child to an alien landscape."[6]

If color was one means by which the second iteration of *The French Chef* could appear hip by tapping into the seductive pop visual style of the 1960s, another was an expanded mode of editing that promised an opening up of the enclosed space of the kitchen, in which the chef moved inexorably along her narrative trajectory, to new spatialities and new temporalities. Specifically, as planning for the new *French Chef* series extended through the later years of the 1960s, Child began to imagine a version of the show filled with flashbacks and in which there could be crosscutting between her kitchen and other sites of culinary interest. In a late memo to Lockwood (June 24, 1971), Child went as far as to suggest that a new style invigorated by editing might obviate the impression of an unfolding reality caught live and, significantly, she approved this potential break from a naturalism of presentation: "If we had more money, it would be so useful to overshoot, and be able to edit out with dissolves to indicate time lapses—and no pretence that it is a live show." Significantly, she added a parenthetical comment that indicated that the experiment with editing should only go so far: "An interesting use of bad cutting, we thought, was *Death in Venice* [1971] where they abruptly cut to flashbacks with no warning, and you got confused. . . . But well worth seeing."[7] (Knowing of the corny puns Child used for the titles of many of her episodes of *The French Chef*, a friend of mine says she should have done one called "Death in Venison.")

Ultimately, though, for the 1970s series, the kitchen scenes of *The French Chef* would still be filmed live and in observance of chronological time. But the transition from one camera to the other was now often done with dreamy dissolves rather than straight cuts, and there would be flashbacks out of the kitchen, although they were carefully introduced by Child so that they didn't intrude on the narrative (as was often the wont of art cinema editing at the time). In addition, the color episodes frequently used zooms to move in and out of close-ups, modifying somewhat the filming strategies analyzed earlier (in which

European art?: Julia Child and Gustav von Aschenbach on the Mediterranean.

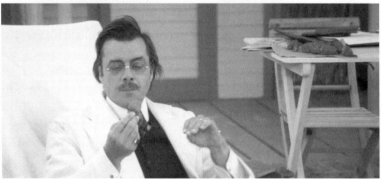

camera movement often brought about the change of scale) and doing so in ways that fit the visual dynamism of film and television in the late 1960s and early 1970s. (Take, for example, the zoom-ins on dancing women covered with words in *Rowan and Martin's Laugh-In*; the zooms in *The French Chef* are, to be sure, certainly much less frenetic than that but they are no less a visually evident formal technique imposed on the content being filmed.)

Soon after the final season of the black-and-white version of *The French Chef* aired, Child had started considering various pedagogical structures for the next iteration of the series. One idea she had was to concentrate certain episodes not on a particular food or food item but on one or more basic techniques or practices. For example, after cooking and stuffing a chicken at Simca Beck's house during her summer vacation, Child got the idea for a two-part poultry show in which one episode would deal with issues of deboning and initial preparation and the follow-up would concern stuffing and poaching. She also thought about episodes in which kitchen skills might be used to very particular ends. One idea, for instance, was for an episode on cooking in very small kitchens. In a memo to Lockwood in 1971, she suggested that episodes could concentrate on fundamental techniques and the variations that could be spun off from them while, at the same time, she expressed caution that the show should not concentrate on basics to such a degree that the more serious and ambitious home cook would find the level too low (especially if that viewer had already been following her from the black-and-white days of the show).

Ultimately, the format that Child found most enticing as a way to innovate the new program was the one she had bandied about with Lockwood in which *The French Chef* would be opened up beyond its studio-set kitchen to the larger culinary world of France. The idea evolved into footage of Child touring gastronomy-related venues in France—shops, farms, sites of fabrication, and so on—interwoven with scenes of Child back in her kitchen applying the experience to her own cuisine. There would be two levels of inter-cutting. On the one hand, there would be episodes largely devoted to the sojourn in France paired with ones that concentrated on Child primarily in the kitchen back home. Thus, an episode in which Child in her kitchen prepared a bouillabaisse could be preceded by one in which she was visiting Marseilles to show off, according to publicity material, "the old port and Chateau d'If; fish types and Marseilles types, Restaurant 'Brasserie des Catalans' and bouillabaisse." On the other hand, individual kitchen episodes themselves might include cuts to scenes in France that would serve as flashbacks to Child's memory of that country and its culinary ways. For example, when in the bouillabaisse episode she mentions the bounties to be had in the open-air market at Marseilles, sequences devoted to Child making her way through that market are quickly inserted. Similarly, her "Whole Fish Story" episode has two scenes of an expert fishmonger teaching her in Paris how to filet various fish; this instruction is inter-cut with scenes of Child back in the U.S. studio applying the lessons learned. Certainly, this sort of inter-cutting would not have the artsy abruptness of, say, Luchino Visconti's memory-driven flashbacks in *Death in Venice*, but it still would open up *The French Chef* in ways that seemed in keeping with the increasingly adventurous visual style of the period. When it was finally ready to air in one set of thirteen episodes, the new season was described in WGBH publicity material this way: "Julia will show her viewers the France she knows as cameras follow her from the sophisticated dining rooms of Paris' great restaurants to the tiny, cluttered kitchens of country inns." For another set of episodes, the publicity material stated, "Julia, in her kitchen, will reconstruct the recipes and demonstrate the techniques which she introduced in the programs produced in France."[8]

Curiously, however, Child's producer, Ruth Lockwood, had toyed for a while with the idea of minimizing the French presence in the new iteration of *The French Chef*. The year 1968 was a fraught moment in geopolitics, and the U.S. government was encouraging a cooling of Franco-American relations. Faced with the nation's global balance-of-payment deficit, exacerbated by the expenses of the Vietnam War and of social programs at home such as the War on Poverty, President Johnson had even called for Americans to curtail foreign travel, especially to a country like France, which notoriously was resisting American hegemony at the time.[9] As Lockwood wrote to Child, "These invitations to travel abroad have caused me to take a long hard look at our proposal for a new *French Chef* series. My feeling is that with world conditions as they are, especially our present relationship with France, and President Johnson's plea to keep our dollars in the United States, it is the wrong time to consider doing part of our series in France." At the same time, Child herself was considering episodes that would deal with cuisines other than the specifically French (although, of course, she would still adhere to the French model of theme, method, and controlled variation). But in the event, the idea of straying too far from the Gallic underpinnings was dropped, and WGBH and Child together began intensive planning of a new, still Frenchified version of the show (which nonetheless did end up including a few non-French episodes, such as a curry show).

Final contractual arrangements for the new *French Chef* were signed by all parties in August 1970. (Interestingly, this was done *after* sequences in France, where Child went regularly for the summer, had been shot; this is a sign, certainly, of WGBH's awareness of Julia Child's importance to the station.) Child would receive $500 per show plus 20 percent of the gross earnings from foreign and commercial rebroadcasts. If she published a book or articles that centered on recipes from the show, WGBH would be considered proprietary, and Child would receive 20 percent of the royalties once a threshold of $20,000 to WGBH had been reached. Significantly, the contract spelled out that this arrangement directly applied only to a new *French Chef* cookbook, not to the second volume of *Mastering the Art of French Cooking*, which was about to come out. (The profit from that book went to Child and Simca Beck, not to WGBH.) At the same time, Knopf, the publisher of *Mastering*, signed an agreement with PBS to allow the educational network's stations to sell copies of the volume in their promotional campaigns and fund drives. While Knopf—and Child, to a degree— were insistent that *Mastering* represented a literary venture in cuisine that was of a different cultural sort than the televisual *French Chef*, they clearly also realized the financial benefits that could accrue from synergy between the two ventures.

Importantly, the contract specified that WGBH would pick up all expenses for out-of-studio filming—consequential in this case because of the costly sequences that had been shot in France. A budget breakdown from the period gives a sense of the expenses involved. For the in-studio episodes, estimated salaries for the crew were $33,787; production costs were $30,119; and indirect costs were $16,729. The corresponding amounts for location shooting were $89,963 for salaries; $167,894 for production; and $106,341 for indirect expenses. This is a much different context from that of the several-hundred-dollar episodes of the black-and-white seasons.

Scenes in France were shot over four weeks in May–June 1970, with Paul and Julia Child and the production team traversing the country from Paris to Cannes and Nice, Marseilles, Burgundy, Normandy, and Brittany, and back again to Paris. In advance of the trip, Paul and Julia had determined the sites to visit and the people to see (for instance, the oldest sommelier in France, Monsieur Hénocq of the Le Grand Vefour in Paris, "now in his 8os," as Child put it in a memo, "but still, evidently, doing his work—a wonderful character with great charm and, of course, knowledge"). Much of this planning was based on Paul's and Julia's experience in going to France for a break every year. Some of it, however, also came from their oldest, cherished memories of the France they discovered together after the war, and those memories did not always hold up to the ravages of time (Monsieur Hénocq, for example, turned out to be too old, frail, and senile to make the footage of him useable).

Close to two hundred PBS stations had signed up to carry the new show, and it was advertised through the late summer and into the fall with the phrase "The French Chef Returns." Frequent mention was made also of the fact that the new version would be in color. (Typical was a declaration that the show was "in glorious shades of eggplant, spinach, and strawberry.")

In two other ways, the new iteration of *The French Chef* would look forward to new experiments with electronic visual media from the 1970s on. First, the new series became the first PBS show to be proposed for home purchase through the new video technology that would come to define a consumerist and domestic lifestyle ethos from the 1970s into the 1980s. Select episodes of *The French Chef* were made available for personal purchase through a technology known as Cartrivision, which entailed purchasing a player for $795 and the cartridges themselves, which sold for $7.95 (half-hour capacity) or $11.95 (one-hour capacity). The production expense for a cartridge was pegged at about $5.50. Child participated in promoting the system in 1972 when she went to a convention for audiotape and videotape dealers and autographed copies of *The French Chef* cartridges. But Cartrivision never really took off, and the fact that the first royalty payments to Child (in 1973) amounted to only $184 confirms the lack of interest the system inspired among consumers.

More consequential was a second experiment that *The French Chef* was involved in: it became the first PBS show to be captioned for the hearing-impaired. The venture began to be put together in early 1972 for the upcoming fall season, and Child filmed promos in March to announce the new project to viewers. The idea, she said, was that the *French Chef* team was "going to try and reach some people we may have missed."[10] Episodes ended with printed titles that invited viewers to write in to their local PBS stations and give their impressions of the experiment.

The venture involved a pilot project of eight episodes being broadcast with captions running over part of the image. The venture had funding from the Bureau of Education for the Handicapped in the U. S. Office of Education and had some underwriting from Polaroid. Importantly, all of the episodes that were captioned had already aired and were in reruns. In at least one case, this meant that the words in the captions ended up diverging in content from what Child had said in the original. For example, in the original broadcast of episode 255, on how to make a good loaf of bread, Child had declared that one way to know whether a loaf was done was to knock one's fist against it and see if it made a thumping sound. Because most people with hearing impairments couldn't employ that technique, it was decided to have the captions offer substitute advice—namely, that one could check color (the loaf should have a nice brown color), texture (the loaf should be crusty), and size (the loaf should have shrunk slightly from when the dough went into the oven).

The hope in limiting the experiment to reruns was that, if viewers didn't like the captioning, they might continue to watch the series anyway with the promise of seeing fresh episodes that hadn't been altered. Nonetheless, there still was discontent among some viewers that their show, as they asserted, had been messed with. Unfortunately, it seems that the captioning technology hadn't been perfected and was jumpy and unsteady, inconsistent in its placement on the screen (some viewers wrote to complain that at certain moments, the captions were superimposed over Child's face), abrupt in the speed with which new phrases came onto the screen, and out of sync with what Child was saying at any one moment.

Some of the letters that came in show a strong degree of insensitivity. For example, one viewer declared, "We feel there are far more viewers with good hearing who watch this show than people who are deaf. Deaf people, the few who do watch this, can always turn up the audio."

Another suggested that PBS simply send hearing-impaired viewers "a pamphlet on lip reading." On the other hand, some viewers without hearing impairments liked the captions for their own reasons. One viewer noted that captions could aid in the pedagogy of culinary preparation because it made the recipes easier to follow. Another wrote to say that the captions helped in language instruction for those viewers for whom English was a second language. And as noted earlier, at least one viewer wrote to say that the captions reminded him of European art films and made the experience of watching the new series feel like participating in an avant-garde work of trendy experimentation.

Complete with a new musical score, the 1970s version of *The French Chef* brought a whole new set of viewers to the series, and for many people it is the later version they remember when they think about the show. It is, for instance, the version that Dan Ackroyd referred to in his sketch on *Saturday Night Live*, with its pastel colors splattered with vividly red blood. Certainly, the 1970s seasons portray a Julia Child who was becoming more performative, especially in the pre-credit sequences, which often involved complex interactions between her and the kitchen gizmos and foodstuffs on hand. (She also started to use funny titles for the episodes, such as one on lamb called "Waiting for Gigot.") She seemed much more outgoing and willing to horse around. At the same time, ironically, the inter-cutting could make her seem more subdued, as it led to sequences of her simply walking through French markets or meeting with figures from the French cooking world or even moving off-screen as those figures demonstrated specific cooking skills. The color seasons of *The French Chef* looked forward to her later television series, in which Child often served merely as the host or even as an onlooker to the activities of others (including some chefs who would later have shows of their own, like Emeril Lagasse). Bit by bit, she was already stepping aside for the food television that would succeed her.

The levity that Child put into *The French Chef* in the 1970s might give the impression that she was fully enjoying herself. It is clear, however, that, as the decade progressed, she began to weary of the effort to do a regular television show of this sort. Some of her reluctance to continue came from personal factors. This was the period in which the maladies that ultimately led to Paul's decline set in. (He had a heart attack and a series of debilitating strokes starting in 1974). One also senses fatigue in Child, who had reached her sixties by this time. Some of her impatience derived from the limits of the somewhat repetitive in-studio format, in which a recipe was worked through from beginning to end. Clearly, the search for a new mode of presentation that would lead to the opening up of the new *French Chef* was not something that the episodes and sequences set in France satisfied for her, and she continued to bandy about other ideas for new formats, such as themed and special-situation shows. As early as the end of the 1971 season, she imagined a scaled-back version of the show that wouldn't involve French scenes and instead would concentrate on very practical concerns the cook faced in the average kitchen. She nicknamed this possible series "The French Chef Faces Life" and imagined episodes on such topics as how to find time to cook when one was working full time.

Finally, there was frustration at the battles that PBS was waging with the Nixon administration, which saw public television as one of the primary media venues for anti-administration attacks and was trying to cut its funding. Clearly, *The French Chef* had no anti-establishment content, but as a steadfast liberal, Child engaged with great commitment in the fight for PBS's future. Her primary contribution was to make herself as available as possible to local PBS stations when they conducted fund drives, a process that became more fraught in the face of the Nixon administration's threats to terminate government financing of educational television. Child's promos did not directly address the political context. Instead, they played on aspects of her seemingly apolitical status as a professor of the kitchen. One sort of commercial imagined the funding of educational television as itself a recipe that viewers could follow to successful completion. As the dialogue in one promo put it: "Here's a marvelous recipe for good public television, and it's very simple. Start with these ingredients: one great big wonderful idea. Add a very talented producer, and one clutch of fascinating personalities. Combine with camera, lights, sound. Now layer in generous sprinklings of your financial support, and up, like a soufflé, pops the kind of great programming only public television can give, but it can only do so if you lend us a hand. Here's how." Another promo played on Child's distinctive personality and emphasized her all-Americanness: "I'm Julia Child. You think perhaps I'm a leetle teeny Franch woman [spelling in original]? Well, I'm not. I'm a great big Sunkist product, born and raised in Pasadena. And I must say it's good to be back in Southern California on *The French Chef*. . . . You can cook in the French manner anywhere, especially here in California, where you have all the wonderful fresh foods to cook with. . . . So if you like to cook and love to eat, join me next time on *The French Chef*. Either Monday evenings at 8, or Tuesday at noon, on [name of station]. This is Julia Child. Bon appétit."

But it is clear that, by 1974, Child wanted either a very new sort of show or an exit altogether from regular, episodic television. Significantly, to the degree that she continued to be tempted by the idea of ongoing engagement in the production of a cooking show, she began to think outside the format of a *French Chef*-like show. For example, she considered a suggestion from a WGBH administrator that she turn the show into a sort of cooking workshop with interaction from a studio audience, whose members could ask questions or pose cooking problems. But in mid-May 1974, during her vacation in France, Child wrote to Ruth Lockwood, "After due reflection, we have decided we do not want to commit ourselves to any series which would involve us in four or more months of program work, since that is just what we are now happily free of. . . . The end-result of long and serious discussions is that we have decided to bring to a conclusion our television life."[11]

Even so, she didn't give up. First, in a memo to Lockwood in June, Child proposed a reduced *French Chef* that would have just three episodes and include guests (a return, again, to that old idea). One of her suggestions was to have Graham Kerr—or, as she put it, "even old Galloping (whom Jim [Beard] says is charming)."[12] Nothing came of the idea, but in 1975, with the U.S. bicentennial one year away, she entertained the possibility of a special or even a series on American cooking that she would co-host with James Beard. Ultimately, though, Paul's illness made her demur, and she wrote to PBS executives that Beard was larger-than-life enough to handle the show himself. (It never did get produced.) When Exxon, which had originally offered to underwrite new seasons of a *French Chef* series that might join Child and Beard, definitively said it was not interested in an American-themed show, Child expressed relief: "We shall withdraw from the project entirely, and this is our formal resignation. Much as we have enjoyed working with WGBH, our active series-television days with you must come to an end. We shall, of course, always support Public Television in general, and WGBH in particular."[13]

In fact, there would be other television shows for Julia Child, some of them on PBS, and many of them realizing her earliest dream of bringing in other chefs and personalities to interact with her or to take over the stage fully with their own presence. But this meant that, bit by bit, Child's own embodied presence seemed to slip away. On television, the later Julia Child appears much more passive, more a listener than a doer, even (for all her original strapping size) more and more diminutive.

Other chefs would come along on U.S. television, and many would seem inspired by Julia Child's joy in opening up cooking instruction to energetic expressions of fun. Already in the late 1960s, Graham Kerr, the host of *The Galloping Gourmet*, had furthered Child's dynamic takeover of the space around her by making the whole studio, not just the kitchen set within it, the domain of his seductive antics as he cavorted with the audience and camera crew. Kerr's insistence on having a fundamental cooking lesson within all the zaniness harkened back to Child's belief in the seriousness of the mission of cookery, but he also looked ahead to celebrity-driven "cooking" shows in which shtick and performance increasingly would become subjects in their own right. In 1993, the Food Network was launched on cable television. It filled up its original six-hour slots (repeated four times a day) with reruns of Julia Child's programs and with programs hosted by her acolytes, including Sara Moulton, a former cooking assistant of Child's, who continued the visual tradition of the chef in the kitchen doing his or her thing at a kitchen counter. Soon, however, the Food Network moved beyond talk-filled cooking demonstrations of the basic "dump and stir" variety, and new formats emerged, such as travelogues, game shows, science shows, postmodern parodies, vaudeville and musical numbers, and so on. All of these had been anticipated by Julia Child's own mixing of pedagogy with entertainment, but they also went in directions she would not have foreseen and, in their frequent lack of interest in the actual work of cooking, would not have approved. *The French Chef* had had its place in television history and in American history, and nothing ever again would be like it.

8 Kitchen Drama

In early lines of a long essay in an anthology he co-edited on the 1960s, the cultural theorist Fredric Jameson asserts that the decade "had to happen the way it did."[1] That may be so, but the 1960s that Jameson then theorizes, and that the rest of the admittedly rich volume presents, is strikingly bereft of any consequential mention of popular culture. It's as if there was no culture industry in the period (rock music does make it in but only as part of a *counter*-culture.) There is no mention, for instance, of Julia Child, let alone broadcast television more generally. This downplaying of mainstream culture in the 1960s is perhaps in keeping with a collection of writings that wants primarily to chronicle the formation in the decade of radical consciousness and active opposition *to the mainstream*. But this emphasis pretty much rules out any sense that mainstream culture itself might be a site in which to look for contradiction or signs even of hope and desire and change. One consequence of this is that the volume reinstates a public-domestic split in which what is going on in the streets is deemed political and what is going on in, say, the bedroom or in front of the living-room television set or in the kitchen is deemed less so. As the introduction to the volume puts it, "The '60's is merely the name we give to the disruption of late-capitalist ideological and political hegemony. . . . In the 60s, this had become a struggle over turf with the seizing of streets."[2] This street-savvy way of conceiving politics gives domestic space little concreteness, little presence, and little political salience. The home is not part of the turf in this version of the decade.

At the same time, conversely, perhaps we shouldn't rush to imagine that any act of domestic assertion of the self turns into a political act of the highest kind. The flip side of downplaying popular culture and domestic everyday life as sites of politics shows up for me in the grandiosity of the mention of Julia Child as a politico in an obituary notice for the neighborhood activist Jane Jacobs offered by Jason Epstein in the *New York Review of Books*: "The twentieth century also produced an extraordinary group of revolutionary women whose accomplishments improved life for others: Rachel Carson, Betty Friedan, Rosa Parks, Julia Child, and Jane Jacobs. . . . No one could teach these women what they knew. Perhaps for this reason they could penetrate the miasma of professionalism that shielded institutionalized malpractice. What these women had in common was a genius for the day-to-day arrangements on which everything else depends, arrangements which their male counterparts did so much to destroy."[3]

One certainly can understand and sympathize with the impulse that leads Epstein to include Julia Child among a list of influential women who made changes in and to America in the second half of the twentieth century. He's no doubt right to see their sphere of action as that of the day to day, which they demonstrated was a realm that mattered. But it is still possible to feel that there is something extravagant in such a conjoining (Julia Child next to Rosa Parks!), one in which the way all these women mattered is framed as a revolutionary, heated battle against the powers that be. It could be argued, for instance, that if Child did penetrate "the miasma of professionalism" by countering the dogma that said that classy French food had to be done only one way (and generally by men), she didn't necessarily make what for Epstein is the related step of assailing "institutionalized malpractice." Indeed, Julia Child was quite in thrall to the big industrial food firms, relied on them constantly for advice, and often took their pronouncements as givens. She was, for instance, a strong proponent of genetically modified foods from multinational corporations.

To comprehend a period like the 1960s, we might indeed need to understand how Julia Child was a key icon of and for it, but this cannot come without a reasoned analysis of what she *specifically* and *irreducibly* offered to her times. Turning her into a political revolutionary is no more helpful than imagining that the turf of the home is a lesser realm of politics than, say, the street. In this respect, let us follow for a bit Epstein's conjoining of Child with Jane Jacobs and see where it might lead. Jacobs's groundbreaking critique of urban modernism, *Death and Life of Great American Cities*, came out the year before the pilot episodes of *The French Chef*, and both women did become icons of the complicated decade that was the 1960s. No doubt, then, there are parallels. Both women, it could be said, were about refusing dogmas transmitted from on high, and both argued instead for a knowledge acquired through direct, local, and down-to-earth levels of experience. That indeed is very much of the time.

The comparison of Child and Jacobs is perhaps not as fanciful as it might seem at first glance. Their worlds come together, for instance, when the famed Philadelphia restaurant magnate Steve Poses recounts that his first venture, the French-inflected bistro Frog in the early 1970s, was an attempt to use food culture to influence urban culture: "I thought [Frog] would be an extension of the coffeehouses of the fifties. A place where people could discuss issues of the day. Hopefully, come up with solutions to the issues of the day. . . . I picked a neighborhood . . . one that no one had defined as a neighborhood. And I decided that my restaurant would function like the corner candy store. That's Jane Jacobs . . . a candy store for our generation."[4]

Both Child and Jacobs, then, were about empowering ordinary citizens through social experience and communal activity. And like Child, Jacobs was about finding the fun in such experience. Much depressed her about what was being done to cities, but she also took great delight in the immediate pleasures of the street, the sidewalk, the neighborhood. (Not for nothing does the book's title put *Life* after *Death*, since hers is a book about street-festival forms of joyous optimism).

But Jacobs also was about building a public sociality within cities that itself tapped into collectivist impulses of the 1960s. For her, the sidewalk was a place of interpersonal interaction—strangers and neighbors came together to watch out for one another, even as they respected one another's private spaces—and from this one could build the larger networks of interconnection needed to fight the powers that be. In contrast, while Julia Child's teaching certainly had its own versions of human connection (the viewers watching the show, the friends and family to whom those viewers might end up serving great food, with great conversation around it), it would be hard, I think, to imagine them as public processes of the same collective-building sort. Child's sense of interpersonal sociality is twofold. On the one hand, there is the social bond fostered between Child as television figure and those (the viewers) who, by watching, share vicariously in the visual experience of cuisine and the elements of its experience. This, however, is at best a virtual collectivity, built up out of mass media's seriality of viewership in which many people do the same thing at the same time but apart from one another in the private space of the home. On the other hand, for those viewers who then applied Child's pedagogy to their cooking, there could be the promise of the social bond fostered among everyone who would then be sharing in a good meal and in all the elements of its experience. For Child, food was a communal practice filled with good talk and good pleasures, and she hoped her pedagogy would lead to social occasions that were rich in quality and conviviality. There no doubt was something adventurous here, something about moving beyond the limits of a conventional way of life and, hopefully, bringing others along on the voyage. But it was also a journey whose terms were fixed (there were only so many paths between failure and success for a recipe) and whose sphere of impact (the kitchen, the dining room) was deliberately circumscribed. Indeed, there was something risky here, but the risks were within a structure that generally was fundamentally comforting and reassuring.

One way I've found useful for thinking about the politics of reassurance fostered by the contained world of the studio kitchen on the cooking show—and on Julia Child's first cooking series, in particular—is to refer to the "drama of the box," a concept that the cultural critic Raymond Williams articulated and then applied, in several writings, to the specific medium of broadcast television. By "drama of the box," Williams meant, first, the history of staged (and, later, televised) drama, which had to do in large part with a moving indoors of the subject matter of plays. As Williams saw it, the bourgeois theater of the eighteenth and nineteenth centuries increasingly came to deal with people in rooms interacting with one another, but often bracketed off any attention to a larger social world beyond their own private intrigues, their own private lives. The "box," then, consisted of the three walls of the theatrical set as it was presented to the audience, but it was also the four walls of the self-contained rooms that this theatrical set was supposed to be representing. As Williams describes it, "It is perhaps a particular stage of bourgeois society, in which the decisive action is elsewhere, and what is lived out, in these traps of rooms, are the human consequences: in particular, the consequences of a relatively leisured society."[5]

For Williams, this turn inward began to be challenged at the end of the nineteenth century and into the twentieth as adventurous playwrights set out to open up theatrical experience to the world at large. Now, characters might try to reject the bourgeois experience and leave it for the world at large (take, for example, the resounding sharpness of the slammed door at the end of *A Doll's House*, when Nora makes a break for a new, proto-feminist way of life), but they also might find that the world beyond their walls impinged on them with a new insistence (for example, the resounding sharpness of the ax at the end of *The Cherry Orchard* to signal an inescapable modernization). In his inaugural lecture in 1974 for a distinguished professorship in drama at Cambridge University, Williams described the process by saying that the new dramatists "created, above all, rooms; enclosed rooms on enclosed stages; rooms in which life was centered but inside which people waited for the knock on the door, the letter or the message, the shout from the street, to know what would happen to them; what would come to intersect and to decide their own still intense and immediate lives."[6] In other words, the new experimenters might still be representing lives lived in boxes, but they also began to hint at forces—ranging from personal yearnings to inevitable social pressures at large—that pushed those lives into a larger social arena.

And, Williams went on to argue, television, the twentieth century's mass form of dramatization, picked up that hint: "There is a direct cultural continuity, it seems to me, from those enclosed rooms, enclosed and lighted framed rooms, to the rooms in which we watch the framed images of television, at home, in our own lives, but needing to watch what is happening, as we say, 'out there.' Our lives are still here, still substantially here, with the people we know, in the similar rooms of our friends and neighbors, and they too are watching: not only for public events or from distraction, but from a need for images, for representations, of what living is now like, and for this kind of person and in this situation and place and that."[7] Television, in other words, would serve as the privileged venue in which ordinary citizens, isolated in boxes of their own (the domestic setting so central to an ideology of individualized family life), could go beyond their own worlds and tap into the experience of others. In *Television: Technology and Cultural Form*, Williams termed this "mobile privatization"—so many people retreating into the private space of hearth and home but gaining an impression of transport through all of the worlds that the box of the television set could give them glimpses of.[8]

I find this idea of multiple boxes—the space in which a drama is performed, the medium in which it is represented (in this case, the television set), the space in which the representation of the performance is witnessed (the home)—useful for thinking about the genre of the televised cooking show. The cooking show gives us a version of, to pick up one phrase from Williams, "what living is now like." Think of *The French Chef*. Into the space of your home comes the drama of someone personally unknown to you who lets you share for a time in her domestic activities and, by the end, has you feeling that, indeed, you know her quite well. Within the stage set of the enclosed kitchen, Child had a space of action to herself, one that she could control, one that worked according to a self-imposed logic, one that was essentially closed off to larger changes going on in the world beyond the set. This was a popular culture that for the most part spoke of nothing dire—a culture that comforted by imagining a cheery special place untouched by anything catastrophic out there in the world.

When, for example, Child claimed in an episode on paella in the mid-1960s that differing views about the authentic version of the dish had led to "terrible arguments, worse than politics, if that's possible," her comment was, of course, a light and fanciful one, but that's the very point. It sets up measures of relevance between culinary discourse and political discourse and banishes the latter to a realm of impertinence. The kitchen set of *The French Chef* had a window that pretended to look out onto the world (or some part of it), but it was still just a set, and it created a self-enclosed place where one strong-willed woman made her own reality and thus could bracket out any reality beyond its frames. The buoyant optimism of the cooking show offered, in its own way, a tale of comfort.[9]

Narrative genres, whether in literature, film, television, or other media, work by what Fredric Jameson terms "world reduction"—that is, they select certain elements from the larger world, leave out others, and construct a space with its own rules and rituals.[10] For example (a minor but revealing one), film noir takes a real world that contains, among other things, blondes and brunettes, and reduces it to one in which brunettes are generally perfidious and blondes are generally domesticated alternatives to the brunette spider woman.

In *The French Chef*, the work of generic reduction is, I think, manifold. First, the world is narrowed to Julia Child in her kitchen, face to face with the ingredients of the day. No other people are here; no inter-social experience needs to be mastered. True, the viewer has a certain inter-social status as an interlocutor whose presence is implied and taken into account in Child's performance of guileless intimacy. But, as noted earlier, there is a hierarchy of roles, and Child is at the top. The viewer may be watching so that he or she can eventually cook like Child, but the immediate and present activity is still one of watching— of being outside Child's world and invited in to participate in it voyeuristically and vicariously at best. It is true too that Child frequently anthropomorphized foodstuffs, which might imply an inter-social world, but the relationships she set up were hierarchical after their own fashion, with Child handling (sometimes literally) the food in ways that asserted the superiority of her personality over it. For example, the famous "chicken sisters" from the color series may have been given personal identities, but they were still there to be manipulated bodily by Child, the lord of this generic universe. Or, as Child put it in the archived script for an early episode on soufflés, the point was "how to use your head so the egg won't use you. In other words, conquer the egg, and you are master of the kitchen."

As a second reduction, the overall tone of *The French Chef* is invariably one of cheerful optimism. This is a world where things generally will turn out all right and will do so to such a degree that narrative endings can be announced at the beginning. That is, this is a world that is lorded over by a confidence—Child's exuberant faith that the world of cooking has a logic—so strong that it can begin with the declaration of the ultimate success that will be had at the end. Thus, a finished tarte tatin can be shown off in the first moments of the episode devoted to that dessert, and Child can then boldly put the completed dish out of sight so that it then functions as both a memory trace and a dream of the future to be achieved in the next half-hour. From the start, there is an affirmation of success in the showing off of the finished offering before the cooking has even started.

Not everything in this circumscribed world is predictably immutable and guaranteed full success. Clearly, there is always potential for a kitchen disaster. But it is confirmation of Child's forceful identity that she can meet the challenge, can always soldier on and do so with gusto. She is so confident that, in at least one case, she could even acknowledge the inevitability of disaster before it occurred. In an episode on Hollandaise sauce and Béarnaise sauce from the color series of *The French Chef* in the 1970s, she directly announced that one was likely to fail in initial attempts to make these sauces. Perseverance, self-confidence, and faith in Child as the guide not only allowed the disaster to be acknowledged, but also affirmed that it inevitably would be surmounted and relegated to a past that no longer could threaten future ventures into the sauce world.

The cooking show, then, offers a particularly formalized and purified (or, in Jameson's term, reduced) sort of narrative. The end is virtually guaranteed at the beginning. There are codified steps by which that end is achieved. (Thus, even if the television cook talks about alternative versions of a recipe, they are logically determined variants that can be specified and taught to the viewer.) The world is reduced to a single actor and a single realm of action, and that action is of a very particular sort (cooking and little else), with the discourse around it speaking about it in very circumscribed ways—for example, as the personal, if vicariously inter-social, pleasures of food preparation and food consumption.

Here I've found it useful to forge a passing comparison to a seemingly different icon of the early 1960s, the nuclear strategist Herman Kahn, as anatomized in Sharon Ghamari-Tabrizi's excellent, quirky *The Worlds of Herman Kahn*.[11] Like Child, Kahn, who worked at the Rand Corporation, was a physically imposing figure who resonated a larger-than-lifeness that could almost seem like caricature and that he put to good use in lectures/performances that were curious mixes of buoyant (and often bad-taste) humor, visions of the worst that could happen, and confident demonstrations of ways to make the worst (the unthinkable, in the parlance of the day) never happen. But unlike Child, Kahn formulated scenarios of the future based in science fiction. They were not about finding the one logic (or one logic and its logically derived variants) that could move one from an initial premise to a guaranteed narrative conclusion, but about imagining as many logics, as many narratives, as many paradoxes and unpredictabilities as possible, all the better to generate solutions for each and every one. In the box that was the Rand think tank, Kahn's mission was to proliferate what-if stories (which is why Ghamari-Tabrizi can talk about him as directly part of the 1960s avant-garde), whereas Child's was to reduce what-ifs to much more localized, manageable sets of narratives whose logic was set out in advance.

In Ghamari-Tabrizi's reading of the early 1960s, the anxiety of annihilation was an essential condition, a social unconscious with which everyone lived, even if only in the deepest, unacknowledged recesses of the mind. Some citizens let the awareness come in too strongly and lived lives of edgy neurosis, but others escaped into the palliatives of sedation (the use of tranquilizers was at an all-time high) or into the hope of a higher metaphysics (the Billy Graham brand of religious salvation was at an all-time high). The worry always existed, though, that everything might disappear in a flash. In the CBS show *The Twilight Zone*, for instance, which debuted at the end of the 1950s and continued into the 1960s, the very coordinates of one's existence—including the very fact that one had indeed existed—could be eradicated in the blink of an instant.

Significantly, the nightmare here isn't always about total annihilation. It can also be about being uprooted from the security of one's material world and the comforting objects that fill it up. This fear is as much social as it is metaphysical, and it expresses itself in *The Twilight Zone* (and elsewhere) in narratives about men and women who cease to matter to those around them; and in narratives about people who are suddenly like strangers to everyone else, who can't fit in, who find that the system has no place for them, who find that their material possessions seem alien. What a science-fiction film of the 1950s allegorized as the plight of the "Incredible Shrinking Man" would be literalized in subsequent decades by the term "downsizing."

The cooking show holds at bay all of this anxiety about traps, unanticipated change, and the potential for everything one cherishes to be taken away in a flash. The generic universe of the cooking show is one in which there is one logical path to an end (or, at best, variant alternative paths); in which that end is inevitably a happy one, a cause for celebration (literally so in that the meals rendered by the narrative are to be consumed in communal festivity); in which there is an ever available abundance of material goods to work with and a comparable abundance of tools and instruments with which to do that work; in which the objects of the world can never resist the control of the protagonist for too long (this or that gadget may break down on *The French Chef*, but a battery of other tools in which to take comfort is always available); in which the field of action is reduced to that protagonist and those objects, with no other people around, but without that absence being a bad thing (unlike so many episodes of *The Twilight Zone*, in which being alone means being in a nightmare of isolation); and in which the protagonist is always going to go again (recurrently, weekly) into the kitchen to perform accomplished acts and receive public accolades for them.

Here it's worth looking at the one unpredictability that does threaten to break into the comforting space of the kitchen set and risk disrupting its confident hold on the future: the figure of the unexpected guest. One recurrent narrative twist or trope in American popular culture of the 1950s and 1960s is the last-minute invitation made to the boss by a man who then alerts his wife that she must make a wonderful meal to land a desired promotion, and sometimes *The French Chef* picks up on this. No doubt, in the age of what Vance Packard in 1959 termed the "status-seekers," real-life fates were decided in such a fashion, but the narrative conceit is so widespread that it takes on the aura of mythology. (The TV show *Bewitched* carried this to an extreme in the 1960s with endless scenes of Darren bringing the boss, Larry, home, and Samantha having to renege on her promise not to use magic to generate a wonderful meal.) As fanciful as the trope is, its persistence seems to say something about the real precariousness of work in the postwar world. Again, as *The Twilight Zone* hints in its own allegorical way, everything can be taken away from you in capricious fashion.

The idea that a boss might fire you if your wife serves a bad meal suggests that the kitchen also was freighted with more anxiety than the feminine mystique of the kitchen as an inconsequential piece of domesticity might suggest. In *Something from the Table: Reinventing Dinner in 1950s America*, Laura Shapiro delineates the trappings of what she trenchantly terms "the literature of domestic chaos," in which housewives frantically try to keep the domestic sphere in operation while juggling multiple tasks and dealing with the varied demands of diverse family members. If one pulls this off, there is great reward (and great comedy along the way whether one pulls it off or not). Child described success with the drop-in guest in episode 133, "Piperade for Lunch," this way: "Very attractive lunch, I think, could very well serve it to boss's wife or boss himself. While he is finishing his aperitif, you pop eggs into oven. And if you serve him sparkling wine with the dessert, you deserve that raise." Numerous episodes of *The French Chef* play on the trope of the last-minute guest and then suggest how one can confidently prepare—and, more important, triumph over—that eventuality. The most striking, because it is the most theatrically set up and dramatically played out, occurs in episode 75, "Ham Dinner." The narrative begins in the pre-credit sequence with Julia receiving a call from Paul (shown on-screen) to say that he will be arriving in a half-hour with two guests and would love it if she could prepare one of her elegant dinners—perhaps that ham feast of which he is so fond. She explains to the viewer that she had been planning to make ham anyway, and it will be easy to change the recipe to feed four people instead of two. (She also confides to the viewer that her trickery in pre-planning without Paul's knowledge, which is how she manages her kitchen, will make her seem like a genius in her husband's eyes.) Child then reiterates how she can meet the challenge of the unexpected guests by having fundamental elements always available in her kitchen. She talks about the usefulness of cards on which the plans for several meals can be written down and vaunts her confidence by displaying a timer that she set when Paul called and that ultimately shows her beating her deadline by thirty seconds. The world beyond the box of the kitchen impinges, then, with a disruptive threat, but it does so only to be contained and controlled by the mastering chef who has logic, reason, and a few well-seasoned tricks on her side.

At the same time, Julia Child's insistence on perseverance against the odds as a personal ethic perhaps might offer life lessons that could resonate with the openness of the 1960s to new ways of being. The genre reduction in the cooking show certainly implies disengagement from some of the things the social world means, but it can also involve a homing in on values that, by being emphasized to the exclusion of others, come to gain new interest, new salience, and new and compelling visibility and thereby foster new perceptions on which to build. By concentrating on the task at hand, for instance, the drama of the kitchen offers a can-do pragmatism that, clearly in Julia Child's case, could be empowering and potentially productive of new relations to the world at large. As one fan wrote to WGBH in 1965, "It is so great to see and hear about international things I have known about only through literature and plays."[12]

As noted, what Child offered was un-dogmatic instruction that was about empowering home cooks to learn enough fundamentals, to understand and agree with the logic behind them, that they could set out on their own. Basic knowledge, passed on by the caring instructor, could be built on in creative, expressive, and self-satisfying fashion. As Child put it—somewhat confusingly, perhaps—in a moment of "Introducing Charlotte Malakoff" that provides an overhead shot into a mixing bowl as she makes sponge-cake batter: "You see, this is a very simple system . . . and the thing, the reason that you look, probably that most people look at people cooking is, uh, to find out the method of doing things and once you've found out the method you can edit any recipes you see. In other words, don't take things literally, use your own, use your ingenuity once you've known the proper method of doing it." The framework imposed by the thirty-minute format might itself mimic the segmented rationality of instrumentalized work, but in Child's hands, the time constraints became a mere springboard for flights of creativity, delights of performative play, displays of ingenuity, and odes to self-directed and self-willed resilience and resourcefulness in the service of a creative cookery whose utility is that it adds taste, pleasure, fun, vibrant visuality, and so on to the workaday world.

As a revealing contrast to the cooking show with its particular blend of leisure and utility, take, for instance, amateur radio, another typical leisure pursuit of the 1950s and 1960s that often seemed to the general public an odd way for grown men to pass their time.[13] True, radio gadgeteering contained traces of the American tradition of craftsmanship, which assumed that any kind of tinkering could have value if it built character and diligence. Like cooking, amateur radio was a homebound activity (except in the case of the station shared by men at their clubhouse) and, like cooking, it required know-how and revolved around tools and tricks of the trade.

But the activity's fit into suburban life was always a bit awkward and even fraught. Except in exceptional times (such as the emergency that required ham radio operators, as they were called, to step in to establish communication links), amateur radio was not necessarily a "social good." The ham often removed himself, or was banished (by his spouse), to a garage or basement or spare room or even a separate building out back—what the hams themselves termed "shacks," as if in recognition of the structures' inelegant misfit with shiny, streamlined suburbia. In the shack, away from family, the ham engaged in strange activities that, although they involved long-distance contact with other men, could seem infantile (why were grown men playing with gizmos?) or emasculating (why were these men spending time with gadgets and not with their loved ones?) or subversive (just what foreigners might a ham be talking to?). Not coincidentally, one of the characters in the famous *The Twilight Zone* episode "The Monsters Are Due on Maple Street" (1960) is a man who spends a lot of his time in the basement with his home-built radio and is suspected by his neighbors of being an alien who is trying to aid in the invasion of suburban America. The ham brought little benefit to those around him and created a space within suburbia that potentially was downright anti-domestic and antisocial. True, there was communication with other men, but it was all about jargon and technical detail—that is, nothing that mattered beyond a coterie of like-minded isolates.

Cooking instruction, in contrast, is all about the benefits. For this reason, it could be lauded as not just an idle pastime. The benefit to oneself could range from higher social status to pride in a job well done to, as was the case with Julia Child, gaining pleasure from the sheer fun that playing around (but in serious fashion) in the kitchen could provide. To others (such as family and guests), the benefits might range from better nutrition to food that offered new qualities of taste and, perhaps, even a glimpse of exoticism through gastronomic contact with other cultures and ways of life.

The cook might appear to be alone in the kitchen, but the activity he or she engages in is at its best eminently social, and the cook is always thinking of the pleasure of those around him or her. It matters, as we've seen, that the set for *The French Chef* contained both a kitchen and a dining room, where Child ended each episode by miming for viewers the appetizing meal they could share vicariously with her. She is in a community, even if only symbolically. In contrast to the ham who goes off by himself to talk to faraway strangers about nothing socially consequential, the television cook feigns being alone (as Child famously said to the viewer when she dropped a potato pancake on the counter, then put it back in the pan, "You're alone in the kitchen—who's going to see?") but, in fact, speaks usefully to others and makes wondrous offerings (if only vicariously) to them. The ham engages in a sort of meaningless chitchat that stereotypically has been assigned to the province of women, while the TV cook makes every bit of patter seem useful because it is in the service of higher ends (gustatory pleasure in Child's case and in that of her viewers).

To be sure, postwar cooking could frequently seem to be a form of social entrapment, when, for example, it was about status and thereby served as a form of seeming leisure paradoxically geared to the hard labor of inter-social success. Revealingly, the sociologist David Riesman offered the explosion of cookbooks and cooking crazes in the postwar period as one symptom of how Americans were becoming increasingly "outer-directed" and bowing to social pressure. As Ries- man saw it, an abundance of new and varied foodstuffs made it easy for Americans to be adventurous with their cooking, but it also increased the social pressures on them, because widespread availability of in- gredients meant that everyone had the same opportunities, and each would-be cook had to find a way to differentiate himself or herself. Hence, the claim to being "gourmets" among ever larger parts of the population; the attempts to find esoteric specialties in what one was whipping up in the home kitchen (known today as "signature dishes"); the seeking out of the exotic (which could include returning to re- gional, antiquarian cuisines as a reaction to modern mass-produced blandness); and the desperation that came from believing that the en- joyment of food had unflaggingly to be worked at (since others might see you as soulless if you didn't enjoy gourmet cuisine, both its prepara- tion and its consumption). Riesman wrote, "As tossed salads and garlic, elaborate sauces, dishes en casserole, *Gourmet* magazine, wine and liqueurs, spread west from New York and east from San Francisco, as men take two-hour lunch periods and exhibit their taste in food and wine, as the personalized cookbook tends to replace the Boston School type—in all these signs of the times we see indications of the new [outer-directed] type of character."[14] Amusingly, Riesman compared the cookbook craze to that for sex manuals but noted a more matter- of-fact, instructional tone in the latter whereas the cookbooks were often overrun with sensual language. Both forms of instructional litera- ture, however, were about making instrumentalized people feel they could still stand out and could give meaning to what was essentially the routinization of everyday life.

Nonetheless, for all its standardization of the drive to success, gour- met cooking also supposed personal expression and the honing of indi- vidual talent. The ideological message of this socially driven gourmet cooking was not unambiguously about making cooks slaves to the kitchen. The kitchen could offer the promise of a site in which socially ambitious cooks could resist the standardization and outer-directed- ness that convenience foods implied and discover their own ways to be creative, even artistic.

The Twilight Zone and other paranoid narratives reveal conservative

Julia Child's kitchen at the Smithsonian Institution

worries about sudden change and immersion in unexpected circumstances. *The French Chef*, by contrast, is all about the salutary resonances that new worlds of cooking and eating and enjoying can bring to one's life (and the lives of others who are transported to new realms by one's culinary success). In the context of the 1960s, when so much was about being new and different and up to date, Child's show offered a temporality that was as oriented toward the future as toward the past. It was, for instance, about going beyond a stultified American cookery into new realms of pleasure. Part of her talent lay in making the new and the unknown not threatening but inviting and desirable. Like, say, space-voyage science fiction, whose investment in new life worlds comes with imaginings of new social practices, new tools, new material objects, and so on, Julia Child's kitchen was one in which new foodstuffs, new gadgets, new flavors, and even new social practices were brought to the consciousness of everyday Americans. And they were introduced by a figure who could seem to embody and offer the image of difference: a woman taking over the realm of French cuisine and making it available and accessible to ordinary Americans.

In conclusion, I will turn one last time to "Introducing Charlotte Malakoff." Predictably perhaps, nothing of the turbulent times of the 1960s seeps into the boxed-in world that the kitchen set on *The French Chef* constructs. And it's perhaps silly to have imagined that world history ever could have broken into that special place (although, as we've seen, some episodes do contain joking references to beatniks and recalcitrant children). Yet even without direct political representation, *The French Chef* is so much of its times. "Introducing Charlotte Malakoff," for instance, contains

—Suspicion about mass-production (homemade is to be preferred to store-bought whenever possible) and the deleterious effects commercial plugging can have on pedagogical integrity (even the brand name on common salt is covered up).

—An attempt to promote manual arts while coming to grips with new technology. A few years later, Kubrick's *2001* would trace human history from the holding of the first prosthetic tools to the computer and beyond.

—An avant-gardist fascination with the look of unfolding temporality (a mixer that whirs on and on and a hand whisk that beats on and on) and with moments of purely vibrant spectacle (a cloud of sugar that explodes out of the mixing bowl). A few years later, Michelangelo Antonioni's film *Zabriskie Point* (1970) would imagine the end of middle-class commodification as endless, psychedelic, slow-motion explosions that blow everyday products into powdery nonexistence.

—A challenge to conventional gender roles and expectations (a woman doing hefty work and playing with gizmos), as well as a challenge to conventional *television* wisdom about gender (a woman who was neither a young beauty nor a homey maternal figure but a wild and somewhat unruly figure who fit into no easy classification and yet was worthy of celebrity).

—A promotion of acts of doing that involved choice rather than slavish obedience to dogma (the alternatives of spooned-out dough and dough from a pastry bag).

—An American can-do spirit that perseveres against all setbacks. "Never get upset," Child advised when she couldn't properly unmold the Charlotte.

—A boundless energy and enthusiasm (dramatized by the editing and camera movement that tried to keep up with Child and didn't always succeed at the task).

—An irreducibility of personality (that voice! that posture!). She was almost freaky in a decade that came to valorize the eccentric, weird, and wildly wacky.

—The cultivation of pleasures. When Child tasted her Charlotte's chocolate-and-liqueur filling, she swooned with delight.

—A generosity of spirit that wanted others to partake of its cheery can-do optimism and, most of all, an investment in the notion that all of this was about having fun. Even turning a tray of sticky dough upside down and seeing that it didn't fall off was "rather fun" for Child, and there is far from anything wrong with that.

The French Chef is not merely instructing in the ways of French cuisine, then. It is making a cultural argument that is not about cooking alone and that relies instead on recurring tropes and figures and narratives of suspense and resolution. Through its forward-moving temporality; its emphasis on the can-do physicality of the strapping figure of action; its concern with structure and planning, tempered by a boisterous investment in the sheer fun of effective performance; its faith that one can change tired conventions of everyday life and get others to share in it, *The French Chef* takes up an assertive position in its historical context and makes an argument for a particularly Americanized—and Americanizing—way of being in the world.

Notes

Chapter 1. The Difference She Made

1. A note on periodization: At various points in this study, I will either call Julia Child's historical moment the 1950s and 1960s (or just the 1960s when I want to emphasize how she may have fit in with the seeming new adventurousness of that decade) or refer to it more broadly (and perhaps riskily) as the "postwar" period. I know that "postwar" has its ambiguities (and covers a lot of ground), but I welcome that. I want to keep in mind how Child does very much seem to belong to an adults' culture of social entertaining and classy consumption rituals that seems typical of the 1950s. For example, it's appropriate that she would have a stiff drink (bourbon) after returning home from studio tapings of *The French Chef.* That habit (both the habitualness and the fact that she regularly drank hard liquor and not, say, wine) seems easily of a time in which adults regularly considered that the thing to do, whether alone or with company. But (and I'll return to this in chapter 6) it also seems appropriate that episodes of her show emphasized which *wine* to imbibe with this or that dish. Wine was about adding classy, Europeanized distinction to a meal, but, by the 1960s, it was also about opening America up to new taste sensations. A stiff drink might be the alcoholic beverage of choice for one's parents, but the youth generation preferred wine, and here (as in other ways, as we'll see constantly) Child straddled the decades and the generations. By blurring the postwar into the 1960s, I intend to catch some of Child's status as a liminal or transitional figure between worlds and ways of life.

2. This is as good a place as any to address what one might term "the question of naming." It is typical in writings on Julia Child, no matter how serious or scholarly, to call her "Julia," and the gesture is understandable. It intends to capture the sense of familiarity, of intimacy, of unpretentious authenticity that Child offered in her public persona. But the fan writing

thereby courts the temptation of assuming that a woman's accomplishments are less consequential than a man's and can be treated informally. For this reason, I will refer to her as "Child" (or "Julia Child" when distinguishing her from her husband, Paul).

3. Judith Jones, "The Story of 'Mastering' at Knopf," in Child et al., *Mastering the Art of French Cooking*, xvi.

4. The transformative taste moment for an American who samples French food for the first time is indeed common in the discourse. Take, for instance, the way in which food writer Melissa Clark frames her recipe for "pomegranate-rose cream meringues" within a tale of memory and epiphany:

> When I was young and studying in Paris I had a friend, Stéphanie, who helped demystify some of the more intimate aspects of French culture. A chic gamine, she taught me the delights of forthright flirting, the art of knotting a silk scarf just so and perhaps, most important, how to make a sublime dinner-party dessert in five minutes flat. . . . When I first saw the glass bowl filled with matte ivory flecks swirled into a snowdrift of cream dotted with scarlet raspberries, I was agog—even more so when I tasted it. The meringues melted on my tongue like sugary air, at first sharp and solid, then poof!, they were gone. . . . Like my semester in France, the dessert was magical, and very mysterious.

All of the standard motifs are here: the French as elegant in so many domains (from fashion to flirting to food), cooking as a social activity (the dinner party), the rendition of the comestible as a dreamy aesthetic entity (how often does anyone ever use the word "flecks" to refer to food?), and the ethereal and mysterious and magical nature of it all. Melissa Clark, "From Paris, with Hustle," *New York Times*, February 13, 2008, F3.

Julia Child offers this account of her own epiphany around a Dover sole in Rouen that "was perfectly browned in a sputtering butter sauce": "I closed my eyes and inhaled the rising perfume. Then I lifted a forkful of fish to my mouth, took a bite, and chewed slowly. The flesh of the sole was delicate, with a light but distinct taste of the ocean that blended with the browned butter. I chewed slowly and swallowed. It was a morsel of perfection." Child, *My Life in France*, 18.

5. Bracken, *The I Hate to Cook Book*.

6. Paddleford, *How America Eats*.

7. See Alexander and Harris, *Hometown Appetites*, xxiii.

8. Shapiro, *Julia Child*, ix.

9. Arendt, *Eichmann in Jerusalem*, 48.

10. For Amy Trubek, the distinctiveness of French cuisine has as much to do with the promotional activities of its practitioners as with its actual taste, and these include the very manner of spectacle by which the dishes are

supposed to be brought out from behind closed doors and then presented to an admiring public, whose appreciative members consequently become further proselytizers for food crafted in the glorious French manner: see Trubek, *Haute Cuisine*.

11. In this study, I talk about Julia Child as participating in an American pragmatism, and I would clarify that I am not referring at all to Pragmatism (with a capital "P")—that philosophical articulation of principles of activity that had its own base in Cambridge, Massachusetts. It is amusing, though, to note that William James's house in Cambridge is just a few doors down Ivy Street from the Childs' house, which itself was once the pragmatist Josiah Royce's abode. James's house bears a plaque from the Cambridge Historical Society, whereas the Childs' does not (at least at the time of my writing these lines), as if Julia Child did not matter to American history in any consequential fashion. In my own invocation of pragmatism, I mean to talk of an American celebration of physical action and bodily engagement as a concerted means of getting things done.

12. Shapiro, *Julia Child*.

13. *Knox On-Camera Recipes*, 1. I owe my encounter with *Knox On-Camera Recipes* to Jessamyn Neuhaus, who mentions it in *Manly Meals and Mom's Home Cooking*, 183, and offered further thoughts in e-mail correspondence with me.

14. There is now, for instance, a growing sub-literature in food and cultural studies on the significance of Jell-O in the Rosenberg spy case (the secret sign between spies was a Jell-O box cut in two). In most cases, the scholars argue that by resorting to a mass-marketed, shortcut product such as Jell-O, the Rosenbergs were seen by their critics as participating in kitsch values of their time and thereby betraying both the depths of their political commitment and their own ethnicity: see, e.g., Nathan Abrams, "'More than One Million Mothers Know It's the *Real* Thing': The Rosenbergs, Jell-O, Old-Fashioned Gefilte Fish, and 1950s America," in LeBesco and Naccarato, *Edible Ideologies*, 79–104.

15. In an insightful essay, Rebecca J. DeRoo analyzes comparable images—what she terms the iconography of the "serving hand"—from advertising and articles in women's magazines in France in the 1960s. In her words, "these women's hands—and by implication, their owners—were intended to represent the fulfillment available to women in domestic life. . . . These magazine ads make a direct appeal to the reader, emphasizing the positive effects of the product when used for the reader's own family. . . . To complement this advertising, the magazines often featured articles that emphasized housewives' skills again by using the convention of close-up images of

women's hands to demonstrate the series of steps involved in cooking a meal or completing odd jobs around the house": DeRoo, "Unhappily Ever After," 197–98. My thanks to Richard Neupert, who suggested that DeRoo's essay offers a useful parallel to my analysis of the Knox cookbook and thereby implies commonalities in the postwar selling of an ideology of women's domestic labor.

16. Child et al., *Mastering the Art of French Cooking*, 585. I do not want to underestimate the user-friendliness of *Mastering*. It is a very accessible book and written in a welcoming style; it's just that it's not presented as a personal account. The sociologist Richard Sennett offers a perceptive analysis of the qualities that make *Mastering the Art of French Cooking* an inviting entry into French cooking for the (relative) novice. Sennett finds the virtues of the volume to lie in such qualities as its recognition and admission of what is foreboding about the seemingly complicated process of French cooking (so that readers constantly are put at ease by seeing that problems have been anticipated, identified, and provided with remedies); its concomitant empathy for the reader/cook and what he or she needs to know (and probably doesn't already know) to bring a French recipe to fruition; and its recourse to loose analogy (for instance, cutting a chicken sinew is somewhat like cutting a string), with the analogical component enabling the reader to compare new experience with the already known and with the looseness allowing the reader to be ready for what will be different in the culinary process. As Sennett notes, many of these virtues are also on display in Child's television performances. For instance, when on one episode she holds her knife in the manner that experience has taught her is most effective for the tasks at hand, she takes time both to show and explain what she considers the right way and to demonstrate what is in fact wrong about the wrong way. In Sennett's words, "Practice has led her to that decision [about the right way of holding the knife]; the practice has given her confidence; she bones without hesitation. When we wish to instruct, however . . . we have to return emotionally just to the point before such habits were formed, in order to provide guidance. So for a moment Child will imagine holding the knife awkwardly. . . . This return to vulnerability is the sign of sympathy the instructor gives": Sennett, *The Craftsman*, 186.

17. See Child, *From Julia Child's Kitchen*, xv.

18. The letter, which I'll return to at greater length in chapter 4, is archived in folder 486 of the Julia Child Papers at the Arthur and Elizabeth Schlesinger Library on the History of Women in America, Radcliffe College, Cambridge, Mass.

19. Julia Child notes in folder 499, ibid.

20. The earliest episodes of *The French Chef* were shot in borrowed kitchens (for reasons I will clarify in chapter 4), and in some cases, there are moments in which the camera crosses into Child's space. In particular, the very first venue she used for the show had a long counter behind which, and parallel to which, there was the long back wall of the kitchen. Child stood between wall and counter while the primary of the two cameras used on the show (more about this in chapter 6) would be positioned in front and thereby offer a flat, laterally composed image of her against the wall. Perhaps because of the geometric drabness of this flat composition, the second camera would sometimes try to move away from a straight angle on the action, and this meant that in some cases the cameraman would be so adventurous as to pass behind the counter and film Child from the side (i.e., ninety degrees from the frontal view). The effect is dynamic, no doubt, but it also seems jarring and even weird as we suddenly see Child from an extremely different point of view—one, moreover, that seems to invade her intimate space rather than maintain cozy distance/proximity to it.

21. Perhaps it is a central talent of popular television that it catches personal mistakes but frequently makes of them a site of learning. The capacity of television for everyday revelation often has to do with its airing of ordinary foibles and failings as potential paths to learning. An academic friend of mine observes that he learned a lot about effective classroom method from watching David Letterman, who often turns a bad joke into a new joke on the joke— or, as my friend puts it, turns a *failed* joke into something successful, something that is effective with an audience.

22. Shapiro, *Julia Child*, 111–12.

23. Gelber, *Hobbies*, 278.

24. The food critic Gael Greene certainly saw it this way. "Everything I wrote [in her new job in 1968 as the food critic for *New York* magazine] would be feeding the fever of foodism, ultimately turning on susceptible taste buds to what would become a contagion, a cultural delirium. After all, this was the mind-bending sixties, a time of unbridled experimentation and flaunting the rules": Greene, *Insatiable*, 5.

25. See, e.g., John F. Kennedy, "The Vigor We Need," *Sports Illustrated*, vol. 17, July 1962, 12–15.

26. Scott Bukatman, "Brushstrokes in CinemaScope: Minnelli's Action Painting in *Lust for Life*," in McElhaney, *Vicente Minnelli*, 297–321.

27. Spigel, *Television by Design*, 45.

28. One exception is Shapiro's excellent biography, which devotes a chapter to the television work. More recently, Kathleen Collins has chronicled Child's place in the history of cooking shows: Collins, *Watching What We Eat*.

29. Powell, *Julie and Julia*.

30. On the denigration of gustatory taste in the Western intellectual tradition, see Korsmeyer, *Making Sense of Taste*.

31. Take a coincidental but revealing example. In the days I was writing these pages, I was reading for class preparation a book by that demanding philosopher Theodor Adorno, *Philosophy of New Music*, which he wrote to defend modern, experimental music while he was living in exile in an America that he saw as the extreme of kitsch cultural baseness. At one point, in a revealing phrase, Adorno contrasts the rigorous logic of serial music à la Schoenberg to a degraded mass music which, he claims, wallows in "culinary pleasure." That is, it is easily digested and its appeal is physical, not intellectual. The gustatory metaphor is offered in passing but it is precisely its thrown-off quality that is significant: Adorno can assume as given that the appeal to taste (rather than higher logic) is by nature vulgar; that culinary taste is below rigor and logic; and that the culinary is obviously a low and easy form of pleasure. The ready acceptance of commonplace denunciation of the culinary by this intellectualizer of higher things is little different than claims about popular culture's easy self-evidence by anti-intellectualists who assume that any attempt to analyze that culture is a betrayal or overkill of it.

32. Barthes, "The Myth Today," 152–53.

33. Sartre, *Search for a Method*, 56. It might be worth saying something here about my own methodology in this regard. Throughout the present study, I offer comparisons in passing of Child to other personalities and practices of the 1960s: for example, Jackie Kennedy, Jane Jacobs, James Bond, and so on. Of course, the results are for the reader to judge, but my intent is not at all to indulge in an eclecticism where historical elements are conjoined willy-nilly. To my mind, in attempting to explain how any one phenomenon (Julia Child, say) fits into its times, it is necessary to take into account other phenomena that those times likewise enabled—not so much to ask what does it say about the 1960s that the decade could give rise to Julia Child, but to ask what does it say about the period that it could give rise to Child *and* Jacobs and Bond and so on at the same time?

An apt example of such conjoining occurs in a study by Nancy Lutkehaus of how the anthropologist Margaret Mead became a key American cultural icon. Noting that Mead and the journalist Janet Flanner died within a week of each other, Lutkehaus mentions that one news correspondent, Paul Greenberg, wrote a single, combined death notice for the two women but then added Julia Child (who was still alive at the time) to the brew by saying that Mead had "handled abstract sociological theories like Julia Child working on a good slab of meat." Lutkehaus expands on the comparison, writing, "Greenberg's reference to Julia Child alluded to another quintessentially American woman who had also become an icon. . . . [A]ll three women represent the hard won achievements of independent, career-minded American women": Lutkehaus, *Margaret Mead*, 241. One could deepen the comparison and note how, as celebrities of the 1960s, Mead and Child became darlings of the new visual medium of television (where they benefited especially from the aura of cultural uplift that came from constant appearance on PBS); how their achievement of iconic status was confirmed by the extent to which cartoons in mass periodicals started to include allusions to them; how their increasing public authority meant that fans often would turn to them for general commentary and lifestyle advice beyond their original areas of specialization (thus, Mead was increasingly enlisted as a commentator on modern American mores, a role she readily welcomed and even cultivated, while Child served as a voice for liberal causes such as Planned Parenthood); and how their media fame made them objects not merely of veneration but, at times, of fans' pilgrimage. Thus, devotees would trek to the Museum of Natural History to seek out Mead as if it were a shrine, and acolytes still make ritual journeys to Child's house in Cambridge. Indeed, as an article in the *Boston Globe* amusingly recounts, the new owners of her house—who are self-professedly far from being foodies—have been besieged since the release of the film *Julie and Julia* by pilgrims who leave offerings such as sticks of butter: Billy Baker, "No Beef with Julia's Kitchen: Her Home's Current Owners Lack the Bone Appetite," *Boston Globe*, August 31, 2009, B1. All of this tells us something about the celebrity of strong-willed, cultured, and intellectually adept women from the 1960s.

Chapter 2. Television Cookery

1. One place you can glimpse footage of early television cooks is in anniversary promotional films made by this or that TV station to celebrate its history. Regarding scholarly works, above all, see Collins, *Watching What We Eat*, which appeared as I was finishing the research for this book. I have included further readings (selected bibliography) of the critical literature on the cooking show, including historical studies, at the end of the present volume. For one excellent scholarly analysis of an individual early cooking show that builds from oral history, see Williams, "Considering Monty Margett's *Cooking Corner*." A number of early television cooks published tie-in books linked to their shows: see, e.g., McCarthy, *Josie McCarthy's Favorite TV Recipes*. McCarthy had a popular cooking show on WRCA in New York City in the mid-1950s. In the latter part of the decade, she offered short demonstrations as part of Shari

Lewis's popular show *Hi Mom!*. One such presentation is available on *A Shari Lewis Christmas* (DVD, S'more Entertainment, 2008). An early and revealing mention of cooking shows comes in an enlightening reportage on viewing habits among early adopters of television for the home. Published in 1947 in the *New Yorker*, the piece sets out to describe what programming was available to these first, intrepid viewers and what they typically made of the viewing experience. The account is useful generally as a depiction of the early days of postwar television and includes several pages on a WNBT cooking program, *In the Kelvinator Kitchen*, which seems quite minimalist in its aesthetic indeed (much of it appears to involve still images of food with voice-over). See Robert Rice, "Diary of a Viewer," *New Yorker*, August 30, 1947, 44–55. The discussion of *In the Kelvinator Kitchen* appears on 51–52.

2. Pennell, *Women on TV*, 39.

3. Richardson and Callahan, *How to Write for Homemakers*, 134–36.

4. Ibid., 135.

5. Wartime programming in the hospitals is discussed in Baughman, *Same Time, Same Station*, 29–31.

6. Dupuy, *Television Show Business*, 74.

7. Anon., "Food Tips to Homemakers Televised," *Extension Service Review* 21 (April 1950), 59, 62–63.

8. McKeegan, "Techniques of Presenting Homemaking Television Programs."

9. Cassidy, *What Women Watched*, 27.

10. Copies of McNall's collation of recipes show up from time to time on eBay and other such websites.

11. "Second Helpings, Please," 6.

12. "The Mayberry Chef," a 1968 episode of *The Andy Griffith Show*, literalizes the idea of the auntie-as-television-cook. In the episode, Aunt Bee (played by Frances Bavier) is chosen, on the reputation of her wondrous home meals, to be the host of a homey cooking show, and Andy and his son, Opie (Ron Howard), try to make do with Andy's dismal attempts to provide dinner while Bee is off at the evening show's live shoots. Eventually, Bee decides that caring for her family is more important than a public career and returns home. The episode seems to merge the image of the warm, intimate, auntie-cook with something of Julia Child (as even the episode title suggests). Bee has a warbling voice somewhat like Child's, and she makes on-air mistakes that end up being endearing to the viewing audience and seem a proof of her authenticity.

It is perhaps also worth noting how, in the 1970s, *The Mary Tyler Moore Show* deconstructed the benign image of the caring auntie, homemaker TV instructor through the character of Sue Ann Nivens (played by Betty White), an acerbic, husband-stealing, self-centered shrew.

13. Endrijonas, "No Experience Required," 23.

14. Birkby, *Neighboring on the Air*. Broadcasting from Sheridan, Iowa, KMA was founded in 1925 by the owner of the local feed-and-supply store as a way to promote his wares. The link from radio to television cooking pedagogy in the 1950s was, on at least one occasion, direct. Bettie Tolson hosted a demonstration about Swedish Christmas sweets by KMA's radio homemaker, Florence Falk. For a photo of Falk's appearance in Tolson's studio kitchen, see ibid., 215.

15. This structure is described in Pennell, *Women on TV*, 99.

16. For background on the sponsors' impact on daytime programming, see Stole, "Televised Consumption."

17. One kinescope survives of a cooking demonstration by Edith Green. It was donated to the Cinema Studies Department at New York University by Green's son Don, who shared useful recollections of his mother with me. For background on Green, see Wooden, "Edith Green," and for background on the nature of commercial television in San Francisco in the early days when Green's show aired, see Eliassen, "Cooking on Air."

18. Green with Bayer, *Kitchen Strategy*.

19. Kaufman, *Cooking with the Experts*.

20. Kaufman, *Cooking with the Experts*, unpaginated gallery.

21. Ibid.

22. There's a profile of Guy and comments by her on cooking on television in Pennell, *Women on TV*, 91–92. The Film and Television Archive at the University of California, Los Angeles (UCLA), possesses an episode of *Cooking with Corris* from 1969 in which she does multiple plugs for Helms Bakery, including showing off Helms cakes and breads to go along with the tagliarini recipe she is cooking.

23. Marsha Cassidy, who researched *The Kate Smith Hour* for *What Women Watched*, graciously shared her description of one cooking demonstration, in this case with the actor Arthur Lake, who was well known for playing Dagwood Bumstead in Columbia's film adaptations of the comic strip. Smith presented Lake and his spouse, Pat, and the couple went to a kitchen set, introduced by a dissolve. Arthur tried to make one of his famous oversize Dagwood sandwiches, but Pat deemed it a "monstrosity." It was indeed so large that Arthur had to tie it together with spaghetti. Meanwhile, neighborhood dogs were eyeing the concoction and eventually stole it as Arthur/Dagwood cried at the misery of it all. The scene dissolved back to Kate Smith, who laughed deeply at the outcome, applauded the dogs, and

thanked the Lakes for appearing on her show. For Cassidy's overall study of *The Kate Smith Hour*, see Cassidy, *What Women Watched*, 49–74. See also Inger L. Stole, "*The Kate Smith Hour* and the Struggle for Control of Television Programming in the Early 1950s."

24. For Barbara Angell's *What's Cooking?*, see the entry at "Yesterday's KPTV," website, available online at http://kptv.home.comcast.net/~kptv/Shows/cooking.htm (accessed November 6, 2010). This site usefully provides many photographs of Angell in the studio kitchen and thereby confirms the typicality of the standard setup: woman at counter with kitchen behind her as cameras catch her demonstrations.

25. I offer more detailed analysis of the television work of this important gastronome in "James Beard's Early TV Work."

26. The surviving episode of *Chef Milani*, along with a later one in which another cook takes his place while Milani is on vacation, is housed at the UCLA Film and Television Archives. For contemporary accounts of the series, see Ray Kovitz, "When It Comes to Food, Chef Milani Cooks It, Talks about It, Sells It—All Successfully," *Los Angeles Times*, August 29, 1952, 22; Bob Work, "Chef Milani Lives by His Stomach and the Recipe Pays Off in TV Fans," *Los Angeles Times*, August 9, 1959, G4. There is also a wealth of Milani lore at the website of a collector, available online at http://www.weddingspinster.com/Chef_Milani.html (accessed November 6, 2010).

27. "Doucette Returning as TV Chef on WNBQ," *Chicago Daily Tribune*, August 22, 1954, A10.

28. A bit of footage of Zelayeta with Billy is available at http://diva.sfsu.edu/collections/sfbatv/bundles/189406 (accessed November 6, 2010).

29. Quoted in Kay Houston, "Jessie DeBoth and the Detroit News Cooking School," *Detroit News* (on-line version), May 20, 2000, http://apps.detnews.com/apps/history/index.php?id=93 (accessed November 6, 2010).

30. Jessie De Both, Kate Smith, and Julia Child were all brash, bold female performers who employed their seemingly awkward size to perfect and project larger-than-life personalities. (One could add Ethel Merman and Martha Raye to the list of iconic, energetic women of the 1950s.) Julia Child may have had Pasadena wealth behind her, and she may have put it in the service of a French cuisine, which is often considered too upper crust, but she also emerged from an earthy, bawdy tradition of big-boned women who use their very embodiment in the assertion of potentially undignified, un-dainty, assertive self-identity. The unwieldy bigness of person and personality were no small part of her appeal. Take, as a point of contrast, Jeanne Carroll, the TV and stand-up comedienne of the 1950s who passed away while I was finishing this manuscript. As her obituary notes, although Carroll paved the way for

later female comediennes such as Lily Tomlin and Joan Rivers, her beauty and classical elegance seemed surprising in stand-up, where female comics more often were expected to be misfits in some way: "When Ms. Carroll came to prominence, no woman was expected to sustain a comedy act by herself . . . nor was she supposed to be hugely attractive: the combination of feminine wit and beauty seemed too potent a cocktail to foist on the American public." *New York Times*, January 2, 2010.

31. Rico, *Kovacsland*. I thank Diana Rico for sharing further thoughts in e-mail correspondence with me.

32. As *How to Write for Homemakers* had already put it in 1949, "You might use a man as a 'stooge,' but use an intelligent one": Richardson and Callahan, *How to Write for Homemakers*, 135.

33. Quoted in Rico, *Kovacsland*, 74.

34. Today, on the Internet, one can find examples from later in his career of Kovacs's antic parodying of cooking. Two clips show his performance as the Hungarian "Chef Molnar," one of the many characters he created for national television. One clip is a mere fragment, a demonstration of un-bridled anarchy in which Chef Molnar, accompanied by a pretty assistant, tries to hack a piece of frozen meat with a cleaver, only to have the tool break in his hands, which then leads him to use the meat like a baseball bat to smash fresh eggs all over the room (and all over the assistant, who, appearing not to be acting, implores him to stop). The clip currently is available on YouTube at http://www.youtube.com/watch?v=-8ZnSjoWACs (accessed November 6, 2010).

In the other, longer clip, Chef Molnar makes what he terms "Chicken Molnar," which entails stuffing one caper inside one olive inside one kielbasa sausage inside one chicken, over which he pours scotch, bourbon, rye, and wine, only to then toss away the chicken and drink the alcoholic sauce. The clip shows a sharp awareness of the conventions of the cooking show. There is, for instance, a re-creation of the standard diagonal composition of some cooking shows, with Molnar posed toward the corner of the kitchen as the main camera faces him straight on and a second camera giving closeups of his manual activities on the various foodstuffs. But in this case, the walls behind Chef Molnar are a quite evident rear projection, which makes the kitchen space seem flat and unreal. There is also a moment that presciently antici-pates Julia Child's admission that it's OK to make a mess in the kitchen, since no one is there to see your mistakes. Chef Molnar says that a recipe calls for a "fresh carrot," but the one he picks up is wilted and floppy, and he offers the consolation, "It's only television. Nobody cares." Finally, in recognition of demonstration television's liveness, the clip has the floor manager, headphones over his ears, come onto the set to tell Chef Molnar they're running out of time and need to speed things up, only to back away in dismay when he gets a whiff of the whole clove of garlic Chef Molnar has just masticated. See http://www.youtube.com/watch?v=zc7UdCrJRKI (accessed November 6, 2010).

35. See the profile on Hanford at the "Broadcast Pioneers of Philadelphia" website, available online at http://www.broadcastpioneers.com/tvkitchen .html (accessed November 6, 2010). All of the quotes and information in this paragraph derive from that website. A clip from 1956 of Hanford demonstrating how to make a chocolate pie is currently available online at http://www .youtube.com/watch?v=pdUvy4cfE8k (accessed November 6, 2010).

36. Perhaps one shouldn't insist too much on the use of standardized products in Hanford's case. At least one fan, the children's writer Jill Wolfson, offers a remembrance on her blog that emphasizes Hanford's concern for home-spun authenticity:

> There were many Wednesdays when I faked being sick so I could stay home from school, blanket to my chin, cup of tea on my nightstand, to watch Florence Hanford's TV Kitchen. It was one of the nation's first cooking shows. There was something so comfortably Philadelphia and still so otherworldly about Florence P. Hanford—her tightly-controlled hair—no strand ever getting into the food—and constant fast patter, her seriousness about the perfectibility of a meal. And the dishes she created! It wasn't that my mother was a bad cook; she was just such a predictable cook. Chicken, always broiled, on Mondays. Spaghetti and meatballs on Tuesdays, etc. Mom was also "modern" in that early 1960s sense, meaning that so many of her ingredients came out of cans and the freezer. Not Florence! Chatting away with her viewers, Florence diced and stuffed and chopped and mixed and whipped and poured and rolled and used so many fabulous utensils that I never knew existed—lemon juicers and garlic presses and wire whisks. I practically swooned over her rubber spatula, the slurping, sloshing sound it made while moving viscous cake batter out of the metal bowl into the cake pan—a pan that had already been buttered by Florence's confident and efficient hands. (See http://jillinsantacruz.blogspot .com/2007/01/cooking-with-florence-and-isa-and-terry.html [accessed November 6, 2010]. I also thank Wolfson for e-mail conversations about Florence Hanford.)

37. For a profile of Mary Wilson, see "Head in the Clouds," TV Radio, July 1955, 8.

38. For contemporaneous accounts of Lucas's television work, see "Airborne Recipes," Time, vol. 51, no. 23, June 7, 1948, 61–62; and "Cooking for the Camera," Time, vol. 65, no. 22, May 30, 1955, 69. Several episodes of

Lucas's culinary television efforts of the 1950s survive at the Arthur and Elizabeth Schlesinger Library on the History of Women, Radcliffe College, Cambridge, Mass. Kathleen Collins finds perfect language to describe Lucas's schoolmarmish televisual style (*Watching What We Eat*, 46–59).

39. "Television Reviews," *Variety*, March 3, 1948, 35.

40. Berry, "The Dione Lucas Cooking Show." For another look back at Lucas, see Jane Salzfass Freiman, "Before Julia, There Was This Great, Unheralded Teacher," *Chicago Tribune*, October 8, 1979, E1.

41. Levenstein, "The American Response to Italian Food."

Chapter 3. French Cuisine, American Style

1. For a sharp and concise history of the beginnings of the CIA, see Andrew F. Smith, "Frances Roth and Katharine Angell's CIA," in *Eating History*, 211–16. More broadly, see Ryan, "The Culinary Institute of America."

2. Kuh, *The Last Days of Haute Cuisine*. See also, e.g., Levenstein, "Two Hundred Years of French Food in America." For contrast, see Levenstein, "The American Response to Italian Food," which argues that Italian food in America was often seen as lowly, urban fare for immigrants and not a cuisine of uplift and distinction.

3. Of course, in this ideological battle over value systems, the reverse of affluence could also be held up as a virtue. There were critiques of American abundance as leading to a sedentary or slothful wastefulness, individualistic excess, and general decadence. The image of affluence would need to be tempered by the sense that such richness be gained by hard work and, to a large degree, be maintained by hard work. A specifically American tradition of can-do pragmatism contributed to the image of the American lifestyle as something to be labored at rather than luxuriated in slothfully. In this respect, for all her invocation of pleasure, Child stood also for pragmatism and appreciation of applied, diligent effort. There would be fun, but there would also be sweat and effort, and this was key to what being in the kitchen was all about.

4. The anticommunist liberal Arthur Schlesinger spoke of liberalism as taking up a necessary position in what he termed the "vital center" of American life. In the center, one eschewed all extremism while allowing rational discourse across the political spectrum to find an auspicious meeting ground where mannered dialogue and debate and discussion might take place. Schlesinger, *The Vital Center*. Metaphorically, one might suggest, the goal of the perfect postwar host or hostess was to constitute himself or herself as a "vital center," providing guests of all stripes with the sense that their opinions mattered and that their needs, as long as they were not excessive, would

gently and liberally be met. As Letitia Baldridge, Jackie Kennedy's secretary, put it in a book about the lifestyle at the White House in the 1960s, "My great wish is that our readers will receive from her [Jackie's] example a dose of inspiration and start entertaining at home. . . . A host helps cheer up those who sit around her table. A host disseminates information and happy gossip, finds solutions to problems, gives everyone many opportunities to laugh or at least smile, and creates a setting where new relationships can evolve into lasting friendships." See Baldridge with Verdon, *In the Kennedy Style*, 139. Verdon was the famed Frenchman who served as White House chef.

5. For structural analysis of spying, see, e.g., Umberto Eco, "Narrative Structure in Fleming," in Eco and del Buono, *The Bond Affair*; and Roland Barthes, "Introduction to the Structural Analysis of Narrative." Barthes uses *Goldfinger* as the example on which to build a theory of narrative and narration. For a concise structural analysis of cooking, see A. J. Greimas, "Basil Soup, or the Construction of an Object of Value," in Perron and Collins, *Paris School Semiotics*, 1–12.

6. "In Ian Fleming's fictional world, Britain was on equal terms economically and politically with the United States, and food was an unlimited pleasure": Biddulph, " 'Bond Was Not a Gourmet,' " 132.

7. A few years earlier, in 1958, *Playboy* magazine had offered its own cosmopolitan men's pedagogy into the differences between red and white wine in an article that, combining sexual and gustatory prowess, mixed advice on wine with photos of seminude red-headed and blonde women: cited in Fraterrigo, *Playboy and the Making of the Good Life in Modern America*, 65.

8. One of the most extreme figurations of 1960s spying as an activity of intrusion or insertion into an alien or foreign territory is the film *Fantastic Voyage* (1966). In it, miniaturized scientists and secret agents from both sides of the Cold War go inside a man's body and fight out his fate. Here the idea that spying is a bodily immersion into the corporeality of the other is directly literalized.

9. Letter from Child to WGBH program manager, Bob Larsen, December 18, 1962, *French Chef* archival files, WGBH, Boston.

10. For a demonstration of the centrality of narratives of spying to television in the 1950s and 1960s, see Kackman, *Citizen Spy*.

11. Spigel, *Make Room for TV*.

12. Laura Shapiro recounts that the pancake incident "became legendary and then apocryphal. . . . Julia dropped a chicken, Julia dropped two chickens, she dropped a turkey, a twenty-five pound turkey, a pig, a duck, and in each case blithely return[ed] them to their platters—all fantasies, but people recalled them joyfully." The legend—both the fact of the original event and then

its expansion into endless new versions—becomes legendary itself, so that the retelling generates further tales. This impulse to offer more and more stories about Julia Child is another mark of her larger-than-life impact within her culture: Shapiro, *Julia Child*, 119.

13. Sartre, *The Critique of Dialectical Reason*.

14. Hess and Hess, *The Taste of America*.

15. Fussell, *Masters of American Cookery*, 48.

16. This sort of translation of common fare into something more exotic through cosmetic touchups is doubly at work in an episode of *The French Chef* on paella (1966). On the one hand, Child justifies including the dish on a French cooking show by noting that it has been mastered by the French (and, as she notes in an aside, it's in France anyway that she first got a taste of paella at its best). On the other hand, she suggests that by putting mussels into the dish against the sunny backdrop of saffron-infused rice, one will be creating "lovely dark accents." Cooking here is the invention of a language, complete with basic phrases to which diacritical marks can be added.

17. In more complicated, even perhaps contradictory, fashion, the press release for episode 39, on cassoulet, asserts that it is nothing more than "the French version of that New England favorite—Boston Baked Beans." The script for the show promises: "I'm going to give it the full dress French treatment, no half measures or compromises." Here we witness the balancing act of the cultural translator or mediator in full force. On the one hand, there needs to be some degree of possible transformation between cultures; on the other hand, these cultures need also to maintain their separate identities. French food is somewhat like other cuisines but it still possesses something special and offers something privileged that thereby demands that one jump in and give it "full dress" treatment without shortcuts. Likewise, Child's instructions for a dish to impress guests, "Veal Prince Orloff" (from an episode in 1964), assert that haute cuisine is "just fancy cooking which takes longer to do than ordinary cooking," but she then declares that if one offers this dish, "that's immortality." Again, there's both nothing unique and something quite special about French cuisine, and it's the work of the mediator to enable the student cook to perch between those two possibilities at once.

18. Shapiro, *Something from the Oven*. For another take on the Friedan–Child coincidence, see Hollows, "The Feminist and the Cook."

19. At the same time, deliberately using convenience foods and shortcuts might also be an act of self-assertion in its own right if those ingredients were used to counter ideologies that assumed women should spend a lot of time in the kitchen, whether they wanted to or not. As a minimally demanding culinary activity conducted without deeper emotional engagement and without

aesthetic intent, the recourse to convenience foods might offer its own form of challenge to the feminine mystique that saw the kitchen as the prime site in which women should express their sentiment for their families through carefully crafted meals that were supposed to be labors of love. To *not* spend time cooking for one's family might be a betrayal of the mystique in the eyes of the mainstream, but to the woman who resorted to such shortcuts, it could have a hint of the deliberately subversive about it insofar as it entailed her preference for her own control of time over slavish duty and devotion. Think, for instance, of the advertisements typical of the period in which a husband extols his wife's cooking while she hides some package or can behind her back and accepts his compliment while winking at the spectator. She's managed the double-edged task of pleasing the family while saving time for herself. No doubt, as Laura Shapiro chronicles, such ads play to postwar industries' massive selling of mass convenience and commodification to women, but they also perhaps tap into a desire on the part of the women to give themselves some control over kitchen time. Maybe it's not creative to open a can, but it can be a crafty way to deal with the constraints of domestic labor (especially if one passes it off as in fact a creative act—for example, the industrially produced meal that tastes like it is homemade and deceives its consumers).

20. Maines, *Hedonizing Technologies*, 122.

21. Maines notes that fun activities can start to become de-hedonized when they begin to seem too demanding (of time, of resources such as money, and so on) and thus appear as a burdensome necessity. And in the case of French cuisine for middle-class Americans, we should remember that it was often not even fully "hedonized" in its initial guise. From the start, it served functions of social status and distinction, and this could be utilitarian in its own way. That *The French Chef* is all about getting French cooking into a half-hour format suggests that not everything was about taking one's time for one's personal pleasure and that pressures, social obligations, and realms of necessity were at work too.

22. Fussell, *My Kitchen Wars*, 159, 164.

23. Brown, *Sex and the Single Girl*. For analysis of the book within the cultural context of the 1960s, see Jennifer Scanlon's biography of Brown, *Bad Girls Go Everywhere*.

24. Ibid., 128.

25. To bring things full circle, the cookbook *Saucepans and the Single Girl* came out in 1965, with its title clearly punning on Brown's tome. A few years later, the cookbook led to two pilots for a proposed television series, also entitled *Saucepans and the Single Girl*, hosted by the perky Joann Pflug. The

show was not picked up as a series, but the pilot episodes survive in the UCLA Film and Television Archive and demonstrate the extent to which the series was envisioned as a hip and comic instruction in swingin' singles '60s lifestyles. In bellbottoms or miniskirts, brightly colored shirts, and multicolored aprons, Pflug energetically moves around her bachelorette pad to prepare captivating meals for men, accompanied by a bouncy bongo beat and a laugh track. In one episode, she makes a peanut butter spice cake for Tommy Smothers, who is taking her on a picnic date. (In what he terms her "groovy kitchen," he watches her cook and tells her he trained at the "Gordon Blue" Cooking School in Paris and the "Jack in the Box in Anaheim.") In the other episode, aided by Michele Lee, Pflug makes a curry for a millionaire she met while (deliberately) looking helpless in the "gourmet section of the supermarket," since that's a great way to meet exotic (and potentially rich) men. In an e-mail to me, Jinx [Kragen] Morgan, the co-author of *Saucepans*, shared her recollections on the book's relation to the show: "My husband at that time, Ken Kragen, was managing the Smothers Brothers and producing their first show, a situation comedy. [The *Saucepans* series] was directed at an audience of young working women who didn't know much about cooking. The recipes were simple and straightforward and the show had elements of a situation comedy (though without any real plot). The tone of the pilots was an attempt at the same lighthearted quality as the book, but it didn't follow it precisely."

26. Friedan, *The Feminine Mystique*, 67.

27. A seeming counter-example, but one that perhaps confirms the general rule, is the un–James Bond spy film *The Ipcress File* (1965), in which the secret agent Harry Palmer (played by Michael Caine) is preoccupied with fine foods. For example, the opening credits have him grinding his own coffee beans and using a French press to make espresso; a later, famous scene has him extolling the virtues of "champignons" to his boss, who evinces little appreciation for such things. Palmer's masterly preparation of an omelet contributes in no small measure to his successful seduction of a sultry spy (Sue Lloyd), who has herself been assigned to seduce him. But it is important that the film (and the series of novels by Len Deighton on which it is based) carefully delineate how Palmer's investment in gourmet cuisine derives from his anxious class status. Palmer is trying to rise from a working-class background into the ranks of those noteworthy British "scholarship boys" to whom the powers at the top allow *limited* social advantage and social mobility. Gastronomy, then, might look cool, but it is really a gambit to give one an air of sophistication, albeit a fraught one. For one analysis of the tactics of class mobility in the film and of the contribution of gastronomy to Palmer's quest for status, see Miller, *Spyscreen*, 115–21.

28. Quoted in Osgerby, "The Bachelor Pad as Cultural Icon," 104–5.

29. Editors of *Esquire*, *Esquire Party Book*, 127.

30. Hollows, "The Bachelor Dinner." On *Playboy*'s masculinization of cookery, see also Osgerby, *Playboys in Paradise*, 129–30.

31. Ibid., 150.

32. Letter from Julia Child, July 31, 1963, archived in folder 355 of the Julia Child Papers, Arthur and Elizabeth Schlesinger Library on the History of Women in America, Radcliffe College, Cambridge, Mass.

33. D. Smith, "Global Cinderella."

34. Kaplan, "Taste Wars," 161.

35. For the renovation of the White House interiors that she initiated in 1961, Jackie Kennedy had a French consultant, but the fact was downplayed to the public for fear of seeming un-American in what was being done to the building. Translation is one form for the mediation of cultures; so is a deliberate hiding of the impact of one culture behind the visibility of another, even as one takes inspiration from both. For the White House renovation and the ways it used Frenchness even while obscuring the fact of its influence, see Abbott and Rice, *Designing Camelot*.

36. Unsigned letter, folder 359, Julia Child Papers.

37. Ferguson, *Accounting for Taste*, 30, 33.

38. In passing, it might be worth noting that, even as they promote a conception of cookery as organic narrative in which each step melds together, cooking shows, including *The French Chef*, do generally minimize two stages in the process of food preparation, presumably because they run the risk of seeming less pleasurable. On the one hand, the activity of cleanup after consumption is rarely depicted—and indeed, off-screen assistants busily whisk dirty dishes and implements away during the course of the shoot so that there is no pile up of messiness. In recent cooking shows, this goes hand in hand with the ability of the celebrity cook, when female, to maintain the image of pristineness even when she has engaged in the supposedly besmirching work of cooking. The tight-fitting sweaters that today's sexy TV chefs dress in are about looking seductive but also about showing off the confidence of someone who is never sullied, never endangered by a de-glamorizing stainfulness. On the propensity of today's female celebrity chefs to wear v-neck or scoop-neck, tight, and cropped cashmere sweaters, see Elaine Louie, "Frump-Free Cooking: The Look That Sizzles," *New York Times*, June 27, 2007, F5, which quotes a creative director at Barney's saying that this look avoids the frumpiness or frowziness of Julia Child and Betty Crocker.

On the other hand, the prep work on the cooking show usually starts with all the elements assembled in the kitchen *and with the act of purchasing bracketed out* as if to minimize the potentially sullying reminder of economic exchange and necessity (all this good food would have to be paid for somehow). Some food shows may talk about ways to do things economically—Rachael Ray's series on dining out for less than $40 a day comes to mind—but without the money ever seeming to be a problem. (Ray usually is able to pull it off.) It is noteworthy that, in a sample episode of Giada de Laurentiis's *Everyday Italian*, we see her cruising the stands at the Santa Monica Farmer's Market and the aisles at a Whole Foods grocery store, making choices, and being handed her purchases, but the intermediate step of money being handed over is elided. For what it's worth, *Saucepans and the Single Girl* makes a joke about the availability of bounties of food and kitchen gadgets on cooking shows. Rushing to get things ready for her date with Tommy Smothers (who, we are told, will only eat dishes with peanut butter in them), Joann Pflug finds herself lucky when, with a quick cut, her empty kitchen counter is suddenly transformed into a space overflowing with bounties of food. "Just what every well-organized kitchen needs," she says happily and to the accompaniment of a laugh track: "Gremlins." The moment unveils the convention but still reminds the viewer that the television universe is a special one, where magic can be performed at little evident cost. Might this also be a comment on all those miracle-performing Jeannies and Samanthas who inhabited sitcom life in the 1960s and brought bounty (but also chaos) to domestic life?

39. Fussell, *My Kitchen Wars*, 159.

40. Ibid., 127.

41. Chamberlain, *Clémentine in the Kitchen*.

42. Hemingway, *A Moveable Feast*.

43. Jordi, "'Our Apprenticeship at the Art of Graceful Living.'"

44. Trubek, *Haute Cuisine*, 22.

45. See Macksey and Donato, *The Structuralist Controversy*. I should note that not all of the papers presented at the conference actually offered a canonical structuralist approach. Some, indeed, already manifested the signs of the post-structuralism that would become more widespread in the 1970s. Nevertheless, they were taken to be representative of that approach in their reception in the U.S. in the immediate period of 1966 and after.

For a general intellectual history of "French theory" as in many ways an American phenomenon, see Cusset, *French Theory*.

Chapter 4. Beginnings of *The French Chef*

1. Reardon, *M. F. K. Fisher, Julia Child, and Alice Waters*, 4.

2. Shapiro, *Julia Child*.

3. Julia Child, "About the Television Series," in *The French Chef Cookbook*, viii–xiii.

4. Quoted in Fitch, *Appetite for Life*, 4.

5. Beck makes an on-camera appearance in "The Spinach Twins," a color episode of *The French Chef*. In the kitchen of Child's vacation home in France, which was located on Beck's property in the countryside, Child and Beck prepare spinach turnovers. The sequence offers a relatively passive Child who basically watches Beck show off her expertise with French pastry dough. Child serves as the translator of culinary concepts into the American context, while Beck presents French methods through an appeal to tradition and procedures honed by legacies of experience. Beck even rebels at Child's suggestion that frozen dough can work as well and declares herself too "old-fashioned" to accept that.

6. All quotes in this paragraph from Hudgins, "A Conversation with Julia Child, Spring 1984," 106.

7. Craig Claiborne, "Cookbook Review: Glorious Recipes, Art of French Cooking Does Not Concede to American Tastes," *New York Times*, April 18, 1961, 47.

8. For the influential cover and accompanying article, see Marshall Burchard, "Everyone's in the Kitchen," *Time*, November 25, 1966, cover and 74–87.

9. The correspondence between Child and Avis DeVoto is rich in such descriptions of American television's power: see Joan Reardon, ed., *As Always Julia*.

10. Much of my account of Morash's involvement with *The French Chef* comes from an e-mail exchange and a long telephone interview he granted me. I thank Russell Morash for his graciousness in making himself available for scholarly research.

11. Letter from Helen Peters, November 21, 1966, archived in folder 486 of the Julia Child Papers, Arthur and Elizabeth Schlesinger Library on the History of Women in America, Radcliffe College, Cambridge, Mass.

12. Child, *From Julia Child's Kitchen*.

13. While some of the recipes in *The French Chef Cookbook* were adapted from *Mastering*, Child's lawyers negotiated for her to have full credit on the television tie-in book. (According to Noël Riley Fitch, they argued with Simca Beck that the explosion in sales of *Mastering* was due to Child's TV show and the publicity around it, such as the *Time* cover, and that it was therefore only reasonable to reward Child in this way.)

14. Folder 489 of the Julia Child Papers contains materials from Hills Brothers in regard to their sponsorship of *The French Chef*.

15. Memo from Ruth Lockwood, September 3, 1963, folder 262, Julia Child Papers.

16. Undated note in folder 486, Julia Child Papers.

17. Memo from Julia Child, April 29, 1964, in ibid.

18. Letter of October 26, 1965, in ibid.

19. The third season of *The French Chef* coincided with the release of the folksy comedy *Dear Brigitte*, with Jimmy Stewart, Bill Mumy, and Brigitte Bardot, in which an all-American family goes to Paris and the young son gets to realize his dream of meeting Bardot, on whom he has a crush. Films like this and the beguilingly named *Paris When It Sizzles* from the year before sold an idea of Paris as contributing to the perfection of a consumerist American lifestyle, even when specific products were not being hawked.

Chapter 5. Prepping *The French Chef*

1. Letter archived in *The French Chef* files, WGBH, Boston.

2. Letter in folder 496 of the Julia Child Papers, archived at the Arthur and Elizabeth Schlesinger Library on the History of Women in America, Radcliffe College, Cambridge, Mass.

3. In fact, when the set was overhauled for the color version in the 1970s, even more of a sense of depth was added. While the counter for the set had been angled from the start to wrap around Child and avoid lateral flatness, the first backdrop for the overall scene had still essentially been flat and parallel to the playing field in front of the cameras. The set redesigned for the program in the 1970s had walls that angled away from the action to offer a visual field that moved ever more into the background. The effect of depth was augmented by a door that seemed to enhance the idea that countrified, open spaces lay beyond the enclosed set.

4. Memo from David Ives, September 1966, folder 486, Julia Child Papers.

5. Ibid.

6. Scripted promotion from February 1965 in Addendum Material 93-M178, Julia Child Papers.

7. Ives memo, May 10, 1966, folder 486, Julia Child Papers.

8. The invoice, now in the Child archives, has a note from Ruth Lockwood written on it adding $100 for "talent"—that is, for Child's salary as a performer on the episodes. Child, in fact, made little money from the original seasons of *The French Chef*, and she tended to give her salary back in the form of donations to public broadcasting. But she did make a sizable sum from her cookbooks, and the television series clearly contributed to the public's interest in buying those books.

9. For a profile of the volunteers, see Louise Logan Melton, "KP Can be Fun," *TV Guide*, June 17, 1972, 14–16.

10. Julia Child memo, November 1, 1963, folder 262, Julia Child Papers.

11. *I Love Lucy* is often talked about as having revolutionized the use of multicamera shooting for television, but its contribution to that mode of production was actually quite particular. There were shows before *Lucy* that used more than one camera to shoot a scene; the key innovation of *Lucy* was that its three cameras were not electronic television cameras but traditional film cameras, which not only gave a sharper picture but, more important, meant that all three were running simultaneously (rather than cutting back and forth as the shoot transpired), thereby offering full coverage of the duration of a scene from the three vantage points. Filming with multiple cameras enabled a capturing of comic performers' routines in live time before the studio audience and allowed their comic talents to play out sequentially for best effect. But the fact that all three cameras produced footage simultaneously throughout the entire shoot enabled the film editor *in the post-production moment* to assemble the episode from three temporally identical takes from three different spatial perspectives. Unlike cinema, *I Love Lucy* didn't require new setups for each shot within a scene because the three cameras offered a mix of angles and distances on the scene, and their footage could then be edited to create visual diversity. Like cinema, though, *I Love Lucy* had its final product (the edited episode) built up in post-production from, in this case, all the footage that the three cameras had shot simultaneously. In contrast, *The French Chef* was shot with television cameras, each of which would shoot the action only when the director chose to switch to it. Editing, then, was done in the moment of shooting, not after.

12. In other words, to continue the comparison, if *I Love Lucy* differed from *The French Chef* in providing full, simultaneous footage from *each* of its cameras for the entirety of a scene, the shows nonetheless were similar in that they employed a multicamera shooting method that required them both to use bright, even lighting across the set.

13. See Arthur E. Fetridge, "Gourmet Cook Fascinates Her Channel 2 Audience," *Boston Sunday Herald*, March 26, 1963, n.p.

14. Elizabeth L. Sullivan, "TV Cooking Lessons," *Boston Sunday Globe*, February 10, 1963, 12.

15. Fan letter of February 2, 1966, folder 358, Julia Child Papers.

16. Cleveland Amory, "*The French Chef* (Review)," *TV Guide*, March 30, 1968, 20. As Scott Bukatman put it in an e-mail to me, "I think the history of television is to a large extent determined by people who can actually talk to a

camera as though to a viewer—Carson and Letterman, Paar, and others. Child is part of a grand history here."

17. Niki Strange, "Perform, Educate, Entertain: Ingredients of the Cookery Programme Genre," in Geraghty and Lusted, *The Television Studies Book*, 305.

18. Ibid.

19. Bonner, "Representations of the Female Cook," 66.

20. In his study of the playboy lifestyle of the 1950s and 1960s, Bill Osgerby notes that publications such as *Playboy* not only were full of instructions for men on how to cook in gourmet style but also were aware that this could seem effeminate if not tempered in some fashion. One solution was to promote haute cuisine as a realm in which men might outshine women, because to do it well, one needed to master a complicated lore (men as more intellectual than women) and wield complicated technology (men as more gadget-oriented than women). "Men could confidently plunge into the specialized knowledge and sense of performance associated with the gourmet. . . . With a solidly 'masculine' range of implements at his disposal, there could be no doubting the manliness of the playboy chef. . . . A combination of manful expertise and 'man-sized gear,' therefore, guaranteed the virile attributes of the bachelor gourmet": Osgerby, *Playboys in Paradise*, 130. In this respect, Child upset clear gender boundaries by doing what men were supposed uniquely to be good at. Her shows were all about background explanation and gadgetry, and they eschewed intuition, dainty avoidance of manual activity, fear of technology, and so on.

21. Fitch, *Appetite for Life*, 5.

Chapter 6. Success of *The French Chef*

1. Letter from Julia Child, September 15, 1967, archived in folder 360 of the Julia Child Papers, Arthur and Elizabeth Schlesinger Library on the History of Women in America, Radcliffe College, Cambridge, Mass.

2. Letter from Dorothea Belida, 1965, folder 357, Julia Child Papers.

3. Memo in *French Chef* files, WGBH, Boston.

4. Fan letter from Irene McHogue, 1962, folder 353, Julia Child Papers.

5. Fan letter from Lowell Manfull, October 24, 1966, folder 358, Julia Child Papers.

6. The story originated in Lewis Lapham, "Everyone's in the Kitchen with Julia," *Saturday Evening Post*, August 8–15, 1964, 20. It was then repeated ad infinitum in other profiles of Child.

7. *French Chef* papers, folder 7, National Public Broadcasting Archives, University of Maryland, College Park, Md.

8. Lenny Lipton, "Lamb Scores Again," *Berkeley Barb*, August 26, 1966. I found this clipping without page numbers in the Julia Child Papers.

9. Sontag, "Notes on 'Camp.'" Not all proponents of the avant-garde might find the kitchen to be a site of empowering, adventurous play. In 1975, for instance, the artist Martha Rosler made a short video, *Semiotics of the Kitchen*, in which, in her description, an "anti–Julia Child replaces the domesticated 'meaning' of kitchen tools with a lexicon of rage and frustration." Set in a domestic kitchen and filmed from one camera position, the video depicts a woman in an apron (Rosler) who holds up kitchen utensils in alphabetical order and manipulates them with violence and repetitive gestures. The relation of the woman to the kitchen here is about monotony but also repressed anger that progressively creeps out. For one analysis of the relation of Rosler's video to the genre of the television cooking show, see Brunsdon, "Feminism, Postfeminism, Martha, Martha, and Nigella."

10. Taber, *Judgment of Paris*.

11. For early Chez Panisse as an expression of the times, see MacNamee, *Alice Waters and Chez Panisse*.

12. Fan letter from Jane Cutler, October 18, 1967, folder 359, Julia Child Papers.

13. "From Motion to Mobilism: Twenty Years of Travel, 1947–1967," *Saturday Review*, vol. 50, no. 60, April 22, 1967, 48–49.

14. Terrence O'Flaherty, "The Watched Pot," *San Francisco Chronicle*, December 28, 1963, 77.

15. Craig Claiborne, "Order and Variety Mark Expert's Well-Equipped Kitchen," *New York Times*, March 5, 1964, 28.

16. For one typical example of the French response, see Elisabeth Bourquin, "Julia, prof' de cuisine française, laisse tomber une crêpe devant les téléspectateurs U.S.," *France Soir*, January 17–18, 1965, 5. The French ambivalence over Child continues to this day. Thus, after the release of the film *Julie and Julia*, with its many scenes of Child in Paris trying to master the art of French cooking, the *New York Times* surveyed figures in the French food scene, from journalists to bookstore owners to chefs, and found that most appreciated her attempt to render French cooking precisely and scientifically and lauded her desire to democratize what was often a mysterious and cliquish art. But they also thought she concentrated too much on the clichéd dishes of an overly formal French culinary past (such as boeuf bourguignon). In a backhanded appreciation that would have made Child cringe, the restaurateur Guy Savoy declared that she "explains her recipes like a housewife, but

she knows how to do it and she does it genuinely": Maia de la Baume, "A 'French Chef' Whose Appeal Doesn't Translate Well in France," *New York Times*, September 17, 2009, A6.

17. For an engaging history of public television and its development out of educational TV of the 1950s, see Robertson, *Televisionaries*, which offers extensive interviews with figures from the period. For a more critical view, see Ouellette, *Viewers Like You?*. My discussion in the next pages of *The French Chef* specifically in terms of the educational and public television contexts of the period draws on materials about the series in the PBS Archives, Library of American Broadcasting, University of Maryland, College Park, Md.

18. See, e.g., Percy Shain, "Dick Van Dyke, Bill Cosby, Julia Child Win TV Emmys," *Boston Globe*, May 23, 1966, 15.

19. For a basic history of WGBH, see Glick, "WGBH-TV."

20. Ouellette, *Viewers Like You?*, 54.

21. Ibid., 46–47.

22. On the recourse of the American corporate elite to television as a propitious form for everyday instruction in modern citizenship (including consumer citizenship), see A. McCarthy, *The Citizen Machine*.

23. Spigel, *Television by Design*, 160, 163.

24. Ouellette, *Viewers Like You?*, 49.

25. *French Chef* papers, folder 8, National Public Broadcasting Archives.

26. Ibid.

27. Ibid.

28. *French Chef* papers, WGBH, Boston.

29. Dave Davis to Ruth Lockwood, January 24, 1967, folder 491, Julia Child Papers.

30. From folder 499, Julia Child Papers.

31. Ibid.

Chapter 7. New Beginnings and the Ending

1. Dave Davis memo, March 15, 1967, archived in folder 262 of the Julia Child Papers, Arthur and Elizabeth Schlesinger Library on the History of Women in America, Radcliffe College, Cambridge, Mass.

2. See Westman, *The Beard and the Braid*.

3. For one depiction of folk culture in Cambridge in the period, see, among others, Hadju, *Positively 4th Street*, 16–27.

4. Letter from Hartford Gunn to Julia Child, June 14, 1967, folder 493, Julia Child Papers.

5. Concerted efforts had been made to develop commercially viable color

processes in the 1950s, but, as Lynn Spigel notes, "The color boom did not take place until after the 1966–67 [television] season": Spigel, *Television by Design*, 345, n. 7. Interestingly, some advertisers (food companies such as Kraft especially) shot commercials in color in the 1950s even though there was little way to watch them in that fashion. For the advertisers, it was important to be able to imagine and project their products as dynamically colorful, even if that desire remained a mere fanciful projection into the future.

6. Shapiro, *Julia Child*, 125.

7. Letter from Julia Child to Ruth Lockwood, June 24, 1971, folder 262, Julia Child Papers.

8. WGBH publicity material, folder 493, Julia Child Papers.

9. For one analysis, see the chapter "The Dollar Challenge," in Endy, *Cold War Holidays*. As Endy notes, many American Francophiles (and Child would certainly count in this camp) vociferously resisted Johnson's entreaties.

10. Script for a promo for captioned episodes of *The French Chef*, March 16, 1972, folder 496, Julia Child Papers.

11. Letter from Julia Child to Ruth Lockwood, May 1974, folder 500, Julia Child Papers.

12. Letter to Ruth Lockwood, June 1, 1974, *French Chef* papers at WGBH, Boston.

13. Letter to Hartford Gunn, October 21, 1975, in ibid.

Chapter 8. Kitchen Drama

1. Fredric Jameson, "Periodizing the Sixties," in Sayres et al., *The 60s without Apology*, 178.

2. Ibid., 2.

3. Jason Epstein, "Jane Jacobs, 1916–2006," *New York Review of Books*, May 25, 2006, 53.

4. Quoted in Quinn, *But Never Eat Out on a Saturday Night*, 132.

5. R. Williams, *Drama from Ibsen to Brecht*, 335.

6. R. Williams, "Drama in a Dramatized Society," 14.

7. Ibid.

8. R. Williams, *Television*.

9. In *The Fugitive in Flight*, a study of another 1960s TV series that appeared just as I was putting the final touches on this manuscript, the noted literary critic and cultural commentator Stanley Fish argues that *The Fugitive* is also a work of popular culture that was closed off to the larger currents of the time. Strikingly, and paralleling my own assertion that *The French Chef* is

of both the '60s and the previous decade, Fish suggests that a deliberate bracketing out of broader context makes *The Fugitive* feel very much like a 1950s show, despite the fact that it debuted in 1963, the same year as *The French Chef.* In Fish's words, "I am not going to explore the relationship between the series and the great events that were occurring at the time of its production—war, racism, riots, assassinations. I turn my eyes away from these events because the series does. It refuses to become a vehicle for the dramatization of the social and political issues that filled the nightly news and commanded the attention of editorial writers." Fish, *The Fugitive in Flight,* 15. Even though he ventures from town to town, *The Fugitive's* Richard Kimble (David Janssen) is in his own way no less in place than Julia Child in her kitchen. Kimble is a force of constancy and of ethical steadfastness who brings enlightenment to a recalcitrant world. The show's title may present him as a man on the move, but he is ultimately a rock of ethical purity.

10. Jameson, "World Reduction in Le Guin."

11. Ghamari-Tabrizi, *The Worlds of Herman Kahn.*

12. Fan letter from Veronica Foley, June 3, 1965, archived in folder 357 of the Julia Child Papers, Arthur and Elizabeth Schlesinger Library on the History of Women in America, Radcliffe College, Cambridge, Mass.

13. Useful in situating amateur radio among postwar hobby culture is Haring, *Ham Radio's Technical Culture.* I rely here too on my own experience in the 1960s as a teenage ham radio operator.

14. See Riesman et al., *The Lonely Crowd,* 144–45.

References

Abbott, James A., and Elaine M. Rice. *Designing Camelot: The Kennedy White House Restoration*. New York: Van Nostrand Reinhold, 1998.

Adorno, Theodor. *Philosophy of New Music* (1947). Trans. Robert Hullot-Kenter. Minneapolis: University of Minnesota Press, 2006.

Alexander, Kelly, and Cynthia Harris. *Hometown Appetites: The Story of Clementine Paddleford, the Forgotten Food Writer Who Chronicled How America Ate*. New York: Gotham, 2008.

Arendt, Hannah. *Eichmann in Jerusalem: A Report on the Banality of Evil*, rev. edn. New York: Penguin, 1964.

Baldridge, Letitia, with René Verdon. *In the Kennedy Style: Magical Evenings in the Kennedy White House*. New York: Doubleday, 1999.

Barthes, Roland. "Introduction to the Structural Analysis of Narrative." *Image—Music—Text*, ed. and trans. Stephen Heath, 79–124. New York: Hill and Wang, 1977.

——. "The Myth Today." *Mythologies*, trans. Annette Lavers, 109–59. New York: Hill and Wang, 1972.

Baughman, James L. *Same Time, Same Station: Creating American Television*. Baltimore: Johns Hopkins University Press, 2007.

Berry, Madonna L. "The Dione Lucas Cooking Show: French Food as Agency and Expression in Post–World War II Domesticity." Master's thesis, University of Massachusetts, Boston, 2006.

Biddulph, Edward. " 'Bond Was Not a Gourmet': An Archaeology of James Bond's Diet." *Food, Culture, and Society* 12, no. 2 (June 2009), 131–49.

Birkby, Evelyn. *Neighboring on the Air: Cooking with the KMA Radio Homemakers*. Iowa City: University of Iowa Press, 1991.

Bonner, Frances. "Representations of the Female Cook." *Coastscripts: Gender Representations in the Arts*, ed. Kay Ferres, 63–71. Queensland: Australian Institute for Women's Research and Policy, Griffith University, 1994.

Bracken, Peg. *The I Hate to Cook Book*. New York: Harcourt Brace, 1960.

Brown, Helen Gurley. *Sex and the Single Girl*. New York: Bernard Geis Associates, 1962.

Brunsdon, Charlotte. "Feminism, Postfeminism, Martha, Martha, and Nigella," *Cinema Journal*, 44, no. 2 (winter 2005), 110–16.

Cassidy, Marsha F. *What Women Watched: Daytime Television in the 1950s*. Austin: University of Texas Press, 2005.

Chamberlain, Samuel. *Clémentine in the Kitchen* (1943). New York: Modern Library, 2001.

Child, Julia. *The French Chef Cookbook* (1968). New York: Alfred A. Knopf, 2002.

——. *From Julia Child's Kitchen*. New York: Alfred A. Knopf, 1975.

Child, Julia, Simone Beck, and Louisette Bertholle. *Mastering the Art of French Cooking, Volume 1: The 40th Anniversary Edition*. New York: Alfred A. Knopf, 2004.

Child, Julia, with Alex Prud'homme. *My Life in France*. New York: Alfred A. Knopf, 2006.

Collins, Kathleen. *Watching What We Eat: The Evolution of Television Cooking Shows*. New York: Continuum, 2009.

Cusset, François. *French Theory: How Foucault, Derrida, Deleuze and Co. Transformed the Intellectual Life of the United States*. Trans. Jeff Fort. Minneapolis: University of Minnesota Press, 2008.

DeRoo, Rebecca J. "Unhappily Ever After: Visual Irony and Feminist Strategy in Agnès Varda's *Le Bonheur*." *Studies in French Cinema* 8, no. 3 (2008), 189–209.

Dupuy, Judy. *Television Show Business*. Schenectady, N.Y.: General Electric, 1945.

Eco, Umberto, and Oreste del Buono, eds. *The Bond Affair*. Trans. R. A. Dawnie. London: MacDonald, 1966.

Editors of *Esquire*, with Scotty and Ronnie Welch. *Esquire Party Book*. New York: Esquire, 1963.

Eliassen, Meredith. "Cooking on the Air: San Francisco's Early Bread and Butter." *Argonaut* 21, no. 1 (spring 2010), 50–71.

Endrijonas, Erika Anne. "No Experience Required: American Middle-Class Families and Their Cookbooks, 1945–1960." Ph.D. diss., University of Southern California, Los Angeles, 1996.

Endy, Christopher. *Cold War Holidays: American Tourism in France*. Chapel Hill: University of North Carolina Press, 2004.

Ferguson, Priscilla Parkhurst. *Accounting for Taste: The Triumph of French Cuisine*. New York: Columbia University Press, 2004.

Fish, Stanley. *The Fugitive in Flight: Faith, Liberalism, and Law in a Classic TV Show*. Philadelphia: University of Pennsylvania Press, 2011.

Fitch, Noël Riley. *Appetite for Life: The Biography of Julia Child*. New York: Doubleday, 1997.

"Food Tips to Homemakers Televised." *Extension Service Review* 21 (April 1950), 59, 62–63.

Foucault, Michel. *Politics, Philosophy, Culture: Interviews and Other Writings, 1977–1984*, ed. Lawrence D. Kritzman. New York: Routledge, 1988.

Fraterrigo, Elizabeth. *Playboy and the Making of the Good Life in Modern America*. New York: Oxford University Press, 2009.

Friedan, Betty. *The Feminine Mystique*. New York: W. W. Norton, 1963.

Fussell, Betty. *Masters of American Cookery: M. F. K. Fisher, James Andrew Beard, Raymond Craig Claiborne, Julia McWilliams Child*. New York: Times Books, 1983.

——. *My Kitchen Wars: A Memoir*. New York: North Point, 1999.

Gelber, Steven M. *Hobbies: Leisure and the Culture of Work in America*. New York: Columbia University Press, 1999.

Geraghty, Christine, and David Lusted, eds. *The Television Studies Book*. London: Arnold, 1998.

Ghamari-Tabrizi, Sharon. *The Worlds of Herman Kahn: The Intuitive Science of Thermonuclear War*. Cambridge: Harvard University Press, 2005.

Glick, Edwin L. "WGBH-TV: The First Ten Years, 1955–1965." Ph.D. diss., University of Michigan, Ann Arbor, Mich., 1970.

Green, Edith, with Leona M. Bayer. *Kitchen Strategy: Vitamin Values Made Easy. What? Why? How? to Feed Your Family*. Self-published, 1943.

Greene, Gael. *Insatiable: Tales from a Life of Delicious Excess*. New York: Warner Books, 2006.

Hadju, David. *Positively 4th Street: The Life and Times of Joan Baez, Bob Dylan, Mimi Baez Farina, and Richard Farina*. New York: North Point, 2002.

Haring, Kristen. *Ham Radio's Technical Culture*. Cambridge: MIT Press, 2007.

Hemingway, Ernest. *A Moveable Feast*. New York: Scribner, 1964.

Hess, John, and Karen Hess. *The Taste of America*. New York: Penguin, 1977.

Hollows, Joanne. "The Bachelor Dinner: Masculinity, Class, and Cooking in *Playboy*, 1953–1961." *Continuum* 16, no. 2 (2002), 143–55.

——. "The Feminist and the Cook: Julia Child, Betty Friedan, and Domestic Femininity." *Gender and Domestic Consumption*, ed. E. Casey and L. Martens, 33–48. Hampshire: Ashgate, 2006.

Hudgins, Sharon. "A Conversation with Julia Child, Spring 1984." *Gastronomica* 5, no. 3 (summer 2005), 104–8.

Jameson, Fredric. "World Reduction in Le Guin." *Archaeologies of the Future: The Desire Called Utopia and Other Science Fictions*, 267–80. London: Verso, 2005.

Jordi, Nathalie. "'Our Apprenticeship at the Art of Graceful Living': American Distinction through French Cooking, 1941–1980." Senior honors thesis, Brown University, Providence, R.I., 2004.

Kackman, Michael. *Citizen Spy: Television, Espionage, and Cold War Culture*. Minneapolis: University of Minnesota Press, 2005.

Kaplan, Alice Yeager. "Taste Wars: American Professions of French Culture." *Yale French Studies*, no. 73 (1987), 156–72.

Kaufman, William I. *Cooking with the Experts*. New York: Random House, 1955.

Knox On-Camera Recipes: A Completely New Guide to Gel-Cookery. Johnstown, N.Y.: Knox Gelatine, 1960.

Korsmeyer, Carolyn. *Making Sense of Taste: Food and Philosophy*. Ithaca: Cornell University Press, 2002.

Kragen, Jinx, and Judy Perry. *Saucepans and the Single Girl*. New York: Doubleday, 1965.

Kuh, Patric. *The Last Days of Haute Cuisine*. New York: Viking, 2001.

LeBesco, Kathleen, and Peter Naccarato, eds. *Edible Ideologies: Representing Food and Meaning*. Albany: State University of New York Press, 2008.

Levenstein, Harvey. "The American Response to Italian Food." *Food and Foodways*, no. 1 (1985), 1–23.

———. "Two Hundred Years of French Food in America." *Journal of Gastronomy* 5, no. 1 (spring 1989), 67–89.

Lutkehaus, Nancy. *Margaret Mead: The Making of an American Icon*. Princeton: Princeton University Press, 2008.

Macksey, Richard, and Eugenio Donato, eds. *The Structuralist Controversy: The Languages of Criticism and the Sciences of Man*. Baltimore: Johns Hopkins University Press, 1970.

MacNamee, Thomas. *Alice Waters and Chez Panisse*. New York: Penguin, 2007.

Maines, Rachel P. *Hedonizing Technologies: Paths to Pleasure in Hobbies and Leisure*. Baltimore: Johns Hopkins University Press, 2009.

McCarthy, Anna. *The Citizen Machine: Governing by Television in 1950s America*. New York: New Press, 2010.

McCarthy, Josie. *Josie McCarthy's Favorite TV Recipes*. Englewood Cliffs, N.J.: Prentice-Hall, 1958.

McElhaney, Joe, ed. *Vincente Minnelli: The Art of Entertainment*. Detroit: Wayne State University Press, 2009.

McKeegan, Margaret Lucile. "Techniques of Presenting Homemaking Television Programs." Master's thesis, Iowa State College, Ames, Iowa, 1953.

Miller, Toby. *Spyscreen: Espionage on Film and Television from the 1930s to the 1960s.* New York: Oxford University Press, 2003.

Neuhaus, Jessamyn. *Manly Meals and Mom's Home Cooking: Cookbooks and Gender in Modern America.* Baltimore: Johns Hopkins University Press, 2003.

Osgerby, Bill. "The Bachelor Pad as Cultural Icon: Masculinity, Consumption, and Interior Design in American Men's Magazines, 1930–1965." *Journal of Design History* 18, no. 1 (2005), 99–113.

——. *Playboys in Paradise: Masculinity, Youth, and Leisure-Style in Modern America.* New York: Berg, 2001.

Ouellette, Laurie. *Viewers Like You?: How Public Television Failed the People.* New York: Columbia University Press, 2002.

Paddleford, Clementine. *How America Eats.* New York: Charles Scribner's Sons, 1960.

Pennell, Ellen. *Women on TV.* Minneapolis: Burgess, 1954.

Perron, Paul, and Frank Collins, eds. *Paris School Semiotics.* Philadelphia: J. Benjamins, 1989.

Polan, Dana. "James Beard's Early TV Work: A Report on Research." *Gastronomica* 10, no. 3 (summer 2010), 23–33.

Powell, Julie. *Julie and Julia.* New York: Little, Brown, 2005.

Quinn, Jim. *But Never Eat Out on a Saturday Night.* Garden City, N.Y.: Doubleday, 1983.

Reardon, Joan. *M. F. K. Fisher, Julia Child, and Alice Waters: Celebrating the Pleasures of the Table.* New York: Harmony, 1994.

——, ed. *As Always Julia: The Letters of Julia Child and Avis DeVoto.* New York: Houghton Mifflin Harcourt, 2010.

Richardson, Lou, and Genevieve Callahan. *How to Write for Homemakers.* Ames: Iowa State College Press, 1949.

Rico, Diana. *Kovacsland: A Biography of Ernie Kovacs.* New York: Harcourt Brace Jovanovich, 1990.

Riesman, David, with Nathan Glazer and Reuel Denney. *The Lonely Crowd: A Study of the Changing American Character*, abridged edn. New Haven: Yale University Press, 1969.

Robertson, Jim. *Televisionaries: In Their Own Words Public Television's Founders Tell How It All Began.* Charlotte Harbor, Fla.: Tabby House, 1993.

Ryan, L. Timothy. "The Culinary Insitute of America: A History." Ph.D. diss., University of Pennsylvania, Philadelphia, 2003.

Sartre, Jean-Paul. *The Critique of Dialectical Reason* (1960). Trans. Quintin Hoare. London: Verso, 1991.

——. *Search for a Method* (1960). Trans. Hazel Barnes. New York: Vintage, 1968.

Sayres, Sohnya, Anders Stephanson, Stanley Aronowitz, and Fredric Jameson, eds. *The 60s without Apology*. Minneapolis: University of Minnesota Press, 1984.

Scanlon, Jennifer. *Bad Girls Go Everywhere: The Life of Helen Gurley Brown*. New York: Oxford University Press, 2009.

Schlesinger, Arthur M. *The Vital Center: The Politics of Freedom*. Boston: Houghton Mifflin, 1949.

"Second Helpings, Please." *TV Radio Mirror*, February 1956, 6.

Sennett, Richard. *The Craftsman*. New Haven: Yale University Press, 2008.

Shapiro, Laura. *Julia Child*. New York: Penguin, 2007.

——. *Something from the Oven: Reinventing Dinner in 1950s America*. New York: Penguin, 2004.

Smith, Andrew F. *Eating History: Thirty Turning Points in the Making of American Cuisine*. New York: Columbia University Press, 2009.

Smith, Dina. "Global Cinderella: *Sabrina* (1954), Hollywood, and Postwar Internationalism." *Cinema Journal* 41, no. 4 (summer 2002), 27–51.

Sontag, Susan. "Against Interpretation." *Against Interpretation*, 13–23. New York: Farrar, Straus, and Giroux, 1966.

——. "Notes on 'Camp.'" *Against Interpretation*, 275–92. New York: Farrar, Straus, and Giroux, 1966.

Spigel, Lynn. *Make Room for TV: Television and the Family Ideal in Postwar America*. Chicago: University of Chicago Press, 1992.

——. *Television by Design: Modern Art and the Rise of Network Television*. Chicago: University of Chicago Press, 2009.

Stole, Inger L. "*The Kate Smith Hour* and the Struggle for Control of Television Programming in the Early 1950s." *Historical Journal of Film, Radio, and Television* 20, no. 4 (October 2000), 549–65.

——. "Televised Consumption: Women, Advertisers, and the Early Daytime Television Industry." *Consumption, Markets and Culture* 6, no. 1 (2003), 65–80.

Taber, George. *Judgment of Paris: California versus France and the Historic 1976 Paris Tasting That Revolutionized Wine*. New York: Scribner, 2005.

Trubek, Amy. *Haute Cuisine: How the French Invented the Culinary Profession*. Philadelphia: University of Pennsylvania Press, 2000.

Westman, Barbara. *The Beard and the Braid: Drawings of Cambridge*. Barre, Mass.: Barre Publishing, 1970.

Williams, Mark. "Considering Monty Margett's *Cooking Corner*: Oral History and Television History." *Television, History, and American Culture: Feminist Critical Essays*, ed. Mary Beth Haralovich and Lauren Rabinowitz, 36–55. Durham: Duke University Press, 1995.

Williams, Raymond. *Drama from Ibsen to Brecht*. New York: Oxford University Press, 1969

——. "Drama in a Dramatized Society" (1974). *Writing in Society*, 11–21. London: Verso, 1983.

——. *Television: Technology and Cultural Form*. New York: Schocken, 1975.

Wooden, Wayne S. "Edith Green: Television's Early Cook, 1949–1954." *Western States Jewish History* 19, no. 4 (July 1987), 306–14.

Further Readings on TV Cooking Shows

Adema, Pauline. "Vicarious Consumption: Food, Television, and the Ambiguity of Modernity." *Journal of American and Comparative Cultures* 23, no. 3 (fall 2003), 113–22.

Andrews, Maggie. "Nigella Bites the Naked Chef: The Sexual and the Sensual in Television Cookery Programmes." *The Recipe Reader: Narrative—Contexts—Traditions*, ed. Janet Floyd and Laurel Forster, 187–204. Hampshire, U.K.: Ashgate, 2003.

Ashley, Bob, Joanne Hollows, Steve Jones, and Ben Taylor. "Television Chefs." *Food and Cultural Studies*, 171–85. New York: Routledge, 2004.

Barron, Lee. "From the Kitchen to 10 Downing Street: Jamie's School Dinners and the Politics of Reality Cooking." *The Tube Has Spoken: Reality TV and History*, ed. Julie Anne Taddeo and Ken Dvorak, 47–64. Lexington: University Press of Kentucky, 2010.

Bonner, Frances. "Early Multi-Platforming: Television Food Programmes, Cookbooks and Other Print Spin-offs." *Media History* 15, no. 3 (2009), 345–58.

Caraher, Martin, Tim Lange, and Paul Dixon. "The Influence of TV and Celebrity Chefs on Public Attitudes and Behavior among the English Public." *Journal of the Study of Food and Society* 4, no. 1 (2005), 27–46.

Chan, Andrew. "*La grande bouffe*: Cooking Shows as Pornography." *Gastronomica* 3, no. 4 (2003), 46–53.

Chao, Phebe Shih. "TV Cook Shows: Gendered Cooking." *Jump Cut*, no. 42 (December 1998), 19–27.

de Solier, Isabelle. "Foodie Makeovers: Public Service Television and Lifestyle Guidance." *Exposing Lifestyle Television: The Big Reveal*, ed. Gareth Palmer, 65–81. Hampshire, U.K.: Ashgate, 2008.

——. "TV Dinners: Culinary Television, Education and Distinction." *Continuum* 19, no. 4 (December 2005), 465–81.

Eaner, Ryan Scott. "From Stovetop to Screen: A Cultural History of Food Television." Master's thesis, New School University, New York, 2008.

Frantz, Lurene Jochem. "A Case Study of an Educational Television Series: *The French Chef.*" Master's thesis, Pennsylvania State University, University Park, Pa., 1967.

Gallagher, Mark. "What's So Funny about *Iron Chef?*" *Journal of Popular Film and Television*, 31, no. 4 (winter 2004), 176–84.

Gunders, John. "Professionalism, Place, and Authenticity in *The Cook and the Chef.*" *Emotion, Space and Society* 1, no. 1 (2006), 119–26.

Hansen, Signe. "From Chef to Superstar: Food Media from World War Two to the World Wide Web." Ph.D. diss, Centre for Film and Media Studies, University of Cape Town, 2007.

——. "Television." *The Business of Food: Encyclopedia of the Food and Drink Industry*, ed. Gary Allen and Kenneth Alba, 366–70. Westport, Conn.: Greenwood, 2008.

Hollows, Joanne. "Feeling like a Domestic Goddess: Postfeminism and Cooking." *European Journal of Cultural Studies* 6, no. 2 (May 2003), 179–202.

——. "Oliver's Twist." *International Journal of Cultural Studies* 6, no. 2 (June 2003), 229–48.

Hollows, Joanne, and Steve Jones. "'At least he's doing something': Moral Entrepreneurship and Individual Responsibility in Jamie's *Ministry of Food.*" *European Journal of Cultural Studies* 13, no. 3 (2010), 307–22.

——. "*Please* Don't Try This at Home: Heston Blumenthal, Cookery TV and the Culinary Field." *Food, Culture, and Society* 13, no. 4 (December 2010), 521–37.

Kackman, Michael. "Cooking Shows." *Encyclopedia of Television*, vol. 1, ed. Horace Newcomb, 584–85. New York: Fitzroy Dearborn, 2004.

Ketchum, Cheri. "The Essence of Cooking Shows: How the Food Network Constructs Consumer Fantasies." *Journal of Communication Inquiry* 29, no. 3 (July 2005), 217–34.

——. "Tunnel Vision and Food: A Political-Economic Analysis of Food Network." *Cable Visions: Television beyond Broadcasting*, ed. Sarah Banet-Weiser, Cynthia Chris, and Anthony Freitas, 158–76. New York: New York University Press, 2007.

Lukacs, Gabriella. "*Iron Chef* around the World: Japanese Food Television, Soft Power, and Cultural Globalization." *International Journal of Cultural Studies* 13, no. 4 (July 2010), 409–26.

Mak, Monica. "The Pixel Chef: PBS Cooking Shows and Sensorial Utopias." *Eating in Eden: Food and American Utopias*, ed. Etta M. Madden and Martha L. Finch, 258–74. Lincoln: University of Nebraska Press, 2006.

Manalansan, Martin F., IV. "Cooking Up the Senses: A Critical Approach to the Study of Food and Asian American Television Audiences." *Alien Encounters: Popular Culture in Asian America*, ed. Mimi Thi Nguyen and Thuy Linh Nguyen, 179–93. Durham: Duke University Press, 2007.

Meister, Mark. "Cultural Feeding, Good Life Science, and the TV Food Network." *Mass Communication and Society*, 4, no. 2 (2001), 165–82.

Miller, Toby. "Television Food: From Brahmin Julia to Working-Class Emeril." *Cultural Citizenship: Cosmopolitanism, Consumerism, and Television in a Neoliberal Age*, 112–43. Philadelphia: Temple University Press, 2007.

Moseley, Rachel. "Marguerite Patten, Television Cookery, and Postwar British Femininity." *Femininity, Domesticity, and Popular Culture*, ed. Stacy Gillis and Joanne Hollows, 17–31. New York: Routledge, 2009.

——. " 'Real Lads Do Cook—But Some Things Are Still Hard to Talk About': The Gendering of 8–9." *European Journal of Cultural Studies* 4, no. 1 (January 2001), 32–39.

Mullen, Megan. "Everybody Eats: The Food Network and Symbolic Capital." *Food for Thought: Essays on Eating and Culture*, ed. Lawrence C. Rubin, 113–24. Jefferson, N.C.: McFarland, 2008.

Nathanson, Elizabeth. "As Easy as Pie: Cooking Shows, Domestic Efficiency, and Postfeminist Temporality." *Television and New Media* 10, no. 4 (July 2009), 311–30.

Pearlman, Alison. "Chef Appeal." *Popular Culture Review* 18, no. 1 (winter 2007), 3–24.

Ray, Krishnendu. "Domesticating Cuisine: Food and Aesthetics on American Television." *Gastronomica* 7, no. 1 (winter 2007), 50–64.

Smith, Greg M., and Pamela Wilson. "Country Cookin' and Cross-Dressin': Television, Southern White Masculinities, and Hierarchies of Cultural Taste." *Television and New Media* 5, no. 3 (August 2004), 175–96.

Strange, Niki. "Perform, Educate, Entertain: Ingredients of the Cookery Programme Genre." *The Television Studies Book*, ed. Christine Geraghty and David Lusted, 301–12. London: Arnold, 1998.

Swenson, Rebecca. "*Domestic Divo?*: Televised Treatments of Masculinity, Femininity and Food." *Critical Studies in Media Communication* 26, no. 1 (2009), 36–53.

Versteegen, Heinrich. "Armchair Epicures: The Proliferation of Food Programmes on British TV." *The Pleasures and Horrors of Eating*, ed. Marion

Gymnich and Norbert Lennartz, 447–64. Goettingen: Bonn University Press, 2010.

Wade, Anne Marit, and Ulla Angkjaer Jorgensen. "Haptic Routes and Digestive Destinations in Cooking Series: Images of Food and Place in *Keith Floyd* and *The Hairy Bikers* in Relation to Art History." *Journal of Tourism and Cultural Change*, 8, nos. 1–2 (March–June 2010), 84–100.

Index

Page numbers in italics refer to illustrations

Williams, Raymond, 234–36
Williams-Sonoma stores, 139
WNDT TV (New York), 192, 201
Wolfson, Jill, 260n36
WRGB TV (Schenectady), 46

Yellow Submarine (1968 film), 218
Your Home Kitchen (KRON TV cooking show, Edith Green host), 54–55

Zabriskie Point (1970 film), 247
Zacherly, 12
Zelayeta, Elena, 66

Dana Polan is a professor of cinema studies at New York University. He is the author of several books, including *The Sopranos* (2009) and *Scenes of Instruction: The Beginnings of the U.S. Study of Film* (2007).

Library of Congress
Cataloging-in-Publication Data

Polan, Dana B., 1953–
Julia Child's The French chef / Dana Polan.
p. cm.—(Spin offs)
Includes bibliographical references and index.
ISBN 978-0-8223-4859-7 (cloth : alk. paper)
ISBN 978-0-8223-4872-6 (pbk. : alk. paper)
1. Child, Julia. 2. French chef (Television program)
3. Cooking, French. 4. Television cooking shows—Social aspects—United States. 5. Cooking—Social aspects—United States. 6. Sex role—United States—History—20th century.
I. Title. II. Series: Console-ing passions book series. Spin offs.
PN1992.8.C68P653 2011
641.5944—dc22   2011006505